T0345083

Engaging Scoundrels

Engaging Scoundrels

True Tales of Old Lucknow

ROSIE LLEWELLYN-JONES

OXFORD
UNIVERSITY PRESS

OXFORD
UNIVERSITY PRESS

Oxford University Press is a department of the University of Oxford.
It furthers the University's objective of excellence in research, scholarship,
and education by publishing worldwide. Oxford is a registered trademark of
Oxford University Press in the UK and in certain other countries

Published in India by
Oxford University Press
22 Workspace, 2nd Floor, 1/22 Asaf Ali Road, New Delhi 110 002, India

First published 2000

16th impression 2023

ISBN-13: 978-0-19-564953-6
ISBN-10: 0-19-564953-2

Typeset in Aldine401 BT
by Guru Typograph Technology, New Delhi 110045
Printed in India by Replika Press Pvt. Ltd

for Ram Advani

Acknowledgements

Several friends were kind enough to provide information and to read through draft chapters of this book, and I am deeply indebted to them.

Janet Dewan from Ontario first told me about George Derusett's Cash Book and Basil de Rusett lent me the precious manuscript and gave me the photograph of 'The Barber of Lucknow'.

Mark Havelock-Allan provided additional details on the death of General Havelock at the Dilkusha Palace.

Dr Fakhir Hussain checked my translations from Urdu and gave helpful advice on the proper transliteration of Urdu names into English.

Nawab Mir Jafar Abdullah of Sheesh Mahal, Lucknow, told me several anecdotes about his illustrious ancestors and demonstrated that the *tehzib* of old Lucknow still survives.

Lieutenant General Menezes, PVSM, SC, and Theon Wilkinson, MBE, the founder of the British Association for Cemeteries in South Asia made helpful comments on the 'Bones of Contention' chapter about Christian cemeteries in India.

Mohammed Jamal Rasul Khan, the Raja of Jehangirabad gave me a thoughtful insight into old Lacknavi culture (and its delicious cuisine) during my visits to his palace.

Ian Shepherd of Lucknow not only walked with me around some of the cemeteries but kept me informed of encroachments, and searched out the First World War graves in the Bandariabagh Cemetery.

My kind hosts in Lucknow, Akilendra, Madhu and Prashant Singh provided me with unstinting hospitality as they have done during a friendship of over twenty years.

P.J.O. Taylor sent me illustrations of the royal visit to London and Paris between 1856–8 and shared my excitement when another piece of the jigsaw fell into place.

There is one person to whom I owe an especial debt of gratitude, not just during the preparation of this book, but on every occasion I have visited Lucknow. Ram Advani's bookshop in Hazratganj is a haven for scholars and visitors to the city, where the real conversations about Lucknow take place over a cup of tea. The enjoyment that Ram Bhai, as he is affectionately known, derives from putting like-minded people in touch with each other, and gently guiding them to the books they need, is only matched by the pleasure we get from his company, contacts and erudition. Every scholar who writes about Lucknow, particularly those from overseas, is indebted to Ram, and it is therefore fitting that this book should be dedicated to him.

1. Asaf-ud-Daula

2. Ghazi-ud-din Haider

3. Ghazi-ud-din Haider, *c.* 1820

4. Nasir-ud-din Haider

Contents

List of Illustrations

Introduction

'*Another* book on Lucknow?' said my friends, 'You've already written one!' Well, yes I had, I explained, but that one was about buildings and this one is about people. 'You mean the Nawabs?' they asked. Certainly the Nawabs must feature heavily in any book about Lucknow, for they created many of its spectacular buildings, and influenced most of its culture during the eighty-odd years of rule in the capital. But the Nawabs, who later became the Kings of Awadh, were not the only people in Lucknow, and sometimes not even the most interesting, despite their fabulous wealth. There were others too, British among them, who were keen to extract money from the Nawabs. These were mostly officials of the East India Company, working for the Company, but sometimes on their own account too, with lucrative little businesses. There were also freelancers, men who risked everything to gain employment at Court, and just a few who succeeded and became wealthy themselves. There were people who lost everything too, including the last King, Wajid Ali Shah, who lost his crown, and his mother Janab Alia Begam, who lost her life in trying to win it back. There were rogues and villains, British as well as Indian, and many tragic tales unfolded in the city.

But there is a danger of becoming too serious about Lucknow and its culture. It was, after all, a place of pleasure, of beautiful gardens, extraordinary buildings, music and dancing, exquisite food, theatrically staged events, and above all, parties. There is something rather endearing about Nasir-ud-din Haider, the most dissolute of all the Kings, who when rebuked by the British Resident for some new folly, replied, 'Come what may, he would drink Hip! Hip! Hoora!' And he did.

This book then is not about the political history of Awadh, or its uneasy relationship with the East India Company, but an attempt to explore some of the previously unknown aspects of Nawabi Lucknow. It is the byways of the past that are often the most interesting, those winding alleys that lead off the main streets, away from the crowd, to undiscovered corners of a city's history. What happened in the year *before* the uprising of 1857 seems to me much more interesting than the often repeated story of the siege of the British Residency. Similarly, the journeys of a few Indian travellers *from* Lucknow to England are often more intriguing than the familiar tales of the memsahibs going to India.

Such an approach is not without its rewards, both for the writer, and it is to be hoped, for the reader. Who would have thought Queen Victoria would have written a description in her journal of Janab Alia Begam, which remained unpublished in the archives of Windsor Castle all these years? And how did the Barber of Lucknow, George Derusett, rise from cutting hair to fitting out a luxury sailing ship for his master? His unpublished Cash Book tells the story for the first time, and incidentally presents Derusett in a more sympathetic light than before. Fifty years after Independence stories still surface about how the British left India, in a hurry, as the date of their departure was brought forward. In Lucknow the military in particular were so anxious to make a decent exit, with their Union flag, that they forgot a British soldier imprisoned in Lucknow jail for some misdemeanour, and the poor man was only found and released some months later by a conscientious Indian Army officer.

Though the people of Nawabi Lucknow may seem distant to us, at the end of the twentieth century, they are not mythological characters, as their children frequently prove. Among the correspondents who have kindly provided material for this book are descendants of the Nawabs themselves, the Quieros family, the family of Mariam Begam, the English wife of Ghazi-ud-din Haider, the Derusett family, Dr G.D.S. Beechey on George Beechey (portrait painter to the last four Kings of Awadh), and others. There are many chains that link us to the past, and the exotic world of old Lucknow is no exception.

October 1998   ROSIE LLEWELLYN-JONES

CHAPTER ONE

Entertaining the Nawabs

A king without a kingdom, or a ruler in exile is invariably a pathetic figure, whether he has been removed by civil war, invasion or his own shortcomings. The fate of a monarch in his own country, still nominally a king, but deprived of most of his kingly functions is equally sad. The story of how the East India Company stripped the Nawabs of power, and how the Nawabs themselves relinquished other rights, has become clearer over the last twenty-five years as historians have adopted a more analytical approach to the Awadh rulers, caught as they were between two mutually opposed forces, the dying Mughal Empire and the expanding British one. The history of Nawabi Awadh serves as a useful paradigm for post-colonial writers examining the mechanics of interference and control by the British in discrete areas of India.[1] In spite of the destruction of many invaluable records during 1857–58, both Indian and British, enough remains to chart the comparatively rapid emasculation of the Nawabi dynasty that culminated in the annexation of their kingdom in 1856.

When the Persian nobleman Syed Muhammad Amin (generally known as Saadat Khan) was appointed Governor of Awadh in 1722 by the Mughal Emperor, he travelled to his new province with a clear understanding of what was expected from him. One of the titles bestowed on him by the Delhi Court was that of 'Nawab', the Arabic word for deputy, for the role of Governor, or *Subahdar*, at that period was to deputise for the Emperor himself. Another title, 'Wazir' empowered him to act as Chief Minister, appointing his own deputies and administrators, while earlier, as 'Faujdar', he had been a military commander with his own troops. The well-defined duties of the Emperor and the expectations of his subjects were to be carried out and met, by proxy, by the provincial governors. They were to protect their designated territories against incursions by outsiders and to aid the Emperor when foreign invasions threatened. They were to collect the land revenues as efficiently as possible, and to remit a portion to the imperial treasury. On a personal level they were to hold regular *darbar* or court, at which their own officials attended to receive instructions and to exchange information. An important part of the *darbar* was the offering of gifts to the ruler, and the presentation by him of a robe of honour *(khilat)* and other marks of favour. The rulers were also to be accessible, at certain times, to the people over whom they had authority, and to initiate charitable and religious works.

In the century or so that followed Saadat Khan's death in 1739, his family, who had quickly established themselves as hereditary rulers of Awadh, lost many of the obligations assumed by the first Nawab on taking up the post of Governor. The British victory at Buxar in 1764 had led to annexation by the Company of part of the Awadh territory and the first of many substantial payments and loans by the Nawabs. It had resulted in the establishment of Company troops in Awadh, ostensibly to defend the Nawabs' domain, but necessarily leading to the loss of autonomous military control by its rulers. It had led, in 1774, to the appointment of a British Resident at the Nawab's Court, the start of that 'fatal friendship' of political and domestic interference, the isolation of the Nawabs and a continual, debilitating flow of criticism over how they conducted themselves.[2] The Company, through the Resident, acted like a filter between the Nawabs and the outside world, ultimately curtailing their correspondence and restricting their movements. The Company undermined the Nawabs' authority in numerous ways, sometimes by supporting dissident courtiers against the Nawabs, sometimes by promoting the Residents' ill-defined jurisdiction over people living near the British Residency, and by allowing them to set up a 'rival' *darbar* in the Residency. It persuaded money from the Nawabs to finance buildings that benefited the British, like the Lucknow Observatory, the new road to Cawnpore, or the Iron Bridge over the Gomti river, as well as the maintenance of the British Residency, while at the same time denying the Nawabs things they wanted, like the electric telegraph. It bestowed on the Nawab Ghazi-ud-din Haider the empty title of 'King', severing his (admittedly by now) weak connections with the powerless Mughal Emperor, but then re-inforcing, in an annual 're-coronation' ceremony, his dependence on the British Resident who put the crown on his head again. In short, by 1856, the East India Company had assumed the majority of functions expected of the rulers, and the Nawabs had become like the plaster statues on their own palaces, presenting a gorgeously rich exterior, but almost hollow within. Symbolically the actual crown used at the first coronation in 1819 was designed by the Court artist Robert Home, together with the new King's coronation robes, his throne, and his coat of arms.[3]

The enforced 'protection' by the Company Army meant that the Nawabs would not be called upon again to defend Awadh. The last time Nawabi troops had seen real action was during the threatened Rohilla invasion of 1794, when twelve battalions of sepoys and a thousand cavalrymen were sent by Nawab Asaf-ud-daula to support the Company army under General Sir Robert Abercromby. The Awadh soldiers were led by Major General Claude Martin, who had volunteered for the post of Commander, after personally urging the Nawab to release them from their usual duties of collecting land revenue in the countryside. By the time the Nawab's own smaller detachment had been mobilised and had lumbered across country, the fighting was all over, the Rohillas having been decisively beaten at Katra.[4]

Although a Nawabi army was maintained until annexation, it was poorly paid and worse equipped because the Nawab Saadat Ali Khan 'considered that the maintenance of any troops of his own was not only unnecessary, but would have had the appearance of a separation of interests between the states' (that is, between Awadh and the Company).[5] After this same Nawab had been relieved of part of the Awadh territories by the Company in 1801, his former aide-de-camp Gore Ouseley justified the move by explaining that 'the nabob [Nawab] is now happy and contented, eased of a burden of a part of the country continually open to the Seiks and Mahrattas; his splendor, furniture and houses in a state infinitely more magnificent than they were before; for he has more opportunity of knowing what funds he can bestow on these things'.[6] But this was not how his son Ghazi-ud-din Haider saw it. He complained that 'the artillery which was formerly the most complete of all the establishments, has not for a long time undergone even the necessary repairs so that there remains scarcely anything of artillery but the name'.

The Nawabs occupied an uneasy period in history. They were too late to rule as medieval emperors, carving out and maintaining their territories through war and diplomacy, but too circumscribed to behave as modern nineteenth-century monarchs, interesting themselves in the welfare of their subjects, in promoting trade, industry, agriculture or the arts, and in enjoying the company of other royal families. Because the Company kept them deliberately isolated, official visits of political importance to the Lucknow capital were limited to those of the British Governor Generals, and these were usually made only when the Company perceived a new crisis in the Nawabi management of Awadh. It is not surprising then, given all these restrictions, that the Nawabi rulers became increasingly introverted, until the last King, Wajid Ali Shah spent much of his time inside the new Qaisarbagh palace. Interestingly, this is reflected in the various portraits of the Nawabs, by Indian and European artists. While Asaf-ud-daula is pictured enjoying an elephant ride and Nasir-ud-din Haider is shown on horseback reviewing his troops, contemporary portraits of Wajid Ali Shah show him in the palace gardens, or being driven through its grounds, or in the zenana, lolling on a

5. Wajid Ali Shah with his harem in the Qaisarbagh Palace

divan.[7] Discouraged and disinclined to wander far from Lucknow, the Nawabs eventually became voluntary prisoners in their own capital, exotic birds in the most magnificent of gilded cages.

With real power taken away from them, how did the Nawabs spend their days? Fortunately there are a considerable number of *akhbars* or Court newsletters still in existence which chronicle the daily routine of the Nawabs. Copies of these newsletters were distributed to significant towns in northern India, which is why they survived when the Lucknow Court records were destroyed. Two *akhbar* translations, from 1828 and 1839 convey the rituals and pomp of Court life, but at the same time, purvey a restlessness and feeling of claustrophobia. The first, of 19 December 1827 describes a day in the life of Nawab Nasir-ud-din Haider, who had become King that year. There was an early morning meeting with his Chief Minister Agha Mir at the Farhat Baksh palace, Claude Martin's old town house on the river Gomti. The breakfast *daroga*, or supervisor, was told to prepare the morning meal in the *mahalserai*, the queen's apartments, and after changing his clothes the King sent a messenger to the British Resident to tell him that breakfast was ready. The Resident, Mordaunt Ricketts, was saluted by the royal guards, and greeted by the King and the Chief Minister at the top of the palace stairs. After a sociable breakfast Nasir-ud-din Haider and Ricketts talked in a separate room and parted after the 'Customary Compliment of attar' when rose-water was sprinkled over the departing guest. The King then visited his mother in her apartments and talked with her for some time before taking his mid-day meal with one of his queens in her rooms.

After lunch he returned to the Farhat Baksh where he received a message from Ricketts, returned to his mother's rooms, back again to the Farhat Baksh where he sent for the Resident for the second meeting of the day in 'the Room in Furreh Baksh near the River side'. Ricketts was again sprinkled with rose-water on his departure. *Khilats* (robes of honour) were then presented to some of his officers, who returned the compliment by presenting *nazr* (a symbolic gift), which the King merely acknowledged. Then the royal elephant was ordered and the King 'went as far as the Troop Pultun Ghat' [the soldiers' riverside camp] to enjoy the fresh air. After dinner in one of the queens' apartments he retired for the night.[8]

The second account, eleven years later, relates similar events which took place on 20 June 1839 when Muhammad Ali Shah was King. The previous day he had sent fifty-one covered trays of food to the Queen Mother 'in the name of prayer for Hazrat Ali'. A loan of Rs 80,000 for the wedding expenses of a prince was returned to the Royal Treasury. The *daroga* of the basket department presented the King with some mangoes, and got a shawl in return. Ceremonial costumes were presented, and courtiers and soldiers gathered to celebrate the anniversary of the King's coronation—'the Presence, wearing very distinguished clothes and precious jewels sat on the throne'. The Resident, probably John Caulfield, was welcomed to the palace by a gun salute and embraced by the King. After placing the crown on his head, the Heir Apparent approached his father with a gift of money, and 'fifty joyous discharges' were fired from the artillery park. The Resident got a finely ornamented turban, a ceremonial dress and many other gifts (none of which the East India Company allowed him to keep). The rest of the day was given up to the exchange of presents between the recrowned King and his nobles.[9]

Clearly ceremonial occasions and courtly etiquette took up a great deal of the royal day. Part of the ruler's status depended upon such things, which is why the exchanges of gifts were recorded in such detail. They demonstrated both the wealth of the monarch, in the quality of his gifts, and the *izzat* or honour, that was bestowed by him, through the gifts, on the recipients. The fact that these gifts could, and often were, subsequently sold for cash, did not diminish the significance of their presentation. Similarly the public meals were important social events where honoured guests would be placed close to the King, and be seen in the royal presence. Apart from these official duties recorded in formal Persian in the news-letters, there are other, livelier descriptions of how the Nawabs spent their time, often in enhancing their own status, but sometimes more simply for the sake of enjoyment.

Although money from Awadh was continually 'drained off' by the East India Company, in the form of loans, fines and solicited gifts, it is important to remember that the Nawabs were still immensely, almost unbelievably, rich men. Saadat Ali Khan's *annual* net income, after all his expenses had been paid was estimated to be £1,200,000. Stories of large loans made to Asaf-ud-daula by Indian and European moneylenders are correct, as are the continual complaints by Indian and European servants that they were owed money, but this does not mean that the Nawabs were ever poor men. Even in exile, Wajid Ali Shah, living on a British pension of Rs 12 lakhs a year, was still extremely wealthy, supporting thousands of people on his staff.[10] Virtually unlimited money was poured into Lucknow in the eighty-odd years of Nawabi rule. It was the richest city in India of its time, far outweighing the Presidency seat at Calcutta, where the Company had had to rely on loans, including those from Awadh, for much of the early nineteenth century, to keep it afloat. In March 1858, a conservative estimate of the true value of property seized from one palace alone, the Qaisarbagh, by the Company's prize agents, was £1,500,000. What was destroyed or stolen from the same palace by the victorious soldiers, Indian, British and Nepalese, cannot be calculated.

It should therefore not surprise us that the entertainments of these exceptionally wealthy men should be on a suitably heroic scale, though it is sometimes difficult to appreciate this from the accounts of disting-uished European visitors to Lucknow, literally dazzled by innumerable marble-like palaces, seldom understanding a word of Persian or Urdu, even less of the customs of the Court, and usually putting up for a while at the definitely sober haven of the British Residency. True, some could see that Lucknow was indeed different from other places that they had visited in India, but some seemed deliberately blasé when describing a fireworks party, a royal banquet or an elephant fight, as if to show real enthusiasm would be to admit that a native Court, and particularly the Court of Awadh, was something uniquely magnificent, whatever one's politics. The official visitors, the Governor Generals and their staff, openly criticised what they saw as extravagant living by spendthrift monarchs, wasting good money that could have been used for poor relief, or indeed repaying their large debts to the Company. Many of the things the Nawabs enjoyed were, by their nature, ephemeral pleasures like temporary gardens, boat trips, musical parties and hunts and most have left no trace. It is only occasionally that we get a glimpse of the absolute splendour, and cost, of Nawabi life, sometimes from artists like Johann Zoffani who painted Asaf-ud-daula at a crowded cock-fight, sometimes from an occasional remaining treasure like a dancing girl's earrings of gold, emeralds and pearls.

But an attempt to discover what entertained the Nawabs is not a fruitless task, for in doing so we learn something of the characters of these men, to see them today without the unthinking praise of many Indian writers, or the vituperative criticism of all English ones, in fact to see them as people who on the whole, made the best of the difficult situation in which they found themselves. It is moreover to see them as individuals, people of differing tastes and talents, who though all bound together by blood-ties and their kingly duties, should not be seen simply as a conglomerate—'the Nawabi dynasty'—which detracts from their varied virtues and vices. It is also an opportunity to see whether or not they upheld the traditions of the Mughal Court, to which they, and their subjects, believed they were the natural heirs.

The enormous number of animals kept by the Nawabs and the expensive establishments for them were frequently commented on, especially by the British, who considered that the money could have been better spent on feeding poor people. Almost the first thing that the East India Company did after annexing Awadh was, as we shall see in a later chapter, to auction the last King's animals on the banks of the Gomti. In happier times these royal animals, the king's beasts, had provided transport, sport and amusement for their owners. They carried the Nawabs to their palaces and gardens, to mosques, and out into the countryside on annual tours, hunting parties and pilgrimages to shrines. Asaf-ud-daula has already been mentioned, pictured on an elephant, and there were a number of royal *feelkhana*, or elephant houses throughout Lucknow, like the one at Chandganj, north of the Gomti, which were not attached to any palace, but kept up by the Nawabs. One imagines Asaf-ud-daula, an inveterate collector, appraising a new purchase, and both man and beast, two large yet dignified figures, eyeing each other approvingly. The elephants were, after the Nawab's kitchen, the most expensive item of his household, costing Rs 64,663 a year to maintain in the 1780s.[11] A good elephant could cost as much as Rs 6,000, and was an important symbol of royalty, as the Company clearly recognised by selling them off for a song. Elephants added 'materially to the pomp of a King' said the Mughal historian Abul Fazl, and rulers tried to collect as many as possible. The animals were trained to salute their masters by kneeling before them and touching their foreheads with their trunks in a salaam. Four of the Nawab's favourite elephants were buried behind the palace in the Daulat Khana, laid to rest with great difficulty, one imagines, but not without affection. Their graveyard is today covered by a garden at the back of the Sheesh Mahal, near the river.

During the favourite hunting season from early December to mid-March, as many as 800 elephants were used to transport the royal party, its European guests, the ministers, the courtiers and their baggage. Asaf-ud-daula would be seated on an 'elegantly caparisoned' mount with two spare elephants on either side, one carrying the state howdah and the other with two men loading ammunition into the guns which they handed him. Accompanying them were about 10,000 cavalry and infantry, with innumerable bullocks, camels and baggage carts carrying two sets of elaborate tents and 'every article of luxury or pleasure' including blocks of ice to cool the drinking water and make iced puddings. Singers and musicians on horseback sang and played like medieval troubadors as the huge procession moved on, while the numerous caged nightingales added their own song. Men with hunting hawks on their wrists, and dogkeepers with pairs of greyhounds ran in front of everyone. Others carried different kinds of nets for trapping animals, birds and fish from the rivers. An even greater number of people, possibly as many as 20,000 followed behind, an instant, moving bazaar to supply all the needs of the travellers during the day, and when they stopped for night to strike camp. No wonder the Englishman Daniel Johnson described the endless procession as presenting 'the appearance of a large army going to a field of battle, rather than that of a hunting party'.[12] And like an army, it did not differentiate between cultivated and barren land, but marched straight towards the evening camp, often followed by 'the poor cultivators running behind the Vizier's elephant bawling out for mercy'.

After two weeks or so on the move, a promising spot was decided upon where game could be expected, and everyone settled down. The large double tents would be set up again for the Nawab and his guests, 'some with extensive enclosures made of cloth and bamboo about seven foot high forming a kind of wall round each tent, of 100 yards or more in circumference'. If the ground was muddy or uneven, low wooden tables would be fitted together to form the floor, which was then covered with fine carpets. There were plenty of entertainments before the shooting began. Impromptu horse races were set up 'to amuse the [Nawab] Vizier', and bets placed on the riders. Acrobats would tumble about in front of him, exhibiting 'wonderful agility and skill' and nautch dancers gave evening performances.

In the morning, after an English breakfast of tea and toast, the Nawab and his hunters would set out, armed to the teeth. Although the Company had allowed Asaf-ud-daula to keep his own arsenal, where weapons were manufactured under the superintendence of Claude Martin, the Nawab had a good collection of English guns too. The ammunition elephant to his right carried forty or fifty double-barrelled guns, a number of single barrels, rifles, and even pistols. If a bird fell after the Nawab had fired there were appreciative shouts of 'Wah Wah!' from the courtiers. Two hundred years ago the countryside of Awadh was full of wild animals and offered a choice of hunting from lions, panthers, leopards, wild buffalo and hogs, to deer and jackals. Tigers were especially prized. In the jungle or across the plain, the cavalry would spread out into two elongated arms, then wheel around to form a circle, sweeping the animals before them. As the circle grew smaller, the Nawab would enter, as if through a funnel, and shoot away. He was reputedly a good shot, which was just as well, as he was once seen 'to amuse himself with firing ball from the fort of Allahabad at pots of water carried on the heads of persons passing to and from the river Jumna'.[13] Not all the killing was done by humans. There were hunting cheetahs, who would be brought out hooded and chained, on buffalo carts, then let loose on buck and deer, their natural prey. They had been trained to wait by the side of the animals they had brought down, and were rewarded by raw titbits. There were hunting hawks trained to catch and kill smaller birds in flight, and there were dogs who hunted jackals, the dogkeepers being rewarded with half a rupee by the Nawab for each jackal caught. After a month or so, the whole enormous party would return to Lucknow by a different route, having covered a circuit of about five hundred miles. For those privileged guests who missed the hunting season, small game like antelope were kept in the Dilkusha Park, which was then an area of some three miles or so, and walled all around.

Asaf-ud-daula was the greatest purchaser of fine horses in northern India, so much so that the English complained they could seldom get decent animals in Calcutta. 'We have to thank His Highness', wrote one visitor, 'as the primary cause of horses being scarce, of inferior cast, and high priced.'[14] 'The daily contemplation of the finest horses in the universe, is another source of pleasure to the Vizier, they are led before him richly caparisoned . . .' Indeed he was so fond of the hundreds of horses in his private stud, that not only did they accompany him on hunting parties, with their own tents, but were, by his orders, so overfed that they could hardly walk. Two huge draught horses sent out from England had been eagerly snatched up by the Nawab at Rs 10,000 the pair. 'He delighted in shewing them to the native Gentlemen, calling them the English elephants. For a long time he amused himself daily in seeing what a quantity of grain they devoured at each meal.' Both animals died from overfeeding.[15] By the 1780s the Nawab was reported to have become too fat himself to mount a horse with ease but he kept up his stables across the Gomti, which were described as 'a large square court of buildings, supported on brick pillars, with a view to the admission of air' and stalls for four hundred animals.[16] The habit of painting the horses 'particularly those meant for show' intrigued Europeans—'I have seen them all the colours of the rainbow, some really produce a grand though singular effect, wrote Captain Madan, who bought a beauty, 'bright orange, with a red flaming tail! I have been trying ever since to rub the paint off but without success.'[17] Another English visitor, Lady Nugent, saw horses painted in sweet-pea colours—pink, blue and lilac—with tails to match.

Among the 'List of Expenses for the Table, Wardrobe etc. of the Nawab per annum' during the years 1780–83 are the various provisions for his animals. Apart from the elephants and horses, there were camels, cows, buffaloes, the 'Kennell', leopards, sheep and goats, cats, antelopes, the pigeon house, tigers and poultry. These were mainly working animals but Asaf-ud-daula had also set up, near his first palace, the Macchi Bhawan, a menagerie and aviary. The first contained 'several serpents of extraordinary dimensions', porcupines, flying foxes, African sheep,

Barbary goats and '2 Ramghur Hill dogs'. The aviary had an 'uncommon collection of birds', including flamingoes.[18]

The menagerie accompanied Asaf-ud-daula to his new palace in the Daulat Khana, and it was enlarged by successive Nawabs, and subsequently moved across the Gomti to a *ramna* or park, where visitors found rhinoceroses chained to the trees, and tigers rattling away at the wooden bars of their cages. The main building contained four covered verandahs shading the cages and dens of other animals. Somewhere, roaming about in the park was a wild man, the 'junglee admee'. A visiting chaplain, the Reverend William Tennant noted that some of the Cabul sheep here were 'painted in different colours to gratify the fantastic taste of the natives, a practice which they follow with their bullocks and horses'. It was an age when rare animals were collected both as curiosities and as living symbols which enhanced their owner's image by showing that he was literally 'a man of the world' with his exotic creatures, brought with such labour and expense from foreign countries. Nasir-ud-din Haider was the proud owner of a herd of English cattle, whose unexpected appearance at the Dilkusha park 'when viewed beneath the shade of the tamarinds and banians of a tropical clime [render them] objects of deep and peculiar interest'.[19] The presentation of unusual animals as gifts to other rulers was popular too. The first giraffes in England in the 1830s had caused a sensation, almost equalled by Nasir-ud-din Haider's gifts to William IV and Queen Adelaide, which included a female rhinoceros, that legend has transposed into a Unicorn. The animals were presented by the King to London Zoo.[20] Less exotic animals were kept not only by the Nawabs, but by their courtiers too. A visitor in 1842 remarked on the tigers and bears in iron cages under the domes of the Chattar Manzil palace 'or in the arcades bizarrely painted' and as late as the 1970s two cages built into an elaborate semi-circular gateway on the Sitapur road could still be seen, which had once housed a pair of tigers.[21] Today's Lucknow Zoo, established in a former Nawabi garden, the Banarsi Bagh, is not a direct descendant of the royal menagerie and parks, but has a more interesting pedigree than most of its visitors probably realise.

Saadat Ali Khan, the brother of Asaf-ud-daula had spent twenty years away from Lucknow before succeeding to the *masnad* (throne) in January 1798.[22] His enforced, though by no means unpleasant stay in Calcutta and Benares had allowed him to pick up many western ways and he understood and wrote English, though he found its pronunciation difficult. Before his departure for Lucknow he got an English tailor to measure him for regimental dress, an English admiral's uniform and a parson's outfit, while a wig maker supplied him with pairs of fashionable perukes.[23] He was the first Nawab to abandon the droopy moustaches of the Persian aristocrat that his predecessors had worn, and to adopt something less affected. Not suprisingly he was 'a man much liked by the English, from his so entirely adopting their manners. If you hunt with him, his pack, I'm told is so very well managed that you may fancy yourself with "Lord Fitzwilliam . . ." He always rides in a cap and boots, leather breeches etc. and upon the most capital horses.'[24] The Nawab chose to be painted on a favourite white horse about 1800, wearing his handsome English riding boots. While he had been in exile, implicated in the murder of one of his brother's favourites, he had requested a European huntsman and a 'European instructor' to live with him.[25] On returning to Lucknow he continued to pay for the animal establishments of his brother, but the great hunting parties of the past were scaled down and horse-racing became the favourite sport. The Nawab's pack of fox-hounds which had been praised at Benares now accompanied him on jackal hunts, as he rode out with his English friend and aide-de-camp, the Persian-speaking Gore Ouseley. The elephant houses throughout the city were now joined by stables in the Charbagh, Dilkusha Park, at Gaughat, and Mukaramnagar Park, but the finest was in the heart of the new city, on Hazratganj. It was called the Chaupar Stables, because of its cruciform shape, where a man standing in the centre could look along each of the broad wings to the stalls. Only one arm of the cross remains today, much altered and used as a club, but a glimpse inside shows how handsomely the royal animals were accommodated. Oral tradition says that elephants were housed here, which is quite probable, from the size of the stalls.

Antoine de l'Etang had been in charge of the royal stables at Versailles until the French Revolution, and had then travelled to India where he found work looking after the horses of the Company's Bodyguard in Fort William. He was appointed by Saadat Ali Khan in 1809 as Superintendent of His Excellency's Stud and veterinary surgeon for the mares and foals in the various parks of Lucknow. From his monthly salary of Rs 2,000 de l'Etang had to hire stable assistants and buy medicines for the animals. At the same time he was also expected to superintend the Nawab's Riding School, the little African jockeys known as the *hubshi* boys, and their racing costumes, the troopers of the Nawab's Bodyguard, as well as the horses themselves with their quaint English names—John Bull, Silver Heels, Gold Dust, Jumper, Billy, Ariel, Quaker and Dice.[26]

He had 'to break in and Dress all the Horses of the Stud, whether Saddle or Carriage Horses, and also those for the Menage and the Turf'. English staff were employed too. There was William Bird, who had 'kept a Livery Stable in Calcutta', Stephen Pilcher, jockey, William Kelly, coachman and Samuel Salman, groom. Dr Law, the Residency surgeon, who must have been a good judge of horse flesh, was frequently asked by the Nawab to purchase horses and mares for him. But de l'Etang and the Nawab fell out over the Frenchman's alleged mistreatment of the animals. The Nawab accused him of not properly breaking in a colt, and of allowing three stabled horses to fall down. He complained that the African boys had not been properly trained, neither had the troopers of the Bodyguard. In his defence, de l'Etang said the 'bodyguard' were young boys who had never ridden a horse in their lives, but he could not deny that nearly thirty horses in his care had died since he took up his appointment. It is clear from the bitter exchange of letters between the two men, that Saadat Ali Khan was passionately fond of horses, spending hours at his Riding School where he says, 'I was always in the habit of attending to the horses myself and ordering Medicines for them'. He was horrified to find the old Frenchman pouring neat Spirit of Turpentine down the horses' throats, and purging them by drawing off blood or 'cupping' them. De l'Etang was in his sixties when he took up the post in Lucknow, and it seems likely that he was not abreast of modern methods of horse-care, as the Nawab clearly was. He was dismissed the following year.

The first Lucknow race-course was some four miles north of the city, just beyond the Mariaon (now Mandion) cantonment, and thus conveniently near for the British officers stationed there. It was established by the horse-loving Saadat Ali Khan, and was one of the earliest western-style courses in India, possibly the first, pre-dating the Calcutta race-course by several years. It may have been suggested by de l'Etang, who was reported during his short stay as preparing and levelling the race-course road and getting wells dug along it. Certainly it had been designed by an expert and was described as 'one of the finest a lover of the turf could wish'. Race-courses have always been associated with a certain louche element, as well as royalty, and the Mariaon one was no exception. William Sleeman, the British Resident from 1849 to 1854, took a particular dislike to it and the company it attracted, especially after finding his Assistant Resident, Captain Robert Bird, was spending so much time there. Instead of dealing with this situation himself, as he should have done, Sleeman complained to the Governor General Lord Dalhousie about it. Anything bad about the Lucknow Court was welcome to Dalhousie's ears, strengthening his conviction that sooner rather than later Awadh would have to be annexed. Sleeman's accusations, verging on the edge of paranoia, fell on responsive ground. He reported that 'there was a good deal of talk about one young officer who had been seen drinking, driving and residing in the intimate companionship with his Jockey, and about all Officers being familiar on the Race Course with the Singers and Eunuchs whom the Resident had so often had occasion to denounce to the King as reptiles who were ruining his reputation and his Country'.[27] One of the King's eunuchs, Basheer, was actually building his own stables for his racing horses near the cantonment road. Sleeman wrote Wajid Ali Shah an official letter of complaint, hoping that the races would not take place again, but received no response. This was not surprising as the King himself was a keen race-goer during the season, offering a purse of gold mohurs as a prize in the King's Stakes. Captain Bird continued to live in the cantonments 'during the racing and training season' in a house provided for him by the King, much to the Resident's chagrin. The Mariaon race-course seems to have been abandoned, together with the old cantonment in 1857, and a new one was built in the Dilkusha cantonment for the enjoyment of latter-day Captain Birds.

Perhaps nothing divides us quite so vividly from the world of the Nawabs, with its curious mixture of the medieval and the modern, the barbaric and the sophisticated, as the animal fights of Lucknow. There are so many descriptions of elephant fights, elephant and tiger fights, tiger and rhinoceros fights, cock-fights and quail-fights that they were clearly popular Nawabi entertainments, and moreover were often put on to entertain the Nawabs' European guests. Although British views coincided with the Indian love of shooting, hunting and fishing, these staged animal fights were not considered 'sporting' by the majority of western spectators. 'These fights were invariably accompanied by the same want of fairness towards the animals baited, and in no one instance had they any chance of success or escape,' wrote Major Archer.[28] There were Indian critics too. 'The diligence with which the people of Lucknow applied themselves to this wanton, cruel form of pleasure-seeking and the pitch of perfection to which they brought it could never have entered the dream of people from any other place,' wrote Maulana Abdul Halim Sharar, whose father worked for the exiled Wajid Ali Shah.[29]

The many accounts of animal fights are painful for us to read today, although it would be wrong to condemn the Nawabs without putting these 'entertainments' into context. Many old towns in England contained their bull-rings and cock-pits, and well within living memory performing bears were led from village to village in Wales and the west country. Bull-baiting, where vicious and hungry dogs were loosed at a chained bull, was not banned in England until 1835. Cock-fighting was immensely popular in Regency England, and was patronised by royalty. It was finally made illegal by an Act of Parliament in 1849. Elephant fights had a long history in India and were a favourite Mughal entertainment, held in the presence of the Emperor. At the beginning of the seventeenth century they were noted as taking place twice a week, on Tuesday and Saturday afternoons, in front of the Agra palace. The status attached to these events was so great that 'the fighting of Eliphants is seldome seen but where the King is, and there often used . . .' and the Emperor Jehangir specifically forbade his nobles from holding elephant fights, because they were the prerogative of royalty only.[30] Asaf-ud-daula, with his fighting beasts was following a long tradition, deliberately adopting a Mughal privilege, though this connection seems to have been lost on his European guests with whom he shared this entertainment. Fights between other animals were staged too and Asaf-ud-daula was described as an 'extraordinary man [who] spent the whole of his time in viewing the different things he possessed, or in shooting, cock-fighting, quail-fighting, pigeon flying, or paper kite flying or in witnessing the contest of tigers and buffaloes, or elephants'.[31]

Some fights took place within the palaces themselves, and a European visitor in 1845 was shown a gallery within the Chattar Manzil palace complex 'from which we looked down upon a narrow court, surrounded by walls and gratings'.[32] Viscount Valentia enjoyed a tiger fight in 1803 which took place in 'a space about fifty foot square [which] had been fenced off on the plain, between the Dowlat Khanah and the river, in front of the Sungi Baraderi, a building open in the Asiatic style, raised about twenty feet from the ground, and which is occasionally used as a breakfast or banqueting room'. At the country palace of Barowen, four miles west of Lucknow, animal fights took place in an open air amphi-theatre, and were viewed from 'a spacious verandah on the east side of the palace.'

There were a number of other permanent sites for these spectacles. The one most frequently used was on the north bank of the Gomti, op-posite the Chattar Manzil palace, and home to successive Nawabs for al-most fifty years. The site was called the Ramna Qaisar, the King's Park, and a sandy arena was marked out here for the elephant fights. The Na-wabs and their guests were seated in 'a long verandah' within the palace, looking out across the river to the park. A little further downstream stood the Shah Manzil palace, and here too guests and royalty 'would sit in the shade of elaborate marquees decorated with gold and silver thread, on the upper terrace' watching the fights on the opposite bank.[33] A second large park, the Hazaree Bagh, contained a circular area enclosed with bamboo fences and iron railings, and covered with a net, where the elephants and other animals would perform.

The common feature in all these descriptions was understandably the comfort and safety of the Nawabs and their guests, even if it meant the finer points of the fights could not always be seen. Something as large as an elephant or camel could be made out from across the river, but tiger fights must have been harder to follow even with a spying-glass. There was also the inherent problem of getting intelligent and normally peaceful animals like elephants to fight in the first place. 'They are naturally averse to quarrel with each other,' mused an English spectator and such fights 'must end in the most shocking manner, [they] are very speedily decided, for one is sure to quit his ground after giving and receiving a few blows'.[34] In fact only rutting elephants were used, and they were further enraged by the *mahouts* (riders) who goaded them on with the *ankas*, a spiked iron bar used like a knuckleduster. Large numbers of men were employed in training and controlling the animals, getting them into the arenas before the fights and locking them up again afterwards. 'They were equipped with red-hot, iron-tipped staves and torches with which they could turn the animals in any direction or drive them to any place they wished.' Crackers were let off to supplement the staves and torches and the skill of these men was said to be as interesting to watch as the fights themselves. Nasir-ud-din Haider staged a spectacular show for the British Commander-in-Chief, Lord Combermere, where a group of buffaloes were matched against pairs of tigers, bears and leopards. Other contests were staged between tigers and elephants, tigers and rhinoceroses (which the latter usually won by tearing out the tigers' entrails with their horns), cheetahs, camels, stags, and rams.

Animal fights on this scale were held by the Nawabs alone, because the cost of keeping the beasts, training and controlling them, and protecting the spectators from injury could only be met by the richest men, while bird-fighting could be indulged in for very little money. The Nawabs enjoyed these humbler sports too, though they marked their own superiority by owning the greatest number of birds, and the finest specimens. Asaf-ud-daula was particularly fond of cock-fighting, as we have seen, and he was painted by Johann Zoffani in 1786 at a fight arranged for him by his favourite English companion, Colonel John Mordaunt, himself an excellent marksman.[35] Many identifiable figures are shown among the spectators, both European and Indian, and all clearly enjoying the game and the gossip. The portly Nawab, with his fluttering white clothes, gesturing in front of the Colonel, echoes the ruffled plumage of the birds in the arena. This was a subject which the painter knew would appeal to an English audience, not only for its glimpse into the exotic Indian Court, but because of the popularity of the sport at home. Colonel Mordaunt staged his fight in the open air, under a *shamiana* or awning, but there were permanent cock-pits too, like the one in Qaisarbagh, which though much altered, still exhibits the circular arena at ground level and the viewing area above it where spectators could peer down.[36] Cock-fights could last for days rather than hours, with periods of recuperation for the birds. When the weaker bird fell down, blinded or too badly injured to go on, the fight was over.

Quail-fighting, which Asaf-ud-daula and other Nawabs also enjoyed, became as popular as cock-fighting, if not more so, for it required far less room. '. . . nor does one even need to leave one's house to watch a performance,' wrote Sharar. 'One can sit comfortably in a room on a nice clean carpet and watch the fight.' Quails are small, round birds and the 'button quail' though tiny, was a fierce fighter. Nasir-ud-din Haider was fond of watching quail-fighting on a table set before him. Like the fighting cocks, the quails had their beaks pared down with penknives by their trainers, to make them into sharp pointed weapons with which to blind and rip their assailants.

The Nawabi passion for pigeons is easier for us to understand. These pretty birds were brought from all over the Middle East, and Afghanistan, with names like *shirazi* and *peshawari* indicating where they had first been bred. Like bird-fighting, pigeon fancying was a hobby that everyone could enjoy, as long as the Nawabs had the largest and costliest collection. The royal *kabutar kothi*, or pigeon house, stood near the menagerie and park to the north of the Gomti. Part of it was later incorporated into Lucknow University, which now covers the site. Another pigeon house stood in the main Qaisarbagh courtyard, and one can imagine the royal birds fluttering in and out of it, and almost hear their pleasant cooing echoing across the lovely gardens. Unsurprisingly, Nawabi pigeons came in different colours too, sometimes with floral patterns painted on their wings.

The symbol or badge of arms of the Awadh rulers was a pair of fish, an ancient Persian token of royalty. One of the imperial standards at the Mughal Court bore two golden fish swinging from a staff, and it was natural that the Nawabs should adopt this, with its links to Persian and Mughal nobility. The fish motif was ubiquitous throughout Lucknow and appeared on the spandrels of the Qaisarbagh palace gateway, on the silver coins struck by the Nawabs, on their coat of arms, their thrones and their boats. Claude Martin used it on his own coat of arms that he designed for himself, and one of the most beautiful of the Lucknow paintings, by Francesco Renaldi, shows Martin's favourite Indian mistress, Boulone, holding a fishing rod and standing at the edge of a marble pool full of gold and silver fish. Saadat Ali Khan took Viscount Valentia 'to see a small temple he had built in the gardens [of Barowen], over a bason for gold and silver fish. It was circular, and adorned with paintings, in compartments, of the most beautiful fish, copied from a French work.' Saadat Ali Khan, the most westernised of the Nawabs, enjoyed the harmless sport of fishing, and he had three little 'water temples' built in the Gomti, between the Farhat Baksh and the Dilaram Kothi where 'he used to sit . . . in the cool of the evening and fish with rod and line . . .'[37]

The Qaisarbagh palace gardens contained a number of fishy follies like the merman bridge and the mermaid gateway. There were other whimsical little buildings, too, including the pigeon house, the double spiral staircase that always led visitors back to the spot from which they had started, and the Lanka, a bridge built over dry land. The gardens were

6. Gateway at Qaisarbagh, with the
spiral staircase

not generally open to the public, except for a few days a year, but after
Wajid Ali Shah had gone, European and particularly English visitors,
who saw them were full of scorn. Plenty of Westerners described the
Lucknow palaces as 'theatrical', creating an illusion of something unreal,
a stage-set, the 'Vauxhall Gardens of the East', or, in a kinder moment,
something out of the 'Arabian Nights Tales'. By the mid-nineteenth century English tastes had shifted away from the frivolous structures of
their Regency predecessors. The era of the great spa towns like Bath and
Cheltenham, which had attracted a gay, light-hearted society was passing. The real Vauxhall Gardens, on the south bank of the river Thames,
came to an end when a new railway viaduct, one of the first to be erected,
strode brutally across Glasshouse Walk and New Spring Gardens Walk,
a vivid symbol of high Victorian technology trampling the pleasures of
an earlier generation. These changing attitudes were naturally exported
abroad with the increasing immigration from England to India, and what
might have been acceptable a generation earlier was now condemned as
'the most debased examples of architecture to be found in India'. I have
shown, in an earlier book, how European critics invested the Nawabi
palaces with the supposed characteristics of their builders, so they became
'debased', 'wanting in stability', 'all very degenerate' and much else. Such
criticisms were clearly political in motivation, but some of them were
also to do with a new-found appreciation of the 'serious' buildings of the
Victorian age, their great railway stations, their solid factories, their public
libraries and board schools. 'The Age of Illusion' as the late eighteenth
century has been described, was vanishing, and Lucknow, the prime
example in India, was already out of date as the last stucco mermaid was
being gilded.

This makes it all the harder to conjure up the theatrical pleasures that
the Nawabs enjoyed, the temporary structures put up for weddings and
parties, the instant gardens erected overnight, with silver trees and Chinese lanterns, the firework displays across the river, opposite the palace,
which lit up the night sky, the fountains and statues glimpsed through
the trees of the pleasure gardens, or the paper kites flying above the roof
tops. They are as illusory, yet picturesque, as the Frost Fair held on the
frozen Thames. Even the bridge of boats that crossed the Gomti, the
most transient thing imaginable, had its own little battlements and embra-
zures for cannon, like a miniature fort. Fortunately, as changing values
make us shrink today from descriptions of animal fights, so they allow
us now to appreciate the illusions created by the Nawabs, the theatrical

nature of the gaily painted buildings, the stage-sets in fact, from which the Nawabs, with a fine sense of the dramatic, briefly created a fairy-tale world.

Probably the most glittering event in the whole of Nawabi Lucknow was the wedding of Wazir Ali, the son or adopted son of Asaf-ud-daula in 1795. It passed into Lucknow mythology, becoming a yardstick against which every similar occasion was measured (and found wanting), since no one else could match the £300,000 that Asaf-ud-daula had spent during the three nights' celebration. The marriage feast was held in a 'rich and extensive garden', probably beyond the Daulat Khana area where the Nawab's new palace was nearing completion. A procession of about 1,200 elephants set off, some with silver howdahs, and Asaf-ud-daulah 'mounted on an uncommonly large elephant, covered with cloth of gold . . .' On both sides of the roads 'were raised artificial sceneries of bamboo work very high, representing bastions, arches, minarets and towers, covered with lights in lamps, which made a grand and sublime display. . .' Four hundred dancing girls gyrated on platforms held aloft by bearers, and 'all the ground from the tents to the garden was enlaid with fireworks, and at every step the elephants took, the ground burst before us and threw up artificial stars in the heavens'.[38] In the centre of the garden the wedding guests were entertained in a 'grand saloon adorned with innumerable girandoles and pendant lustres of English manufacture, lighted with wax candles'. The garden itself was 'illuminated by innumerable transparent paper lamps or lanterns' hung on the branches of the trees.

Mirza Abu Talib Khan Isfahani, whom we shall meet in another chapter, and who was one of the few Indian critics of Nawabi extravagance, noted dourly that the 'sceneries' were in fact part of a huge artificial fort, 'five miles in circumference, with regular bastions, towers and gateways, [and] was formed with bamboos and covered at night with lamps which required 20,000 men to attend them'.[39] The idea of imitating buildings in canvas over a bamboo frame is not unique to Lucknow, as anyone who has seen the pandals of Calcutta during Durga Puja will realise, but the conception of carrying out a 'fort' of this size is extraordinary, a masterpiece of design, architecture and engineering that has probably never been repeated anywhere in the world. The bridegroom and his party were housed in expensive wedding tents 'made of strong cotton cloth lined with the finest English broad cloth, cut in stripes of different colours', another form of temporary structure.

Unlimited wealth meant that nearly anything was possible. A privileged English guest, Viscount Valentia, described walking between two palaces in the Chattar Manzil area 'through a lane of double silver branches, with attar placed on stands between each'. The whole complex, with its garden basons of water reflecting the coloured lamps hung around them, 'was the splendour of the Caliph Haroun-ul-Rashid, as described in the Arabian Nights Entertainment' although the Nawabi band playing English tunes off-stage must have struck an incongruous note. These enclosed gardens between two of the palaces, long since bisected by a main road, must have been particularly fine. The Nawabs and their guests would sit on the verandah looking out across 'a spacious tank of water, with sparkling *jets d'eau*, ornamented with marble statues, and illuminated by many coloured lamps. The prospect bore a pleasing and fairy-like effect: the faint manner in which the distant colonnades and statues were lighted up reminding me in some degree of the effect produced in the background of Martin's famous picture of Belshazzar's Feast.'[40] We know exactly where this was because a rather poor photograph, about 1856 and probably copied many times over, still exists. In the background is the imposing columned verandah, which had once been the main entrance to Claude Martin's old town house, the Farhat Baksh. The 'spacious tank', empty and dirty, lies in front, the statues, fountains and Chinese lanterns all gone, for by 1852 Wajid Ali Shah had moved into his new palace of Qaisarbagh. Yet how tantalisingly close, less than a decade earlier, had been the vision of fairy land here. Lady Nugent found an astonishing sight across the Gomti one evening: 'The place that was yesterday only a barren waste, was converted into a beautiful garden, filled with flowers, pavilions, temples, bowers, and fountains, all composed of coloured lamps, and different sorts of lights. A beautiful palace was at the end, the pillars and columns of which were formed of spiral lights, continually turning around. As soon as we were seated, there was a great display of fireworks. At intervals, illuminated balloons were sent up, which, by remaining a considerable time in the air after they were at some distance, looked like so many moons.'

Indeed, no festive occasion was complete without a firework display, the most ephemeral of all the arts, and one with a long, though apparently unwritten, history in India. What the Nawabs' dinner guests saw as they crowded onto the palace verandah overlooking the Gomti, were not just ordinary Indian fireworks with the noisy 'patakhas' and sparkling 'phuljaris', but spectacular set-pieces that took days to set up on the banks of the Gomti by engineers and workmen. 'Long rows of human figures and animal forms of various sorts, were burning in magic fire; lofty palaces of wood and paper, shone, burst and were scattered in flames, and, more beautiful than all the rest, rose some twenty or more air balloons, which having shot up to a great height in the air, showered down sheaves and nosegays of fire . . . '[41] This impressive display was in 1845, and it is interesting to compare it with a similar description, by an Englishman, of a Mughal firework party two hundred years earlier to see how the Nawab's engineers were following a well-established tradition.

In front of the Agra palace 'on a Strand by the River side, under the castle wall and the Kinges windowe, there was a place Rayled in, about half a mile in Compasse att least. In it were placed the fireworkes, vizt, first a ranck [row] of great Eliphants, whose bellies were full of squibbs, Crackers, etts. Then a ranck of Gyants with wheeles in their hands, then a ranck of Monsters . . . All theis being fired (although not att one tyme) innumerable were the Rocketts, reports, squibbs, and Crackers that flewe about and aloft in the Ayre, makeinge the night like day. The noyse was as terrible . . . Mee thought it a brave and pleasant shew . . . Here was Cost and Labour enough, but it wanted it may bee the Arte wee have in Europe of those kinde of workes.'[42] A folio in the Padshahnama actually shows the display that Peter Mundy saw in February 1633, with rows of convincing artificial elephants with rockets for tusks, and the 'giants' with fireworks sprouting from their heads. Clearly the Nawabs were recreating, with contemporary technology like the addition of balloons, the great displays of the Emperors, and the Gomti river running below the verandahs of the Chattar Manzil palace became at such times a fair imitation of the Agra and the Yamuna. Firework displays were the proper accompaniment to festive occasions and the British Resident John Monckton reported to Company headquarters in Calcutta that the celebrations of January 1820, marking the first coronation of Ghazi-ud-din Haider, were to include 'the usual things of Presents, Fireworks and Nautch'.[43]

Viewing fireworks from the riverside verandahs with a glass of champagne in one's hand was not only a Nawabi pleasure, but one enjoyed by Europeans too. Claude Martin put on a fine display in 1797 for Sir John Shore before a dinner held in his house of Farhat Baksh. The Governor General's aide-de-camp, George Cornish, reported that 'a very beautiful display of fire works was let off immediately opposite on the bank of the river and in the middle, at the conclusion after the representation of a splendid temple, a boat was placed from whence issued an immense fountain of fire. This country is the Etna of fire works and although these were the finest I ever saw the General [Martin] apologised for them, he had not time for better. He seemed to think them contemptible and told me I should after seeing the display which the Nabob [Asaf-ud-daula] means to give us.'[44]

There were at least two French firework makers in Lucknow at the end of the eighteenth century, Louis Bourquien, a soldier of fortune, who had 'started business as a maker of fireworks, and in this capacity accompanied one Gairard, the proprietor of the Vauxhall Gardens of Calcutta to Lucknow'. Both men had manufactured arms as well as fireworks, for the two products were then more closely related. Gairard was subsequently employed by Claude Martin to organise his own displays outside the Farhat Baksh, and he lived in Lucknow until 1807, working at times for Saadat Ali Khan. Another employee was the civil engineer J. Munro Sinclair, who among his many other duties, organised firework displays for Ghazi-ud-din Haider, and who was rewarded with a *khilat* on one occasion in 1825 for 'exhibiting . . . some artificial Fire Works etc. made to His Majesty's order'. (Sinclair later reported that the value of the *khilat* was almost the same as the cost of the fireworks, a hundred rupees, so he had not actually made a profit out of his labour, though the workmen lent to him by the King had got a hundred rupees to share out between them.[45]) Several different strands had fortuitously come together in Lucknow to create the spectacular firework displays. The Mughal idea of figurative representations (perhaps themselves influenced by the burning of Hindu demonic images) blended with the more romantic European creations of temples, bowers and boats full of sheaves of fiery stars.

'Hawa khana', literally 'to eat the air' is the descriptive Urdu phase for taking a stroll or a ride in the open air, usually in the early morning or the evening. Lucknow has been called the 'City of Gardens', and though some have been lost to encroachment or development, others remain as one of the most enduring of the Nawabs' legacies. Spectators could watch the Nawabs bowling along in their English carriages, with an English footman in attendance, on their way to the gardens to 'eat the air' with their courtiers. The *baghs*, or gardens, were private areas, surrounded by high walls so that the royal ladies, in strict purdah, could not be glimpsed by passers-by. Many of the gardens' names are still used today, even when later buildings have completely swallowed up the original site, like the Charbagh, with its once 'noble gateway embosomed in a wood' and its 'massive folding doors'. Some of the gardens were created by the

Nawabs' ministers, like the Gulab Bari of Amin-ud-daula, Wazir to Amjad Ali Shah, where English rose cuttings were grafted on to the sweet scented Indian variety. Across the river, which by the 1840s had two bridges, the 'Stone' Bridge (really made of brick), and a bridge of boats, lay several extensive gardens and parks. The Ramna Qaisar and Hazaree Bagh, scenes of the animal fights have already been mentioned, and there was also the Nasiree Bagh, which was 'a small garden in the French style, with a summer-house, adorned, or rather overladen, in a very tasteless manner, with articles of glass, china, bad paintings, copper-plates, and all sorts of bagatelles'.

The Nawabs' gardens, like their palaces, reflected the eclectic tastes of their owners, and Lucknow had a number of foreign gardens. In contrast to the French-inspired Nasiree Bagh, Captain Leopold von Orlich found the nearby Padshah Bagh 'a large and beautiful garden, laid out in the English style, and uncommonly delightful. A bason with many fountains intersects the garden in its whole length [but] the effect of the natural beauties of this spot is spoiled by the many painted statues, models of sandstone after the antique, etc. which, by the King's orders, have been daubed with a dirty red colour, and produce a most disagreeable impression. At the furthest end of the garden are two pretty summer houses with marble baths, and vapour baths, connected with a spacious harem, which consists of a quadrangular building, the windows and doors of which are towards the inner court. This edifice is so situated, that the King can see the amusements of the ladies from the colonnade of the palace. . . .'[46] There were formal Persian-inspired gardens where the central axis 'is usually occupied by a marble tank, in which many fountains are playing, and cypresses alternate with roses in embellishing its margin' and gardens 'in the old-fashioned style, full of orange and lime trees, flowering shrubs, and flowers, all the year round, in sucession, except the hot winds; interspersed with statues and vases'.[47] Asaf-ud-daula's first gardens, within the courts of the Macchi Bhawan palace were 'divided into parterres by walls and fountains. Along the side walls runs a corridor, forming one continued arbour of vines, which shades its whole roof.'[48]

There was a pleasant synthesis in the Nawabs' gardens where the symmetrical Mughal layouts echoed the old French parterres, which were still popular in India well into the nineteenth century. The addition of garden statuary, which was not of course Islamic, was probably inspired by Claude Martin's profuse use of classical figures on his buildings and in his own French garden at Constantia. The eighteenth-century English picturesque gardens with their baroque walks and unexpected vistas, popularised by Capability Brown and Humphrey Repton, were much harder to create in India, with its extremes of climate, and perhaps there was an unspoken idea that this kind of soft, romantic landscape would not convey the right impression for the Company's stern men of duty. True, some British officers, who had been given the Charbagh by Wajid Ali Shah had planted some fruit trees, and made it into a pleasant orchard, but it was the Nawabs who ordered the fantasy gardens and landscapes, two of which must have been particularly charming and imaginative. Near the Dilkusha palace was a short-lived 'English' village of which only the ruins of some mud-huts remained by 1827 and at the Daulat Khana palace there was a Chinese garden, whose tall pagoda was still visible in 1858, similar to the one in Kew Gardens. There were a number of Chinese men at the Lucknow Court; twenty-four were recorded among the Nawab's staff in 1831, and it is tempting to think they may have built the pagoda, at the height of the European craze for Chinoiserie.[49]

Of the flowers themselves, apart from the roses, we can be fairly certain they included sweet scented bushes like rat-ki-rani (queen of the night), jasmine, frangipani, and the ubiquitous poinsettias, marshalled into line by the *malis*. Dr Nathaniel Wallich, the Danish superintendent of the Calcutta Botanic Garden had sent some rare plants up for the King in 1826, but we do not know what they were. A well-meaning attempt by the Resident to get Mr Mitchell, an English botanist, to instruct the King's gardeners foundered after a few months when the botanist left, though other Englishmen were put in charge of the royal gardens by Nasir-ud-din Haider. Their role however was more nominal and these 'superintendents' were not expected to get their hands dirty, anymore than the Nawabs would have been found weeding a flower bed.

Photographs show the Qaisarbagh gardens probably much as the last King had left them, and confirm the description of a newspaper reporter who had got in during the annual fair when Wajid Ali Shah opened the main area to the public for a few days. 'The garden is tastefully laid out with marble statues, arranged in curiously outré groupings, Venus and Cupid and in juxtaposition an English cow, not a bad specimen of the statuary's skill. Then we witness a magnificent marble reservoir where gold and silver fishes disport undisturbed, also fountains of marble which play unceasingly.' Also here was a *barahdari*, a light, open building where musicians and dancers could perform, and a beautiful Mughal inspired marble pavilion. (This was subsequently dismantled by the British and re-erected in Banarsi Bagh where it has recently been nicely restored.)

The Nawabs were quick to realise the potential of steam engines, then being built in England, for their pleasure gardens. In 1812 Saadat Ali Khan wanted a steam engine capable of raising water to a height of 24 feet from the Gomti 'to water his road and grounds during the dry season, to fill Reservoirs for Artificial fountains and such other private purposes', and this was ordered from Birmingham.[50] Unfortunately it did not arrive until after the Nawab's death, because it was part of a larger commission that included the Iron Bridge, designed by John Rennie, and the hiring of four English engineers who were sent out with it, but by the early 1820s there were a number of Nawabi-owned steam engines operating. J.M. Sinclair, who had arranged the firework displays was an invaluable man, not only a civil engineer and architect (when the two professions were often interchangeable), but also a man 'who is perfectly acquainted with the Mechanism of the Steam Engine, having lately erected several with Machines of all kinds attached'. He had spent much of his working life in India, where his father, uncles and brother were employed by the East India Company, spoke fluent Hindustani, and had been personally recommended to Ghazi-ud-din Haider by the Marquess of Hastings. Sinclair kept himself abreast of mechanical innovations and had 'been in correspondence with the most eminent Engineers of the day during the period of his employment with the King of Oude'. He had bought, on the King's orders a 'two-horse steam engine manufactured by Butterly & Co' and a number of other steam engines, machines and engine boilers during 1822 and 1826.[51]

Some of the first steam engines in India had been imported into Lucknow by Claude Martin, who had ordered them from the Birmingham factory of Matthew Boulton and James Watt. Although there were initial difficulties in setting them up (which is why the manufacturers preferred to send their engineers out to accompany an order), one or more engines were certainly working before 1800, raising and pumping out the water at Martin's riverside home. When the Chattar Manzil palace was taken over by the Company after annexation, steam engines were found that had powered the fountains in the marble tank. To meet the new demand for technical information, an English clergyman, the Reverend Perkins had translated a 'Treatise on the Steam Engine' into Urdu, under the title *Bahr-i-hikmat*, which was published in Lucknow in 1847.

The arrival of these engines in Lucknow led not only to increased water supplies and numerous tinkling fountains in the walled gardens but also to the development of steam-powered pleasure boats that chugged up and down the Gomti, bearing the Nawabs and their friends. Standing today on the banks of the silent and deserted river, it is difficult to imagine the scenes of merriment and splendour it has witnessed, to catch an echo of the music that came from the European bands, playing in the palace gardens that ran down to the water, or a whiff of acrid smoke that drifted across from the firework parties. 'The river exhibited a scene of uncommon activity, traffic boats, small barks, and fishing boats, were rowing backwards and forwards; the King's gondola, adorned the forepart with two horses leaping from the jaws of a fish was steering to the Dilkusha Park, in case it might be His Majesty's pleasure to come back by water.'[52] Like the river Thames that was once the most important thoroughfare in London, the Gomti has dwindled in importance to a mere division between north and south Lucknow. It was possible, earlier this century, to take a boat up river from the eastern palace of Dilkusha to the western palace of Barowen, passing en route many of the major buildings, but boat owners cannot be persuaded to make this journey today. Lucknow has always been subject to monsoon flooding, which was only alleviated by the erection of flood bunds in the 1960s, but this did not stop people from building near, or even in, the river. Some structures had their own water gates on to the Gomti, like the Shah Najaf, the Farhat Baksh, the Dilaram and Barowen, so that the Nawabs could make a grand entrance from their boats.

The Nawabs' state barges and pleasure boats get almost no mention in contemporary descriptions of the city or by present-day historians. Yet they were extraordinary creations, perhaps the most imaginative works from the city's craftsmen, rivalled only by the temporary buildings and tableaux in the palace gardens. Fantastic prows, beautifully carved and painted, decorated the boats. Asaf-ud-daula's barge, the *moh punkee*, or 'rowing boat' had a prow of gigantic gilded peacocks, whose tails fanned out around the body of the boat. A flat-bottomed, punt-like boat upon whose narrow deck dancing girls and musicians performed, had an elephant's head and tusks. But the most eye-catching of all was a series of 'fish-boats', vessels that were actually designed to look like fish. Robert Home, the artist at the Court of Ghazi-ud-din Haider wrote in December 1816 that he had been busy 'finishing a model of a Boat three feet long in the shape of a fish, and painting it from nature and manning it . . .' The next month he told his daughter that 'I am now turned Boat Builder. You must know that a particular fish is the principal figure in His Excelly's [*sic*] Coat of Arms. And boats and the sailing on the river His principal amusement. So that my model'of the boat, the exact figure of this fish, pleased him so much that he has desired me to make a large one like it, 37 feet long without its tail, and 2 feet broad.' At the same time, Home was designing another boat for the Nawab in the shape of a swan, which must have been commissioned as a gift for 'His Excellency as yet, I believe knows nothing of the Swan and I expect it will be an agreeable surprize to him'. In January 1818 both boats were launched and Home admitted they gave 'great satisfaction in every respect. I have succeeded beyond my expectations,' he wrote.[53] Home's fish boat, painted from nature, may be the one that appears in Captain Robert Smith's panorama of Lucknow, sketched in 1832. One of the drawings, made near the Stone Bridge, shows a curved fish, its head the prow, its tail the stern, and four pairs of oars poking surreally out through the gills.[54] At any rate, Ghazi-ud-din Haider was so pleased that he appointed Home as 'head of the Board of Works' and the artist was subsequently commissioned to make a carriage, with 'a Fish for the body, similar to the boat' as well as 'A Howdah that is to be on springs . . .'

It may have been J.M. Sinclair the engineer, working with Robert Home who first suggested placing a steam engine inside one of the fish boats to produce a mechanical curiosity that would amuse the King.

7. The King's 'Fish Boat', redrawn from Capt. Robert Smith's
panorama of Lucknow, 1832

Major Archer, who was attending Viscount Combermere on a visit to Lucknow in 1819 spotted an early example in the Daulat Khana area: 'a small boat, in the shape of a fish, with a steam-engine, went backwards and forwards before the palace.' Bishop Heber saw 'a steam boat, a vessel fitted up like a brig of war and other things which show the King [Ghazi-ud-din Haider] to be fond of mechanical inventions' in 1826. The British Resident borrowed one of the King's 'steam vessels' in 1831 'to make an evening excursion on the Gomti' with Nasir-ud-din Haider, when a band of musicians were playing under the palace of the Shah Manzil. The Russian Prince Saltuikov found another boat shaped like a fish swimming around on the large artificial lake near the Daulat Khana, surrounded by stone steps and grotesque statues: 'Sur cet étang, étrangement découpé, circule un bateau à roues qui a la forme d'un poisson gigantesque.' A photograph of 1858 shows the last fish boat, an extraordinary submarine-shaped vessel with a snub nose, fins and a tail, almost like a small plane without wings. It appears to be covered in wickerwork, over a wooden frame, which gives it a proper, scaley appearance.

There were more conventional boats on the Gomti as well as these queer fish. Nasir-ud-din Haider chose an English-made pinnace, which was fitted up for him by George Derusett, the 'Barber of Lucknow' as we shall see, and there were other beautiful pleasure boats, skiffs and budgerows. How the Nawabs would have enjoyed steam-driven trains too, perhaps commissioning their own fish engines and carriages, but unfortunately railways were generally undeveloped in India until after 1857, when the exiled King no longer had unlimited funds nor his own land to lay down a track.

Whether the building of palaces and religious edifices can be seen as an 'entertainment' is a debatable point. Certainly the word 'Lucknow' conjures up a city almost entirely created by the Nawabs, but was this done by them out of duty, need or pleasure? This is not the place for a long analysis of why the Nawabs built as they did, which has been covered in my earlier book, but to find out what enjoyment they may have derived from doing so. Asaf-ud-daula, the collector, and a man 'who could never bear to hear that any person possessed any thing superior to his own' is said to have wanted a replica of every famous building in the world in his new capital. 'For this purpose, he always inquired after what was considered as splendid in other countries,' reported Viscount Valentia. Thus the 'Stone' Bridge over the Gomti was thought to resemble one crossing the Seine at Paris, and the famous Rumi Darwaza, the Roman/Turkish Gate, was supposed to imitate a doorway at Constantinople. The Nawab was however dissuaded from adding a replica of the East India Company's Calcutta military headquarters, Fort William, to his brick menagerie. Abu Talib, his sternest critic, complained of the Nawab's expenditure on his 'pigeon-houses, cockpits, sheep-folds, deer park, monkey, snake, scorpion and spider houses' while his father's relatives went hungry, and claimed that the ruler was spending ten lakhs a year to satisfy his 'building mania'. Certainly no sooner had Asaf-ud-daula embellished the Macchi Bhawan fort to his liking than he began building an entirely new palace, the Daulat Khana, while at the same time erecting the majestic Bara Imambara, which became his last resting place. An architectural competition was held for the design of this Imambara, the winner being Kifayat Ullah, and one imagines the Nawab scrutinising the plans and then choosing the largest and most expensive proposal.

His brother, Saadat Ali Khan was an amateur architect, when the word amateur did not have the derogatory meaning that it does today, and of all the Nawabs, he is the one we can say with certainty, derived the greatest pleasure from his hobby. 'Building is his favourite amusement,' explained Viscount Valentia. 'He ever lived much with the English [and] it has greatly improved his manners and given him his liking for English building vide his different palaces.' His aide-de-camp and riding companion Gore Ouseley confirmed that 'he has a taste for drawing, he is a very good architect: he has a very good taste as to ornaments in houses: he builds palaces with very great taste.' The artist Henry Salt noted that 'His Highness is particularly fond of building, but instead of following the models of Hindostan he prefers the architecture of Europe'. John Baillie, the British Resident reported in 1813 that the Nawab had been 'exhibiting designs for new palaces and decorations of rooms, the execution of which had commenced, and the completion of which, if intended, must occupy and serve to amuse him for a period of several years'. Viscount Valentia was taken to see Barowen, which was built by the Nawab 'after a plan of his own. The architecture is an imitation of Grecian, with many faults, yet a very fine portico, rising the whole height of the house, gives a considerable degree of grandeur to the front. It is a vast pile, but contains only one large room on each floor.'[55]

The true authorship of the now ruined palace of Barowen has long been a mystery, but there have always been rumours of a connection with Claude Martin, who was, among many other things, an architect. Perhaps Major Newell was correct when he claimed in 1916 that the site, known also today as Musa Bagh, 'was originally laid out as a garden by Asaf-ud-daula. The house [Barowen] was added by his half-brother,

Saadat Ali Khan from designs furnished by General Claude Martin who modelled it on the lines of an English manor.'[56] It would be nice to think that there was indeed a brief but fruitful collaboration between these two gifted men, cut short by Martin's death in September 1800. Both were foreigners and anglophiles, both were interested in the new technology coming at that time from England, both were connoisseurs and collectors of fine paintings and both were imaginative architects. If Martin had indeed provided the initial designs (so far no confirmation has been found among his correspondence), then the Nawab's own contribution and enthusiasm must have been considerable. The palace of Barowen was described as 'precisely after the English style, and may be said, perhaps, to be the only facsimile of an English mansion on the plains of Hindustan . . .'[57] There is something touching about an English house, designed by a Frenchman and a man of Persian descent, in an Indian city, which makes the wilful destruction of this supposedly 'protected monument' all the more sad.

Other buildings by Saadat Ali Khan that have survived include the Nur Baksh Kothi in Hazratganj, now the Deputy Commissioner's House, the only remaining house of several built here by the Nawab for his sons. Hazratganj itself was laid down by Saadat Ali Khan to connect his palace of Dilkusha with the city palaces, a processional route lined with his own buildings, and originally barred at either end by two imposing gateways, half Grecian, and half 'Moorish' that turned the area into an exclusive royal enclave.

None of the later Nawabs of Awadh showed the same architectural skill as Saadat Ali Khan, although each one commissioned further buildings to adorn the city, and Wajid Ali Shah added the last great palace complex of Qaisarbagh, which took only four years to complete (from 1848 to 1852), and which rivalled Versailles in size. Strangely, Nasir-ud-din Haider, the most frivolous, and many would say, the most dissipated of all the Awadh monarchs, received a postal packet from England in November 1836 containing 'a Diploma enrolling the King of Oude as a Member of the British Society of Architects signed by Earl de Grey and other packets . . . of two pamphlets on architecture'.[58] Because Nasir-ud-din Haider's ten years reign was conspicuous by his *lack* of building, this seems curious at first, but a little detective work reveals that this was a 'reward' for his finally completing the Lucknow Observatory, named the Taronwali Kothi, or House of Stars, which was pressed on him, with much cajoling, by the East India Company, which wanted an observatory and meteorological office in northern India but didn't want to pay for it.

8. Roshen-ud-daula Katcheri, Qaisarbagh

The harshest criticism by English writers of Lucknow's unique style of architecture came after the annexation and the uprising of 1857, for the majority of visitors before then had usually conceded that its palaces and religious buildings were impressive, if only because of their size and extent, even though other parts of the city left a lot to be desired. But none could appreciate the Nawabi love of decoration that extended to the exteriors of their buildings. 'One of the fancies of the King [Amjad Ali Shah]', sniffed Captain von Orlich, 'consists in having all the houses of the city painted white, or in colours, and covered with scenes of Indian life.' Another sarcastic European, Dr Hoffmeister, noted an enormous building, one of the royal zenanas, with blank walls: 'Something however being necessary to break the dismal monotony of the solid masonry, each niche intended for a window was, with truly Oriental bad taste, filled up with figures as large as life representing men of every age and every rank, painted *al fresco* in the most gaudy colours.' Prince Saltuikov, the most sympathetic of the visitors found that the same Nawab had murals of his favourite servants painted on a garden screen in the palace.

The public rooms of the palaces, as one would expect, were richly furnished, often in the English style, with gilt chairs, chaises longues, dining tables, swagged velvet curtains and a profusion of chandeliers and girandoles. Between the large gilded mirrors hung on the walls were English and French paintings, a radical innovation from a traditional

Muslim house with its chaste calligraphic pictures. Some of the furniture had been specially commissioned by the Nawabs from England,
and other pieces were bought from English people on their departure
from India. One of the Residents, T.H. Maddock, sought permission
from the Company to sell his household furniture, plate, carriages, horses,
camp and state equipage, wines and stores, etc. to Nasir-ud-din Haider
for Rs 98,423, and knowing his anglophilia, almost certainly succeeded.[59]
But these were domestic matters compared to the mania for collecting
curiosities, particularly anything mechanical, which became so notorious
that Europeans would travel to Lucknow especially to sell novelties to
the Nawabs. How many clockwork mice and jack-in-the-box and mechanical singing birds, and weather-vanes, and toy sailing boats and rocking
horses found their way to Court one can only imagine. Daniel Johnson
reported that 'The greater part of [Asaf-ud-daula's] time being occupied
with trifles and trifling amusements . . . he was most delighted with two
pieces of mechanism—two boys, one beating a drum, and the other
playing a tune on a fife', and that he possessed 'some of the finest pieces
of mechanism ever made by man'.

It is no surprise that Asaf-ud-daula's 'museum', which was housed in
the Aina Khana, in his new palace of Daulat Khana, contained the largest,
and most expensive collection of objects ever assembled together in
Lucknow. It was only rivalled by the Farhat Baksh museum of Claude
Martin, who matched the Nawab in acquisitiveness, but outdid him in
taste. While Martin's collection was that of a discerning eighteenth-century connoisseur, Asaf-ud-daula's was a glorious hotch-potch of anything that took his fancy during the twenty-two years of his reign. The
Aina Khana, or Mirror Glass House contained 'English objects of all
kinds—watches, pistols, guns, glassware, furniture, philosophical machines [scientific instruments], all crowded together with the confusion
of a lumber room'. A gold *taziya* which had cost over a hundred gold
mohurs was exhibited there, together with all sorts of jewels, clocks and
watches made by Cox & Co of London. 'A valuable chronometer, or one
which had been sold as such, would be suspended next to a common
watch of the most ordinary description, and which, indeed, had possibly
cost the Nabob as much as the chronometer. Both toys, having equally
amused and deluded the Nabob for a few minutes, were consigned to
this cabinet never perhaps to be seen again' wrote Thomas Twining. The
Nawab 'is absurdly extravagant and ridiculously curious; he has no taste
and less judgement', complained one visitor. 'I have seen him more
amused with a titotum [a spinning top] than with electrical experiments,

but he is nevertheless extremely solicitous to possess all that is elegant and rare; he has every instrument and every machine, of every art and every science, but he knows none.'[60]

This fascination with mechanical toys, models, and indeed anything man-made that could move, was common to most of the Nawabs. Among the items on J.M. Sinclair's shopping list when he went to Calcutta for Ghazi-ud-din Haider were 'toys', telescopes, a 'model of a Water Wheel' and magic lantern screens for the transparencies collected by his father.[61] The ingenious Robert Home reported in January 1818 that he had 'begun a building for Panoramas that are yet to be painted, the centre Temple of which, where he [Ghazi-ud-din Haider] and the spectators are to be, is to turn round by Machinery to save him the trouble of looking behind him. For he must be seated, and all others stand, so that his seat must be raised to place his eyes on a level with the standers' eyes.' The artist was busy painting 'two large transparent pictures, ships at sea, and a ship on fire'.[62] Home was working on the building with an 'English architect', who is not named, but was probably James Lock, newly appointed by the Nawab 'to superintend certain improvements intended to be made in the Neighbourhood of the Palace of Farrah Buksh'.[63] The long-vanished Panorama House, unique in India, may well have been one of the 'improvements', suggested by Home at the Board of Works and designed to impress the Nawab's guests at his forthcoming coronation.[64]

It was Home too who introduced the first gas-lit lamps into Lucknow, at a time when experiments with gas and electricity were regarded as entertaining tricks, rather than potential sources of heat and light. '. . . I have commissioned Bazett to send me out a small portable gas apparatus . . . It consists of three distinct apparatus, a furnace, a purifier and a gasometer or reservoir. I wish for it to amuse His Excelly [sic] and would therefore like it to be neat, and so made that I could easily put it together for use . . . add a pretty chandelier or two, the tubes can be made here to convey the gas; we shall only want the stop-cocks necessary.'[65]

A visitor to the Hussainabad Imambara in the 1850s found, to his surprise 'two wooden figures, which when the pipes that supply the water are worked, move in unison with the pumps, and have quite the appearance of working the machinery'.[66] More entertainment was provided by hot-air balloons, which had first been introduced into Lucknow by Claude Martin, who built them to amuse Asaf-ud-daula. Fifty years later, his great nephew Nasir-ud-din Haider was equally delighted by a mysterious English gentleman who floated past the Dilkusha Palace in a balloon which he had commissioned. 'The king was sitting at the window in the upper story of the Dilkusha house, with some English gentlemen when the balloon passed up close by, and the gentleman took off his hat and bowed gracefully as he passed . . . the king seemed much pleased' and ordered Raja Bakhtawar Singh, one of his officers, to chase after the balloonist and bring him back safely to receive his payment.[67]

Critics and commentators of the Nawabs have naturally tended to dwell on colourful episodes like this, and indeed a lot of the Nawabs' spare time was spent on frivolous, expensive and cruel amusements, like the staged animal fights. Their fascination with machinery and mechanical instruments was genuine, although the innovative technology coming from England at that time was ultimately used only to provide further palace entertainments and not to benefit the citizens of Lucknow. But this does not mean that the Nawabs neglected to meet the expectations of their subjects, nor to fulfil the obligations of a Muslim ruler. Indeed, the grander the palaces, and the more extravagant his way of life, the more powerful the King was seen to be. Authority, especially in India, was intimately associated with pomp, lavish buildings and huge retinues. With the fall of Delhi to the East India Company in 1803, many of the people who had worked at the Mughal Court travelled to Lucknow, and this in turn reinforced the Nawabs' claims as the natural successors to the Delhi kingdom. It was part of a monarch's duty to provide patronage for artists, craftsmen, poets, dancers, musicians, calligraphers, jewellers and even courtesans who were attracted to his Court, not only from other parts of India but from the Middle East, China, and Europe too. Lucknow's rich cultural life, sponsored by the Nawabs, provided an alluring atmosphere where literature, poetry, music and dance could flourish. But its contribution to the visual arts should not be neglected either.

Among Asaf-ud-daula's vast and jumbled Aina Khana visitors had noticed 'the elegant paintings of a Lorrane [Claude Lorraine] or a Zophani', hung promiscuously between paper lanterns and cuckoo clocks. Although artists like Johann Zoffani, William Hodges, Ozias Humphry and the Daniells, have been classed as 'Company painters', a term coined by the art historian Mildred Archer, and indeed at first a useful way of categorising these previously undervalued painters, it is time to move on and see their temporary employment at the Lucknow Court from the Nawabs' point of view. These adventurous westerners were not employed by the East India Company, though they did have to obtain permission from the Company to travel into Awadh, and usually came armed with recommendations from important Company officials. Once they got an entrée into the Court, it was up to them to flatter the Nawabs and their officials into sitting for their portraits, and there is no doubt that the Nawabs found this a particularly gratifying experience, from the number of paintings that still remain. No one has yet attempted a catalogue raisonné of portraits of the Nawabs, so we do not know how many exist, and just as importantly, how many have been destroyed. Previously unknown portraits pass briefly through the auction houses of London and New York, then disappear again into private collections. But perhaps we can begin to estimate the importance of portraiture to the Nawabs from written, if not visual, records.

A painted image of the monarch was equivalent to today's signed photograph of royalty—it conveyed an intimate mark of favour on the recipient, whose own *izzat* was enhanced by the gift. 'As a mark of particular favour' Ghazi-ud-din Haider gave Joseph Quieros, an old employee who had once worked for Claude Martin, 'a fine oil painting of himself done by the Royal Court painter Robert Home, Esq'. This painting was however, returned by Joseph Quieros' son, on the old man's death in 1822, for he had willed that 'the said painting may be returned to his Majesty the King of Oudh with a communication on my part expressive of the very high Estimation in which I ever held it and my grateful sense of the many favours which he was graciously pleased to confer on me during the period I had the pleasure of being in his service . . .'[68] Home also painted miniatures of the King, which would be given as *nazr* to distinguished visitors to the Court. Similarly Sir John Shore (later Lord Teignmouth) came away from a visit in 1797 with a beautiful portrait of Asaf-ud-daula by Zoffani, that he had seen in the Aina Khana 'as a memorial of his friendship'. Rather ungraciously Shore then added that it was *not* set in diamonds but it bore 'a strong resemblance to the Nabob; and for which, to say the truth, I would not give two-pence'.[69] Europeans who entered the royal service like the engineer Lieutenant Crommelin and the surgeon William Stevenson, whom we shall meet again, got the King's miniature, 'set with jewels' to be worn on the breast like a decoration at the compulsory *darbar* attendances.

Ozias Humphry described his first meeting with Asaf-ud-daula on 8 April 1786: the Nawab hospitably rose to embrace the foreigner, who was introduced by the Resident of the time, Colonel Harper. Humphry brought out a little painting of his own patron, Sir John Macpherson 'which was the first time His Highness had ever seen a miniature from Europe.' Two days later the Nawab sat for Humphry for forty minutes

'without any apparent impatience', and the following week there was
another sitting and a discussion on 'the merits of European art'. Mirza
Sulaiman Shikuh, the Mughal Prince who had taken refuge at Lucknow,
also sat for his portrait on the *masnad*, while reading in English a poem
translated from the Persian.[70] During Humphry's visit to Lucknow there
were three other European artists present, Thomas Longcroft, Charles
Smith and Johann Zoffani, the latter working on 'Colonel Mordaunt's
Cock Fight', which was sold to the Nawab. The artist subsequently produced a second version which was bought by Warren Hastings, and is
now in the Tate Gallery in London.

The Nawabs were painted by Indian artists too, but interestingly the
majority of these portraits are clearly influenced by the sitters' contacts
with western art and artists. The traditional Mughal style of portraiture
seems to have dropped out of favour by the end of the eighteenth century.
The medium had changed too, and oils on canvas were adopted by native
painters, like Muhammed Azam, who produced two remarkable portraits
of Ghazi-ud-din Haider and Nasir-ud-din Haider perhaps based on lost
works by the English Court artists, but nevertheless, pictures full of
character.[71] Although completely western in style, Muhammed Azam
could not, or perhaps dare not, resist painting a faint nimbus around
both crowned heads, a reminder of the haloes encircling the Mughal
emperors, to show their status.

Although styles had changed, the importance of the group painting,
showing the Nawab at the centre of an admiring throng had not, as a
number of surviving pictures by Indian artists demonstrate. Ghazi-ud-
din Haider is shown at a splendid table with the Resident Major Baillie,
and at a banquet with the Marquess of Hastings and his wife, hemmed
in by a jostling crowd of courtiers and Company officials. Nasir-ud-din
Haider is at a troop parade near Constantia, dressed in uniform and riding a sprightly horse. He is pictured at a more modest meal, warmly
pressing the hand of a smirking Englishman, who could conceivably be
George Derusett, his one-time favourite. Wajid Ali Shah is seen fondly
embracing the Governor General Lord Hardinge on the latter's visit in
1847, a scene likely to have taken place in the Chattar Manzil. One imagines the Court artists standing by as the Nawabs sat down to enjoy a
good meal, and scurrying about with sketch pads to get the best angle,
for what was clearly the predecessor of today's restaurant photograph.
In a series of lost pictures before 1805, the English Court artist George
Place was commissioned to paint Saadat Ali Khan, his courtiers, and his
palaces, though when Place chose to put the Resident in one of the

Court scenes, the Nawab stopped him, because he had fallen out with William Scott. It is possible that a surviving equestrian portrait of this Nawab (in the Oriental & India Office Collections) is a copy by an Indian artist of one of Place's lost paintings. Some of Saadat Ali Khan's staff were employed in collecting and copying pictures and Viscount Valentia found portraits of the Nawab's favourite English friends and English officers decorating the walls of Barowen. When the Marquess of Hastings visited the newly completed Khurshid Manzil, based on a miniature European castle, complete with moat and tiny drawbridge, he was flattered to find his own portrait artlessly hung in the principal room, opposite that of Madamoiselle Parisot, copied from a French print.

George Place was working in Lucknow during the reign of Saadat Ali Khan, with Charles Smith and Thomas Longcroft who had established themselves there during his brother's time. None of the three men were formally employed by the Nawab, but each received commissions from him and from other wealthy men which enabled them to earn a good living. Place got between £5,000 and £6,000 for a single portrait of the Nawab, which was negotiated through Gore Ouseley. Robert Home, whom we have already met, had painted Saadat Ali Khan in Calcutta, at his Garden Reach home. 'I had a great liking for that man', Home wrote 'a fluent English speaker . . . ' One of the artist's first tasks on arriving in Lucknow in 1816 was to complete a huge painting of the Lucknow *darbar* of the late Nawab (who had died the previous year) and which had been started, but not finished, by George Place. It depicted the Nawab's ministers, his European attendants and 'personages of note' in Lucknow. A similar painting was begun of the first *darbar* held after Ghazi-ud-din Haider's coronation in 1819, but this dragged on for several years as ministers and attendants were dismissed or appointed and had to be painted in, or out, depending on the royal favour. When the new British Resident, John Monckton, was appointed, Home grumbled that if *his* portrait was to be included, then someone else's would have to be rubbed out to make room.[72] Important guests at Court including Sir Edward Paget and Bishop Heber were sent along by Ghazi-ud-din Haider to Home's studio to be captured in oils, as a memento of their visit. Home painted numerous portraits of the Nawab, many now destroyed or untraceable today, but one that survives shows the new King shortly after his coronation, a shimmering figure in cloth of gold, ermine and silk velvet, laden with jewels.[73] The artist retired in 1828, a year after his patron's death, on the pretext of failing eye-sight, though he continued to paint in retirement in Cawnpore until his death in 1834. Nasir-ud-din

Haider, the next King and possibly the vainest, was thus without a European Court artist for much of his reign.

George Duncan Beechey was the son of Sir William Beechey, portrait painter to George III and Queen Charlotte. The English King was godfather to George Duncan, who learnt his craft at his father's'side, but who then, perhaps wishing to move out of his father's shadow, arrived in Calcutta in 1826. There he met the French landscape artist A. Dufay de Casanova, described as 'a person who draws views', who went to Lucknow and was working for the King by 1832. George Duncan Beechey followed him three years later and became official portrait painter to the last four Kings of Awadh. He lived in Lucknow for the rest of his life, with his Indian lady Houssiana Begum and two other consorts. The loss of the majority of Beechey's paintings at sea in 1851 is particularly sad because it included portraits not only of the Kings, and Wajid Ali Shah as a young man, but of the royal ladies too. One bright young thing insisted on being painted as Cleopatra, and although this particular portrait survived and was given to W.H. Russell, the Irish journalist, during the sack of Qaisarbagh, it was subsequently lost.[74] Beechey was a valued artist, who received a monthly salary of Rs 1,300, and who was promised Rs 10,000 for each portrait he completed of his first patron Nasir-ud-din Haider. Beechey set up his studio in the British Residency and the King used to enjoy talking to him while he worked. Beechey's august family connections would have given him considerable status, for the Awadh Kings were keenly interested in the English royal family, especially when flattering comparisons were made between the two Houses. A large oil painting by Casanova, who had temporarily abandoned his 'views', was among Nasir-ud-din Haider's gifts to William IV and Queen Adelaide. It depicted a meeting between the Awadh King and the British Resident Colonel John Low, though presumably before the two had fallen out over the King's drinking habits.

A fine bronze bust of Nasir-ud-din Haider exists, made by an unknown European sculptor, but this is the only three-dimensional Nawabi portrait, although figurative marble and plaster statues were immensely popular. The Nawabs also developed a taste for allegorical paintings from Greek and Roman mythology, of the kind that decorated grand country houses in Europe, and Robert Home wrote in 1816 that he was painting two life-sized portraits of four of Ghazi-ud-din Haider's wrestlers 'two in the character of Hercules and Achelaus, the other two Hercules and Antaeus'. The useful Mr Sinclair was further ordered to provide an oil painting of Zeus in 1823. I recently found two curious souvenirs of this fancy in the unlikely setting of the Royal Engineers Officers' Mess at Chatham in Kent; a pair of 'classical' paintings of naked cherubs, scantily dressed men with antique bronze helmets and women in Grecian robes, which had come from the throne room of the Qaisarbagh palace in 1858 and which were presented to Sir Colin Campbell, the officer who led the recapture of Lucknow, and who in turn presented them to Chatham.

There were some paintings which could not be hung on the walls. Asaf-ud-daula's remarkable collection of illustrated Mughal manuscripts were described as being 'preserved in large port-folios'. These included the spectacular Padshahnama, which the Nawab had generously pressed on Sir John Shore during his visit, as well as the Zoffani portrait already noted. Although Shore would not take the manuscript for himself, he thought it would be an acceptable gift for the Royal Library of George III, and it was delivered, with five other illustrated manuscripts in 1799, after the Nawab's death. Asaf-ud-daula was said to have paid the equivalent of £1,500 for the Padshahnama, and it is tempting to think that some of the scenes depicted in it with such detail may have inspired him to recreate a second Agra in his new capital.

If Saadat Ali Khan had been the most visually talented of the Nawabs, with his architectural skills, then Wajid Ali Shah, the last King, was the most literary and musical member of the dynasty. In a city full of poets, and poetry recitations, both sacred and secular, the King was considered a gifted writer, working under the *takhallus*, or pen-name of Akhtar (Star). The English writer John Pemble has said that 'If he had not been such an unsuccessful king Wajid Ali Shah might have been remembered as a successful man of letters. Literature and music were the ruling passions of his life and his talent as a writer was real.'[75] Appreciation of the written word was one of the attributes expected of a prince, and it was a royal prerogative and indeed a duty to encourage writers, commission histories, and establish libraries. (There is a touching picture of Asaf-ud-daula teaching one of his young sons to write Arabic and Persian words.) The Nawabs were themselves entertained by professional performers who practised the lost art of *dastan goi* (story-telling), and who knew the trick of painting vivid pictures in the air, with tales from the old Persian classics like the *Bagh-o-Bahar*, or Saadi's *Gulistan*, which was a particular favourite of Saadat Ali Khan. They were briefed on current events by their *harkaras* (news messengers) and spies, but amused by extracts from the gossipy English papers published in Calcutta.

Asaf-ud-daula's *kitab khana*, or library, which was housed in the Daulat

Khana, attracted only the very modest sum of Rs 2,000 for its upkeep during the year after his death, and it was not until 1835 that we hear of it again, when it had become 'very extensive and valuable . . . both Oriental and English'. An Englishman, Edward Cropley, was appointed as librarian, and dismissed within a year, wreaking a slow but terrible revenge, as we shall see later. After this episode the third King of Awadh, Muhammad Ali Shah ordered that 'all the Books, English, French and Persian, purchased from time to time by his predecessors, to be collected and assorted with the view to form a Library for the convenience of those, without distinction, who may be disposed to frequent it, and that he [the King] has appointed a French Gentleman of the name of Fortier who at one time was on the personal staff of the late King [Nasir-ud-din Haider] to be the librarian'.[76]

Ten years later the library had been split into three different collections, and the best books and manuscripts housed in an 'out office of the Motee Mahall Palace'. The largest part of the library, containing more than 6,000 books, was housed in the Tope Khana, the arsenal near the British Residency, which was 'an extensive building including a large square which is filled with guns'. Not surprisingly the books were subsequently found to be in poor condition, stored upstairs in the north wing of the arsenal, above dusty rooms filled with old military supplies. The third library, of 300 books, was in the Farhat Baksh palace, collected there by Amjad Ali Shah. Aloys Sprenger, who had been sent to Lucknow by the East India Company, published *A Catalogue of the Arabic, Persian and Hindustani Manuscripts of the King of Oudh* in 1854 and found, to his sorrow, that though there were many unique volumes in the collections, they were in a bad state. The only job of the 'librarian' had been to count the books, not catalogue them, and it was clear that some valuable volumes had been misappropriated and replaced with worthless ones. Many manuscripts were in 'Chogatay (the mother of the present Turkish or Ottemanly)' which had been studied in the Delhi Court up to the time of Aurangzeb and which may have come into the collection at the same time as the Padshahnama.[77] Of the French and English books we know little, though it is possible that these included some of the 5,000 odd volumes from Claude Martin's own eclectic library, which was auctioned on his death. Sprenger found that several books had been translated from English to Persian, for Ghazi-ud-din Haider, and that his physician, Dr Gibson, used to amuse him with stories from English books, including Quain's *Elements of Anatomy* and other medical books. The books were magnificently embellished with the royal coat of arms, which had grown from Robert Home's modest design and now incorporated mermaids, tigers, fish, an anchor, a dagger, necklaces, rosettes, a garland, two banners and the royal *chattar* or parasol shading the crown. Underneath is printed 'Royal Library of His Majesty the King of Oude'.

9. A book plate from the King of
Awadh's library

The fate of the royal libraries after annexation is unclear. 200,000 volumes of rare books and manuscripts of immense value were said to have been sequestered by the Company on annexation. There are suggestions that some of the books went to La Martiniere School library, and were looted or destroyed during its occupation by sepoys in 1857–58. Others seem to have formed the nucleus of the Amin-ud-daula public library, built in 1882 on the site of one of the garden follies, but the majority, like the royal portraits, have probably found their way to collections in Britain and America.

The first royal printing press was established in 1821, when Ghazi-ud-din Haider founded a 'typography' and published a number of books including *Haft Qulzum*, a two-volume dictionary and grammar of the Persian language. Lithographic printing was introduced nine years later by an enterprising Englishman Henry Archer, who was immediately employed by Nasir-ud-din Haider to set up the King's Lithographic Press in Lucknow. It was however impossible to keep printing as a royal monopoly and within the next two decades at least thirteen other presses were set up, mainly by Muslims, and one by the Company in the British Residency. The King's Press was renowned for its printing of classic *naksh* and *nastaliq* characters, and by 1834 Nasir-ud-din Haider was ordering the translation of English books into native languages, so they could be engraved and printed. His successor Muhammad Ali Shah continued to support the Press, and Colonel Wilcox, the superintendent of the Lucknow Observatory was given the additional task of setting up three more royal presses. These were used to print forms for the King's Revenue Department and 'plates of Bactrian coins' and books patronised by the King, as well as translations of scientific treatises, like Lord Brougham's preface to 'Natural Philosophy'. A surviving book printed in 1849 is 'The Lucknow Almanack of His Majesty's Observatory at Lucknow' *(Taqwin Baitun Sultanate Lucknow)*, which starts with the phases of the planets for the year 1849–50 and then casts the horoscopes of prominent personalities, starting with the Resident William Sleeman, and containing brief histories of the English kings.

A great deal of Nawabi time was devoted to entertaining guests and friends to public dinners, and such emphasis was placed on the royal kitchens that the appointment of kitchen supervisor was an important position. Hasan Reza Khan, who became Chief Minister to Asaf-ud-daula was said to have been originally employed as supervisor in his father's kitchen. The royal women and other royal relatives all had separate kitchens, and the habit of sending each other covered trays of food from different households as a mark of respect was a common one. Lucknow cuisine, as it developed in the royal kitchens was distinguished by its richness, its blending of Mughal and Persian dishes, and its extravagant presentation, with beaten gold foil laid on top of the dishes. Master chefs were allowed unlimited supplies of ingredients, they were humoured and flattered by the Nawabs, and often earned substantial salaries and costly *khilats*. In return they experimented with new dishes that would tempt their royal masters and impress the dinner guests. A long-standing story among local cooks is that the reason for the particular softness and palatability of the Lucknow kebab was because the Nawabs suffered from bad teeth and found it difficult to chew unminced meat. Now this oral tradition can be confirmed by the discovery of a previously unknown description of Asaf-ud-daula in 1787 by Captain Madan: 'His figure is rather a curious one, and put me much in mind of a pair of dutch nut-crackers; very short, fat, and though a young man, has lost all his teeth, this makes him splutter much in speaking which he does without ceasing.'[78]

Some, but not all, of the Nawabs were fond of alcohol, excessively fond at times, and many evenings were frittered away at drunken parties followed by recovery the next day. Western liquor was preferred and one of the first things Asaf-ud-daula did after establishing his capital at Lucknow was to inform the Governor General Warren Hastings, in a letter which is part of the Company's official 'Persian Correspondence' between the two men, that 'he is fond of wine and requests a stock of different kinds' to be sent up from Calcutta. This was the same Nawab who was described as being 'perpetually intoxicated with Liquor—His Evenings are generally devoted to his Orderlies and his Bottle . . . all appearance of decency and decorum is banished' and the British Resident John Bristow reported that during the hunting party of 1776, which was camped at Etawah, the Nawab and his drinking companion Murtaza Khan 'render themselves and the whole Court utterly incapable of business by getting drunk like Beasts'.[79] Saadat Ali Khan was reported as being a generous host that 'gives many things when he is drunk—repents when sober' and Nasir-ud-din Haider was, as we shall see, an unrepentant drinker. In contrast the pious Amjad Ali Shah, when invited to the Residency for breakfast or dinner, would take his own servants, drink only tea, and leave when the English started dancing.[80] Surprisingly, Wajid Ali Shah, for all his sensual appearance, and the English calumnies of decadent behaviour, abstained from alcohol.

Saadat Ali Khan's anglophilia embraced the English belief that French cooking was the best of all, and he brought with him from Calcutta a French chef who provided the banquet described by Viscount Valentia in 1803, when twenty-seven sat down to dinner, sixteen of them Europeans. 'The dinner was French, with plenty of wine' although everything else was English, from the furniture, the girandoles, tableware, cutlery, decanters and wine glasses to the band, dressed in regimental uniform, and playing English tunes while the guests dined. Another guest thought that 'his table, to which all the English of any rank were welcome, had in every respect the appearance of a nobleman's England' with the Nawab enjoying venison and cherry brandy.[81] The French chef also supervised the public breakfasts too, which were semi-formal occasions, when the Resident of the day would be invited. This was a useful meeting place, especially during Muharram when both the Nawabi and residency offices were closed. Public discussions that often extended for several hours, were conducted across the table. When the Resident John Paton objected to these breakfasts on a Sunday, Nasir-ud-din Haider agreed they should not be held on either the Christian or the Muslim days of worship. The breakfasts were often crowded affairs too, as everyone jostled to get near the tables. Major Archer described one occasion where 'fat, insolent knaves of nobles' shouldered aside 'well-behaved English gentlemen, or even a lady' and certainly some of the illustrated dining-room scenes do look terribly crowded. But the guests were soothed by singers who 'gave us some Persian and Kashmirian airs with considerable sweetness and tone', he added.

Meals between the earlier Nawabs, the Residents, and other Europeans like the wealthy Claude Martin were frequent, sociable occasions. Asaf-ud-daula and Prince Sulaiman Shikuh enjoyed a dinner at Colonel Harper's in June 1786, where they 'gave proof of their strength by cutting through buffaloes and sheep with their scymiters'.[82] The Residents were hospitably invited by the Nawabs to attend Muslim celebrations like Eid-ul-Zuha, when breakfast and dinner were held in the Shah Manzil palace, followed by fireworks. In return the Nawabs were invited to Christmas parties by the Residents, where generous gifts were exchanged between hosts and guests. Musicians and dancers provided entertainment for these festive occasions, and as a compliment to each other's cultural tastes the Resident and other Europeans would engage nautch dancers, while the Nawabs got their Anglo-Indian bandmasters and musicians to play English airs, or sing ballads. Mr Braganca, an old Anglo-Indian who worked in the Residency reported that Saadat Ali Khan had recently sent Joseph Quieros to enquire whether he would allow twelve-year-old Master Braganca to go to the palace and play the piano twice a day for him. 'His Excellency is fond of Musick and the Boy plays on the Piano admirably for his age, and there is not another here that can supply his want.' The boy got Rs 200 a month for his performances, which helped his father support his own 'numerous family'. For a time European guests were piped into dinner by Jerry Gahagan, the Nawab's Irish bagpiper.

With the worsening of relations between the Nawabs and the Company, these convivial entertainments ceased. The Residents had not been invited to Nasir-ud-din Haider's noisy, drunken parties, nor would they have wished to go. His successor Muhammad Ali Shah was often confined to his bed through illness, and Amjad Ali Shah, as we have seen, was not a gregarious man in European company. Although there were clearly formal contacts and dinners between Wajid Ali Shah and William Sleeman, the good-tempered humour of the earlier days had gone. At the end of another finger-wagging session by Sleeman, the King must have been only too glad to retire to the zenana to be entertained by his numerous wives, dancers and musicians. Perhaps he was amused by the royal mimics, who would re-enact the events of the day, dressing up in crinolines and Company uniforms to imitate the English officials and their wives, in exaggerated mime.[83]

And so the days passed by pleasantly enough. The growing storm of annexation and revolt seemed no more than a distant rumble of monsoon thunder across the Gomti, echoing through the stables and the parks, making the elephants shift uneasily and the pigeons fall silent. There were many reasons why the annexation in 1856 was so unpopular among the people it was designed to liberate. The Company found it hard to understand that the inhabitants of Awadh might prefer to be ruled by their own Kings, with all their faults, rather than the sober Chief Commissioner, James Outram. Is it true to say that the Nawabs had lost all sense of reality among their gilded palaces and theatrical gardens? Not really, for the obligations of the Nawabs, self-created successors of the Emperors, towards their subjects, were largely met. What often seemed to the Company ridiculous extravagance and meaningless ceremony was seen in quite a different light by the people of Lucknow. There was a general disbelief at the time of annexation that the Nawabs, who had clearly demonstrated their friendship to the English in adopting so many of their ways should be deprived of their country. Perversely, the more anglicised the Nawabs seemed, the more they were disliked by the English, who mocked their well-meaning attempts to flatter the unwanted guests in Awadh. Perhaps the strongest image which remains at the end is that of the rhinoceros in the park, chained to a tree, an incomprehensibly exotic animal, but one that could only wander in a circle prescribed by its masters.

NOTES AND REFERENCES

1. Two good studies are Richard Barnett's *North India between Empires: Awadh, the Mughals, and the British*, published by the University of California Press 1980, and Michael Fisher's *A Clash of Cultures: Awadh, the British and the Mughals*, published by Manohar, New Delhi 1987.

2. See, *A Fatal Friendship: The Nawabs, the British and the City of Lucknow*, by the author, published by OUP, Delhi 1985, for an overview of the relations between the Residents and the Nawabs.

3. Robert Home's designs for the coronation, and the Nawab's boats are in his sketch books at the Victoria & Albert Museum, London.

4. See, *A Very Ingenious Man: Claude Martin in Early Colonial India*, by the author, published by OUP, Delhi 1992, for a description of the Nawab's army.

5. Ghazi-ud-din Haider to the British Resident, 3 October 1823, no. 12, Foreign Political Consultations, National Archives, New Delhi.

6. *The Asiatic Annual Register, or, a View of the History of Hindustan, and of the Politics, Commerce and Literature of Asia, for the Year 1807*, London 1808, p. 176.

7. Untitled painting of Wajid Ali Shah and female attendants in the State Museum & Library, Banarsi Bagh, Lucknow. Ref. no. 59.97.

8. 18 January 1828, no. 17, Political Consultations, Oriental and India Office Collections (OIOC) at the British Library (BL), London.

9. Fisher, op. cit., p. 261.

10. Sharar, Abdul Halim, *Lucknow: The Last Phase of an Oriental Culture*, translated by E.S. Harcourt and Fakhir Hussain, London 1975.

11. The Nawab's Household Accounts 1777–83 (Warren Hastings' Papers), Add 29,093, BL.

12. Johnson, Daniel, *Sketches of Field Sports as Followed by the Natives of India*, London 1822, p. 175.

13. Johnson, op. cit., p. 183.

14. Madan, Captain Charles, *Two Private Letters to a Gentleman in England from His Son Who Accompanied Earl Cornwallis on His Expedition to Lucknow in the Year 1787*, Peterborough 1788, p. 42, BL.

15. Johnson, op. cit., p. 192.

16. Tennant, Reverend William, *Indian Recreations*, 3 vols, London 1804 ii, p. 413.

17. Madan, op. cit., p. 43.

18. *The Asiatic Annual Register for the Year 1800*, London 1801, p. 98.

19. Roberts, Emma, *Scenes and Characteristics of Hindostan with Sketches of Anglo-Indian Society*, vol. I, London 1835, p. 350.

20. Beechey, Dr G.D.S., *The Eighth Child or George Duncan Beechey, Portrait Painter 1797–1852: Royal Portrait Painter to the Last Four Kings of Oudh*, London 1994.

21. Fayrer, Dr Joseph, *Recollections of My Life*, Edinburgh 1900, p. 89. The tigers belonged to the Nawab Moosun-ud-daula, a cousin of Wajid Ali Shah.

22. Saadat Ali Khan replaced his nephew Wazir Ali, whose short reign lasted only four months, from September 1797 to January 1798, when he was deposed by the Governor General. Fearing unrest, the Company brought Saadat Ali Khan from Calcutta in a palanquin, disguised as an Englishman. See, *A Tour Through the Upper Provinces of Hindostan*, by Augusta Deare, published London 1823, p. 102.

23. *The Calcutta Review*, vol. 3, January–June 1845, Calcutta, p. 78.
24. Madan, op. cit., p. 33.
25. *Calendar of Persian Correspondence*, vol. 8 (1788–89), Calcutta 1911, Item dated 30 January 1788, p. 53.
26. 9 February 1811, no. 64, Bengal Political Consultations, OIOC.
27. 13 June 1851, no. 145, India Political & Foreign Consultations, OIOC.
28. Archer, Major E.C., *Tours in Upper India and in Parts of the Himalaya Mountains*, vol. I, London 1833, p. 34.
29. Sharar, op. cit., p. 116.
30. Beach, Milo Cleveland & Koch, Ebba, *King of the World: The Padshahnama*, Exhibition Catalogue, Azimuth Editions Ltd, London 1997, p. 72.
31. Johnson, op. cit., p. 193.
32. Hoffmeister, Dr W., *Travels in Ceylon and Continental India*, Edinburgh 1848, p. 264.
33. Sharar, op. cit., p. 117.
34. Madan, op. cit., p. 44.
35. Colonel John Mordaunt had originally been recommended to Asaf-ud-daula by the East India Company officials as an aide-de-camp, and the two men became good friends. The Nawab was said to have cried like a child at Mordaunt's funeral in 1790.
36. This building is now called Kakori Kothi and there is good architectural evidence that it was used as a cock-pit and was built or owned by Claude Martin, who appears in Zoffani's cock-fight painting.
37. Darogah, Haji Abbas Ali, *The Lucknow Album*, Lucknow 1874, plate 47.
38. *The Asiatic Annual Register for the Year 1804*, vol. VI, pp. 9–10.
39. Abu Talib Khan Isfahani, Mirza, *History of Asaf-ud-daula, Nawab Wazir of Oudh*, translated from the Persian book *Tafzihu'l Ghafilin*, by William Hoey, Allahabad 1885, p. 59.
40. Mundy, Captain Charles, *Pen and Pencil Sketches, Being a Journal of a Tour in India*, 2 vols, London 1833 i, p. 32.
41. Hoffmeister, op. cit., p. 272.
42. Beach & Koch, op. cit., p. 66.
43. 8 January 1820, no. 81, Political Consultations, OIOC.
44. 'A Letter from George Cornish, Aide-de-camp to Sir John Shore, Governor General, during an Official Tour in 1797', in *Bengal Past and Present*, Calcutta 1918, xxvi, Part 2, pp. 105–26.
45. 16 December 1825, no. 27, Political Consultations, OIOC.
46. Orlich, Captain Leopold von, *Travels in India Including Sinde and the Panjab*, translated by H.E. Lloyd, 2 vols, London 1845 ii, p. 96.
47. *The Asiatic Journal and Monthly Register for British India and Its Dependencies*, vol. II, June–December 1816, London 1816, Article entitled 'Recent Notes on Lucknow', p. 578.
48. 'Account of Lucknow from Gladwin's Asiatic Miscellany', reproduced in

The Asiatic Annual Register for the Year 1800 under 'Miscellaneous Tracts 1785', pp. 97–110.

49. *The Asiatic Journal and Monthly Register, etc.,*op. cit., p. 579.
50. 29 February 1812, Report by the engineer Captain Duncan McLeod, Foreign and Political Consultations, National Archives, New Delhi.
51. 12 January 1827, nos 59 and 60, Political Consultations, OIOC.
52. *The Asiatic Journal and Monthly Register, etc.,* op. cit., p. 578.
53. The Home Papers, OIOC. I am grateful to Sally Rynne of the London Institute, who is writing her Ph.D. thesis on 'The Court Arts and Architecture of Lucknow 1770–1850', for telling me about this collection.
54. Captain Robert Smith's panorama of Lucknow, eight pen and ink sketches, 1832, in the Victoria & Albert Museum (Prints & Drawings), London. These detailed drawings show only a small area of Lucknow, west of the old Stone Bridge, and include the Rumi Darwaza, the exterior of the Daulat Khana palace, the Tope Khana and the river Gomti.
55. Valentia, Viscount George, *Voyages and Travels to India, Ceylon, the Red Sea, Abyssinia and Egypt in the Years 1802–1806*, 3 vols, London 1809, p. 146.
56. Newell, Major H.A., *Lucknow, the Capital of Oudh*, Bombay n.d., p. 23.
57. Spry, Dr Henry, *Modern India with Illustrations of the Resources and Capabilities of Hindustan*, 2 vols, London 1837 i, pp. 233–4.
58. 7 November 1836, no. 56, India Political Consultations, OIOC.
59. T.H. Maddock to H.T. Prinsep, Political Secretary to the Government of India, 18 November 1831, Foreign Political Consultations, National Archives, New Delhi.
60. *The Asiatic Annual Register for the Year 1804*, op. cit., Article entitled 'Historical Sketch of the Late Asuf ud Dowlah', p. 11.
61. 19 October 1827, no. 134, Political Consultations, OIOC.
62. Robert Home to his daughter Anne Walker, letter dated 15 January 1818, OIOC.
63. 9 January 1818, no. 3, Political Consultations, OIOC.
64. The Panorama House in Lucknow predates both the Colosseum in Regent's Park, London (1822) and the London Diorama (1823). The Colosseum, designed by Decimus Burton, exhibited a panorama of London, taken from the top of St Paul's Cathedral, while the Diorama, designed by A.W. Pugin, specialised in picturesque subjects, including scenes from nature and ancient ruins. Some paintings were transparent, like Home's ship pictures, and clever lighting added to the effect. The panorama remained stationary, but the Diorama audience of 300 was slowly revolved to face each picture in turn. Whether the London Diorama was based on reports of Home's panorama, or whether the idea originated in Europe but was first realised in Lucknow is not yet clear.
65. Robert Home to Anne Walker, letter dated 25 May 1818, OIOC.
66. Schonberg, Baron von, *Travels in India and Kashmir*, London 1853.

67. Sleeman, William, *A Journey Through the Kingdom of Oude in 1849–1850*, 2 vols, London 1858.

68. Written account to the author, from John Quieros of Stevenage, dated 24 August 1984. Mr Quieros is a direct descendant of Joseph Quieros (1759–1822) whose correct title was Don Joseph Chamois de Quiros Chevalier, and who founded the Lucknow branch of this old Spanish family.

69. *A Journey through India: Pictures of India by British Artists*, Catalogue issued by Spink & Sons, London to accompany an exhibition in November 1996, p. 6.

70. Ozias Humphry's Diary, 5 February –19 June 1786, Photo, Eur. 43, OIOC.

71. *Indian and Southeast Asian Art*, catalogue issued by Sotheby's New York for an auction on 19 September 1996, lot number 193.

72. Robert Home to Anne Walker, op. cit., ref. 62.

73. Portrait in the Metropolitan Museum of Art, New York.

74. Beechey, op. cit.

75. Pemble, John, *The Raj, the Indian Mutiny and the Kingdom of Oudh 1801–1859*, Harvester Press, Hassocks 1977, p. 89. Wajid Ali Shah wrote a large number of books including *Pari Khana (The Fairy House)*, *Diwan-i-Mubarak (A Joyous Anthology)*, and *Tarikh-i-Mumtaz (The Story of Mumtaz)*. See also *King Wajid Ali Shah of Awadh*, by Mirza Ali Azhar, published by the Royal Book Co., Karachi 1982.

76. 3 July 1839, Foreign Political Consultations, National Archives, New Delhi.

77. 2 September 1848, no. 77, Political Consultations, OIOC.

78. Madan, op. cit., p. 37.

79. The Resident John Bristow to Sir Philip Francis, 10 January 1776. Add Mss. 34, 287, BL.

80. Von Orlich, op. cit., p. 94.

81. Deare, op. cit., p. 101.

82. Ozias Humphry's Diary, op. cit., 19 June 1786.

83. See Kincaid, Dennis, *British Social Life in India 1608–1937*, London 1938, pp. 106–7, for a description of this little-known practice.

CHAPTER TWO

A Poorer Class of Person

Not everyone enjoyed the glittering life of Nawabi Lucknow. There were an unknown number of silent spectators who stood outside everything for which the city was famous, excluded by their poverty. They stand outside history too, for nowhere do we find the paupers of Lucknow mentioned, except for an odd sentence from passers-by on their way to the Residency or the palace. One visitor of 1816 even remarked 'with considerable satisfaction, that the loathsome and disgusting scenes of misery and poverty, so conspicuous in every other large city I had visited in India, were here either unknown or studiously concealed. The poorer class of natives seemingly enjoy in Lucknow a degree of liberty fully suitable to their condition . . .'[1] This anonymous writer seems however to have confined himself to the newer part of the city laid out along the southern bank of the Gomti, for there are no descriptions of the Chowk or any of the highly populated mohallas further south and west. These were the areas that usually appear on pre-1858 maps hatched in and simply labelled as 'dense city'. Only after the radical restructuring of the old city by Sir Robert Napier in 1858, when he bisected it with a grid of broad, straight roads, do we find them identified as Rakabganj, Golaganj, Yahiyaganj, Mahbubganj, Kashmiri Mohalla, Deorhi Agha Mir, and so on.

And yet the poor *did* exist here too, and just occasionally they make a voiceless appearance at the edge of the Nawabi stage. The poor have no names either, or names which are hardly ever recorded. In the mortality figures from October 1846 to March 1847 at the King's Hospital only the professions of the deceased and the areas they lived in are noted: a prostitute from the Chowk, a sepoy from Golaganj, three beggars from

Khas Bazar, Khundari Bazar and Meena Bazar, two *syce* (grooms) from Hussainganj and Muftiganj, and a *khidmagar* (table servant) from Aliganj.[2] It is impossible to estimate the number of poor people in Lucknow in Nawabi days. The total population is also unknown, though it was probably around 300,000, a figure far removed from the wildly exaggerated guesses of some Europeans that it was nearer a million. The urban population was likely to increase during times of particular hardship like the great drought of 1791 or the floods of 1840, when people would come in from outlying villages to seek relief. People on a low income could suddenly find themselves sliding into penury where their homes and livelihood were lost.

Quite apart from natural disasters, houses could be arbitrarily demolished on the orders of the Nawabs and their Ministers from greed, or spite, or revenge. Religious disturbances and riots led to deaths and house burnings. With no records of people affected by these events, nor of the substrata who were paupers all their brief lives, we cannot say whether Lucknow contained a greater or smaller number of poor than other Indian cities of similar size. And without records of employment and wages paid it is impossible to define the boundaries between reasonable subsistence and absolute poverty. There are few clues. A *chaprassi* at the King's Poor House called Kuttoo, who lived in Khiyaliganj, got Rs 3 a month to feed his family. Because this was insufficient 'he used to go out a begging in the night, with his wife, and that he and his family always wore filthy clothes'.[3] To be employed was not always a guarantee of having enough to eat. Although epidemics like cholera affected everyone, rich and poor, it was the endemic illnesses like dysentery, measles and bronchitis that often felled the poor, because long-term malnutrition had fatally weakened their resistance.

Poverty is not associated with Nawabi Lucknow. Nowhere in the increasingly large number of books on the city will you find the words 'beggar', 'pauper' or even '*garib log*' in the indices, because poor people generally make dull reading. We have no Indian Mayhew or Dickens to guide us, which is why this chapter is necessarily short. But it is worth looking at the scanty material available, and the charitable measures that were put in hand by the Kings to remind ourselves that there was another side to what was, for nearly a century, the wealthiest place in India.

'Happening to enter the town at the west end, and which contains the poor mechanics and labourers of every sort I never witnessed so many varied forms of wretchedness, filth and vice,' wrote the Reverend William

Tennant in 1798. '. . . vice and poverty are the only qualities that this people uniformly display . . . Amidst all this blaze of wealth and magnificence, thousands of poor wretches are seen on the road to all appearance in real want. There is not, perhaps, in the whole compass of human affairs a more striking display of the inequality of condition, than this scene affords. Extravagant wealth is amassed in the hands of one man, and is confined to the narrow circle of his favourites; and this superfluous store is grinded from the faces of the indigent, who are wallowing in all the filth, of penury and wretchedness.'[4]

Lady Nugent repeated the chaplain's observations fifteen years later, as she watched men scrambling beneath the feet of the Nawab's elephant for coins flung down from the howdah: 'It was impossible not to compare the ostentation and splendour of the Nawab's procession with the half-starved miserable appearance of his subjects.'[5] Major Archer saw the same scenes in 1827 when he noted 'hundreds of men, women and children throwing themselves under the elephants to catch the pieces of money distributed by the noblemen who sat behind in the King's howdah'. Those who did manage to pick up the heavy silver rupees embossed with crown and fish were often forced to surrender them to others more desperate but less foolhardy.[6]

The gulf between the richest Indian Court of its time and the paupers in the streets was bound to seem particularly striking even to an impartial European observer. But as relations worsened over the next half century between the East India Company and the Nawabs, criticism of the contrast between rich and poor was to take on an increasingly shrill note, and the Nawabs' supposed mismanagement of Awadh was given as the principal reason for annexation.

It would be interesting to have comments from contemporary Indian writers on the poverty that seemed so evident south of the line of palaces and *imambaras*, but these are not forthcoming, except from Mirza Abu Talib Khan Isfahani, who accused Asaf-ud-daula of oppressing the poor. The reasons for the omission of something that struck foreigners so forcefully, are probably two-fold. To suggest publicly, in writing, that everything in the kingdom was not perfect, was to invite punishment, as indeed Abu Talib found, and as did a later writer, Kamal-ud-din Haider, who lost his job for criticising the King. Censorship was certainly not confined only to the East India Company. What the ordinary inhabitants of Lucknow thought as they stepped over the shrouded figures of sleeping beggars or distributed small change to those importuning outside the religious buildings, we shall never know. Secondly, there is that useful phrase *shehr ki ankhon*, literally 'city eyes' which means that the spectator very quickly becomes accustomed to sights which only a few days earlier would have seemed shocking. The beggars, 'the halt and the blind', simply merge into the background, an accepted part of the streetscape, 'the poor you have always with you'.

Certainly this is what seemed to have happened to Wajid Ali Shah, who, in refuting the Company's charges against him at annexation wrote: 'Were any impartial individual to see the vast population of the city of Lucknow, the numerous beautiful and magnificent buildings that have been erected there during my reign, there being hardly any thatched or mud houses to be seen—the wealth, ease and happiness of the inhabitants, and the marks of perfect cheerfulness apparent in their faces—[he] would hardly credit that the country had been, as represented, labouring under the most lamentable mis-rule . . .'[7] Yet only three years earlier, in May 1854 a dreadful incident had taken place at 'a house hired from Buchraj, merchant in or near the Chowk' for a marriage feast. There was the customary distribution of money to beggars, a mad rush to collect it, and fifty-nine paupers dead in the crush, with seventy injured. The bodies of the dead were taken to the Gomti and flung in. 'All who perished, or suffered, were beggars or of the very humblest class who subsist upon charity in this great City,' reported the Resident.[8]

Neither did Wajid Ali Shah mention the King's Charitable Fund, though he was probably unaware of the racket that was uncovered in August 1856 when Company officials were trawling through the deposed King's establishments. Mr John Sangster, an Anglo-Indian who had worked for nearly thirty years in the Residency as a clerk, had been appointed Almoner of the Fund about 1842. The Fund had begun with the laudable intention of removing beggars from the streets, by providing them with 'Charity Tickets'. Against these tickets, which could be issued for life, they could get Rs 2 a month, and hand-outs of clothing and bedding. In return they had to promise not to accost passers-by for alms. The tickets were at first distributed to deserving cases, but investigation revealed a pitiful little deception. The wretched Kuttoo, who worked at the Poor House, was found to have been 'selling' the charity tickets and had, over the years, accumulated the sum of Rs 1,104. Three of the beggars had paid Kuttoo Rs 12 each for a life ticket. On becoming Almoner, Sangster asked Kuttoo to bring him the tickets of dead paupers, in secret, so that money could be claimed against them. Sangster and his wife were also found to have stolen thirty *rezais* or quilts intended by some kind soul for the ticket holders. Even when they had got their tickets, either honestly, or by purchase, the beggars still had to overcome another hurdle. Fateh Ali, also employed in the Residency office, and using inside inform- ation, would tip off the poor and the blind when 'the pay was to be dis- tributed and get them their allowances, and thus used to receive some presents from them in return for informing them of the time of the distribution'.[9] Whatever a beggar's bribe was worth, it was certainly useful to Fateh Ali who was paid the meagre salary of Rs 5 per month. The sad- dest thing about the Charitable Fund scandal was not only the exploita- tion by underpaid staff of the very people the Fund had been designed to help, and the fact that it had been going on for years, but the pathetically small amounts of money involved in the scams. While Europeans emp- loyed by the Nawabs were easily picking up Rs 1,500 per month as their basic salaries, not to mention all the gifts and *khilats* while they remained in favour, people outside the palace gates were trying to rub along on a few rupees a month.

The Poor House, or Pauper Asylum as it was later called, was establish- ed between 1835 and 1840 in a building off the Old Cawnpore Road, with two open-air courtyards, surrounded by low, dark rooms. It was 'chiefly supported by the munificence of the King' and its kitchens pro- vided food for the in-patients of the adjoining Khairat Khana, the hospi- tal founded by Nasir-ud-din Haider in July 1831. William Stevenson had been junior surgeon to the Company's 14th Regiment stationed in the Mariaon cantonment until he was spotted by the King and requested 'to attend the Sick poor of this place'.[10] By November 1828 Dr Stevenson was employed by Nasir-ud-din Haider 'in affording medical aid to the native poor of this City' at a dispensary he had set up, where people could receive treatment and be vaccinated against smallpox.[11] When the Khairat Khana was opened, Dr Stevenson was appointed as Superintendent and it is from his meticulous six-monthly reports that much of our information comes. The Khairat Khana was divided into two parts—the Unani or native hospital, where traditional treatment, based on herbal remedies, was given by Indian physicians, and the European hospital, also known as the King's Hospital, where surgical operations were carried out. About 1840 the two hospitals were physically separated. The Unani section re- mained in the city on the Old Cawnpore Road, but the European part was moved into a building 'in the immediate vicinity of the Residency and Palace' though complaints were made of its confined space, and it was initially less well appointed.

During 1839 the Unani section treated 102,276 patients and was

described as a spacious and airy building 'and for a Native hospital remarkably clean'. The patients were given board, lodging and clothing
and a refectory attached to it 'for the accommodation of the necessitous'
fed the poor.[12] Dr Stevenson was paid both by the King and the Company,
getting a monthly salary of Rs 1,500, with an extra Rs 500 for superin-
tending a dispensary which gave 'relief to the poor' and Rs 740 from the
Residency treasury which included money for the vaccination establishment. He submitted his six-monthly bill for expenditure to the King's
treasury, and unlike other Europeans in the King's service seems to have
been paid fairly promptly, or at any rate, did not have reason to complain.
Conscientiously he visited both hospitals daily and reported that 'The
patients that come into Hospital are generally those of all the lowest order
or such as live at a distance and have no means of conveyance.' Occasionally
'respectable individuals' would arrive too, but these were few compared
to the poor of Lucknow. 'A ward is set apart for the women of the Town,'
he continued, noting that 'the Out Patients are in general in better circumstances than those that come into the Hospital'. Out-patients formed the
majority of sufferers treated, 204 in May 1839 against forty-one admitted
and they preferred to take their medicines in the hospital, but return
home after treatment. Of the forty-one admitted patients during that
month six died, eighteen were cured and the remainder stayed for further
treatment.

Staff in the Unani Hospital included three assistants, 'a Brahmin Cook,
a Mussulman Cook', a water-carrier, male and female sweepers, a *dhobi*,
a barber and a *chowkidar*. Medicines bought in May 1839 included seven
seers of castor oil, then popular as a purgative. Monthly expenditure
included atta, daal, rice, sago, sugar, milk, salt, ghee, spice and tobacco at
a cost of Rs 300, and a typical meal for all the eighteen in-patients cost
only 9 annas and 6 pice.

A second surgeon was appointed in 1840 to meet the needs of patients
in the King's Hospital near the Residency. Dr Menzies, the officiating
Residency surgeon, listed his duties as attending on the Resident and his
family, assisting the Residency chaplain, attending all the Residency staff
who fell sick, including the Resident's escort and the city guards, and the
Indian prisoners in the Thug and Dacoit jail, as well as running the hospital and attached dispensary. Between April and October 1840, 1,563
out-patients were seen here, the great majority of them male. Their complaints were not recorded in detail, though two men came in suffering
severe wounds after being attacked by elks. Some complained of swell-
ings in various parts of the body, and these were treated successfully with

what was described as acupuncture, though this is unlikely to have been based on the popular treatment used today, but more likely a simple aspiration to draw out the fluid. Clearly Dr Menzies could not deal with every patient himself, and he relied, like his colleague, Dr Stevenson, on trained Indian doctors, including 'the young Mahomedan Physician educated at Fort William' who was sent from Company headquarters in Calcutta, and Puran Singh, the 'native doctor attached to the Residency'.

On Stevenson's early retirement in 1841, Dr J.S. Login was appointed as Superintendent of both hospitals, and he continued to file the same methodical six-monthly reports as his predecessor. Login suggested that branch dispensaries should be set up throughout Lucknow, because not all who needed treatment could get to the Residency, especially during the rainy season. This was not however adopted because the King, Amjad Ali Shah, was unwilling to pay for the extra costs involved. Login's medical reports make dismal reading. The commonest illnesses were rheumatism, fever, syphilis, ulcers, 'cutaneous afflictions' (skin diseases) and dysentery, with an average of ninety-two patients treated daily. Prisoners in the Thug and Dacoit jails suffered most from fever, ulcers and rheumatism. Leprosy was also common. Six years later the pattern of illness had not changed, for no preventative measures had taken place. Dr Login reported that 'In the Hospital at Lucknow a large proportion of those admitted consists of miserable objects picked up off the streets in the last stage of disease . . . Many of the deaths . . . took place before the Patients had been many *hours* in Hospital and a large proportion within the second or third day.'[13] Login wanted to make a statistical survey of the rheumatism and neuralgia cases, comparing their incidence with the annual changes in temperature, and he proposed to do this in collaboration with Lieutenant Colonel R. Wilcox, Superintendent of the King's Observatory, who had been keeping temperature charts. Wilcox's death in 1848 and the closure of the Observatory the following year, meant that this interesting project never came to fruition.

But other surveys were carried out and the hospital report for February 1850 was grim, spelling out the real cost of the hedonistic life-style that characterised parts of the city. 'Syphilis in its various forms, cutaneous afflictions and rheumatism form nearly half of all the cases included in the present returns,' reported Dr Leckie, the new Superintendent. The latter two illnesses were connected with syphilis 'complicated by Venereal taints'. Venereal disease was not only present in female prostitutes, but in young boys between twelve and sixteen years of age who presented themselves for treatment of syphilis. These were caused, said Leckie by 'revolting practices' and the patients before him were not solitary examples for 'there are Houses in the City, where . . . Boys are professedly kept for the above unnatural purpose'. They were treated with 'Mercury Alternatives, and Iodine of Potassium', both standard though harmful and ineffectual treatments.[14] The fact that syphilis, a contagious disease, was common among prostitutes, and nearly fifty per cent of hospital patients, puts a different gloss on current romantic notions of the doe-eyed enchantresses leaning from flower-strewn balconies in the Chowk.

The doctors' reports concentrated on endemic diseases, but also noted epidemics too, where the poor were particularly at risk through lifelong malnutrition, poor housing and virtually no sanitation. Cholera was a major killer, striking hard in the old, crowded city. As many as a thousand people in a single day were reported to have died in August 1842, and after another outbreak the next year, Amjad Ali Shah had 'a small stock of pills' distributed to police stations in Lucknow, which were to be handed out if the disease struck again. A cholera epidemic in the winter of 1849–50 killed thousands of people, 700 dying on one day alone. A smallpox outbreak at the same time added to the general misery and distress, and although vaccination was available and an effective preventative, an ingrained fear or superstition prevented many from availing themselves of it. Vaccinators at the hospitals were careful only to inject the children of 'approvers'.[15]

Even before the methods of transmission of diseases like cholera, typhoid and malarial fever were known, the Residency doctors had pinpointed the filthy condition of the streets in the old city as a major cause of illness. Dr Login was repeating a frequently voiced criticism when he wrote in 1844 of 'the extreme inattention to cleanliness, ventilation, and drainage, which exists in every part of this most densely populous city, and which is the more to be regretted as Lucknow is in itself extremely good, or at least as favourable as any city in the plains can be expected to be, and admits for the numerous ravines intersecting it, of an easy system of drainage into the Goomtee'.[16] Gullies flooded with floating sewage during the rainy season physically prevented poor people from seeking medical help when they most needed it, for they could not afford a *dhoolie* or palanquin to carry them over the mire to the Residency dispensary.

British attitudes to the treatment of illness in the capital differed widely. Dr William Blane, physician to Asaf-ud-daula thought it was his duty to treat all British subjects too, but not other Indians. When called to render first aid to a labourer who had been badly injured in the Residency when a wall collapsed on him, he refused point-blank. He also refused to treat the Resident's Indian bearer, who died from an unspecified illness in April 1791, saying that natives should use their own physicians. 'I certainly am not competent to decide on the Skill of the Native practitioners,' he added pompously, 'but I believe it is generally supposed that they are full Two Centuries behind us in Medical knowledge and that their Skill in surgery is very contemptible indeed.' When challenged by the Resident, Blane adopted a different attitude and said, even more pompously: 'In a large city like this, where there is a large Establishment of Native Physicians and Surgeons who are employed with confidence by and to the Satisfaction of the Prince [Asaf-ud-daula] and the Nobles of the country, it is to be presumed that they are adequate to the attendance of the class of people I have mentioned' that is, ordinary working-class people. Friction between the Resident, E. Otto Ives, and Dr Blane led to the latter's dismissal the following year, exacerbated by his behaviour to the dying bearer.[17] Another Resident, Colonel John Low lamented that 'His Majesty [Amjad Ali Shah] is one of those persons who unfortunately think more highly of Asiatic than of European Medical Science (admitting only a superiority of European Surgery) . . .'[18]

But there were more humanitarian attitudes among other medical practitioners. It was the success of surgical operations by English doctors that attracted Indian patients. The use of chloroform as an anaesthetic seems to have been first tried in 1849 and then only sparingly, during major operations. Opium pills probably dulled the pain of minor operations which patients were willing to undergo. An assistant surgeon in the Company's Medical Service, Dr Brett got a *khilat* from Nasir-ud-din Haider for performing 'a number of successful and gratuitous operations upon the eye and for the removal of the stone in many of the poor of the city'. It was thought that the King's approval would publicise Brett's skill 'and induce all blind persons in Lucknow (and they are generally amongst the poorest classes) to attend Mr Brett to have their sight restored'. These must have been operations for cataract, common among the poor and malnourished. Other 'surgical operations which from their novelty have excited much interest amongst the people, one of the operations for stone having been performed at the palace by His Majesty's express request' doubtless added to Brett's lustre.[19] Buoyed up by his success, Brett then sought the Company's permission to set up as an oculist in Lucknow, but this does not seem to have been granted, and there is no further mention of this kind-hearted person.

Just as poverty in Lucknow has been generally ignored, so too have civil disturbances in the city, which led to violent death, homelessness, and looting. In 1828 the Resident Mordaunt Ricketts reported that 'The recurrence of the Festival of the Mohurrum has in consequence of the two opposing Parties of Sheahs, and Soonhees, ever been attended at this city with some disturbance and bloodshed.' Six people were killed during that year's *taziya* procession, and Nasir-ud-din Haider, badly advised by one of his Ministers, ordered the destruction of 400 houses belonging to the Sunni Mewatties of his own Bodyguard. The houses were burnt and plundered and the mausoleum of Dhunnay Khan, late Commandant of the troops, was dug up and destroyed. When rebuked, the King said he intended to build a new *ganj*, or market, across the site of the mausoleum, and added airily that Agha Mir, a former Chief Minister 'had in his time pulled down hundreds of Houses and Mosques without any notice being taken', though that is doubtless not what the dispossessed house-owners would have said.[20] This particular Minister had been accused of demolishing houses for their building materials which were then utilised in his own palace, and of knocking down 'thousands of houses' on the pretence of road building. Gangs of men armed with pickaxes would accompany him on his raids. What this meant in terms of human misery cannot be calculated. And this was no isolated whim of a despotic Minister either, for Abu Talib had described equally shameful scenes during Asaf-ud-daula's time, when families would be forced out of their houses which were demolished over their heads, by the Nawab's labourers. 'They are ordered by him [the Nawab] without getting either money, compensation or another house.'[21]

Deliberate actions like the forced requisition of houses without compensation were a clear cause of increased poverty. Another, more subtle, but no less harmful ploy, was the habit of paying wages in arrears, and sometimes holding those arrears over for a considerable period of time. It was a common complaint among Europeans who entered the Nawabs' employ that they had to lay out their own money in providing services, and then present their bills for payment. Claude Martin, Antoine de l'Etang and J.M. Sinclair are only three men from many who paid out of their own pockets for the royal arsenal, the royal stables and the royal fireworks, only to find they were not to be recompensed. Most people who found themselves in this situation wrote to the Resident about it, but there was nothing he could do to interfere in a private contract between the Nawabs and their employees. This miserly behaviour by the Nawabs was not confined only to the Europeans, but extended to Indian employees as well. Troops, bodyguards, palace servants, craftsmen and public employees from the Kotwal down to the men who watered the streets, were all kept waiting at times for their salaries. The many pensioners whom the Nawabs supported could also suffer too if money was late coming into the royal treasury, and thus late in going out. The smaller the amount, only a few rupees in some cases, the meaner it seemed to keep people waiting.

Among the last King's pensioners, the *wasiqadars*, many of whom were descendants of the previous Nawabs or people who had served the Court well, were thirteen Christian pensioners. These were retired Europeans or Anglo-Indians who had worked for the Nawabs, or were the children of former employees now dead. Those who had managed to survive the vagaries of royal employment, and to remain in favour, were remembered, though the fact that they had to apply for a royal pension meant they had accumulated little while in service. Familiar names are here, the Catanias and Bragancas, musicians to the Kings, Mrs Dubois, widow of Colonel Adolphe Phillibert Dubois, former aide-de-camp, Mrs De Silva, widow of Nasir-ud-din Haider's coachman and Miss Charlotte M. Sinclair, daughter of J.M. Sinclair, the engineer and general man about Court. The condition of these 'poor whites', though not of course comparable to the really poor people out on the streets, was still pitiful. Miss Sinclair sent a petition to the new Governor General Lord Canning in September 1856 stating that she had last received her monthly pension of Rs 20 in June of that year, and that she owed Rs 200 to people 'who saved her from starvation to death' during the summer. She begged to go home to England where 'she wishes to lead the life of a Christian instead of being tormented by the Devil and subject to the whims and caprices of many bad men in power at Oude' who were pressing her to settle her debts with them.[22] It was found that pensions for other Christians had not been paid for long periods 'owing, no doubt to the caprice of those officers of the late Government upon whom they were dependent for their pittance', wrote Captain Fletcher Hayes, who as Military Secretary was deputed to sort out the mess. Of necessity, poor whites would run up bills with local tradesmen, then have to apply to Indian moneylenders for credit, spiralling into debts that they could not meet. On their deaths, auctions were held of their few effects, and creditors paid off where possible. One should not lose too much sleep over the moneylenders, but the loss of income to small traders like bakers and butchers, themselves probably living on credit, was a further hardship to people on the margin of penury.

'Europeans of the lower order', as a British Resident described them, were often seen as trouble-makers, with their drinking habits, illicit relationships and the occasional murder. Jerry Gahagan, the Nawab's Irish bagpiper, accidentally shot his 'best friend', the illiterate Stephen Caldwell, with whom he lived, and Gahagan followed him to the grave six months later. John Sangster, a 'needy orphan' of eleven years was the son of George John Sangster, who ran a foundry for Asaf-ud-daula. His mother, who had died shortly after his birth was the daughter of M. Gairard, the French fireworks maker. Too young to earn his living, the boy had been brought up by his Indian grandmother (who herself lived on charity), for the family 'who in One Sense are Natives themselves' had inter-married with local women. The Company, to whom an appeal was sent on the young boy's behalf, declined to help. It was this same John Sangster, who in later life was appointed Almoner of the Poor House, where he defrauded those even more in need.

Inter-marriage between 'Europeans of the lower order' and Indian women was not uncommon in Lucknow before the early 1800s, creating a substantial community of Anglo-Indian families, a few of whom still remain today, dignified and quiet people, often in reduced circumstances. Less common were marriages by European women to Indian men, though these did take place, and a few Muslim families today have a white great-great grandmother, assimilated without trace.

But there was one group of people in Lucknow about whom virtually nothing is known, even less than the paupers in the hospital, or the beggars on the street, and these were the African slaves, imported like so many head of cattle by Arab traders. The extent of the African slave trade into India is only just beginning to be evaluated by historians, but one fears it was considerable.[23] African mercenaries had been employed to fight other peoples' battles in southern India during the turbulent period of the mid-eighteenth century when both the French and the English East India Companies were jostling for power. They seemed to have been used to supplement the Nawabi regiments and Bodyguard, though just as readers will not find poor people mentioned in books about Lucknow, neither will they find any Africans.

Claude Martin had a number of African slaves in his eclectic household, whose names we do know, because he left them small pensions and clothing allowances in his Will. There was Sans Chagrin, Aneeseed,

Dick, Amber the eunuch, and Dyoh Coffice (more properly Coffire, or Kafir). We have seen the little *hubshi* boys trained, rather unsuccessfully, as jockeys to ride Saadat Ali Khan's racing horses by Antoine de l'Etang. Shipments of African slaves are recorded in the Company records of 1831, when eighteen men were landed at Bombay in an Arab ship and brought overland through Jaipur, Ajmer and Agra to Lucknow in covered *hackerries* or carriages and sold to Nasir-ud-din Haider. A proclamation against slavery had been issued by the Governor General from Calcutta in 1789, but the practice could only be discouraged outside British India. The Arab traders were, when closely questioned, clearly fulfilling an order placed for the men, and not just travelling through India on the off-chance of selling them. The fact that the men were secreted in covered carriages added suspicion to the deal. Nasir-ud-din Haider, to save face, after purchasing the men, issued his own proclamation against slave-dealing, but a further contingent seems to have come in two years later. In 1846 Amjad Ali Shah artlessly requested 200 swords for his African troops, which gives us an idea of the numbers involved. How much, or how little, they were assimilated into the population of Lucknow we cannot say, except for an odd reference in 1848 to the daughter of a 'Negro and a native parent' who was being treated in the city hospital.[24] During the uprising of 1857 African soldiers who had been in the King's regiments were found fighting alongside their companions in the siege of the British Residency, but after that they vanish from view, a people who truly have no history.

Lucknow was not, as we have shown, a paradise for all, as some would have us believe. Whether there were more, or fewer, poor people than in a comparable city, is impossible to judge, until more evidence is found, and in any case, what city can compare to Lucknow during its heyday? One could suggest that the immense wealth of the Nawabs and the ease with which they spent it had a trickle-down effect, and generated a substantial number of employees, who in turn had money of their own to spend. But wealthy men attract beggars, charlatans and hangers-on too, which could have cancelled out any possible benefits. It would be fairer to say that there *was* poverty in Lucknow, directly aggravated by the actions of some of the Nawabs, with their wholesale land clearances, and their refusal to address questions of road building and sanitation in the old city but there was also some amelioration with the hospitals and dispensary that they supported. We are left with a flawed, but perhaps now, more honest picture of the city.

NOTES AND REFERENCES

1. Anon, *Sketches of India, or Observations Descriptive of the Scenery etc. of Bengal.* Written in India in the years 1811–14. Black, Parbury & Allen, London 1816, pp. 602–3.
2. 23 October 1847, no. 146, Political Consultations, OIOC.
3. 1 August 1856, no. 68, Political Consultations, OIOC.
4. Tennant, Reverend William, *Indian Recreations*, 3 vols, London 1804 ii, p. 404.
5. Nugent, Lady Maria, *A Journal from the Year 1811 Till the Year 1815*, London 1839, pp. 299–300.
6. Archer, Major E.C., *Tours in Upper India and in Parts of the Himalaya Mountains*, vol. 1, London 1833, p. 14.
7. Wajid Ali Shah, *Reply to the Charges Against the King of Oude*, pub. J.F. Bellamy, Calcutta 1856, p. 37.
8. 12 May 1854, nos 54 & 97, Political Consultations, OIOC.
9. 1 August 1856, no. 68, Political Consultations, OIOC.
10. 11 April 1828, no. 29, Political Consultations, OIOC.
11. Vaccination against smallpox was being carried out on children in the Orphan Society, Calcutta, in 1786, ten years before Edward Jenner began his inoculation experiments in Gloucestershire. See *Chowkidar*, vol. 7, no. 6, p. 128, published by the British Association for Cemeteries in South Asia, London.
12. 2 March 1840, nos 33–42, Foreign Political Consultations, National Archives, New Delhi.
13. 3 July 1847, no. 69, Political Consultations, OIOC.
14. 8 February 1850, no. 150, Political Consultations, OIOC.
15. Ibid.
16. 6 January 1844, no. 105, Political Consultations, OIOC.
17. 4 May 1791, Bengal Secret & Military Consultations, OIOC.
18. 28 June 1841, no. 72, Political Consultations, OIOC.
19. 17 March 1835, no. 48, Political Consultations, OIOC.
20. 22 August 1828, no. 11, Political Consultations, OIOC.
21. Abu Talib Khan Isfahani, Mirza, *History of Asaf-ud-daula, Nawab Wazir of Oudh*, translated from the Persian book *Tafzihu'l Ghafilin* by William Hoey, Allahabad 1885, p. 59.
22. 17 October 1856, no. 129, Political Consultations, OIOC.
23. See the forthcoming article on 'The African Presence in India', by Dr Fitzroy Baptiste, of the University of the West Indies, Trinidad, to be published in *The Africa Quarterly*, Indian Council for Cultural Relations, New Delhi.
24. 26 November 1848, no. 30, Political Consultations, OIOC.

CHAPTER THREE

The Barber of Lucknow

It is now generally accepted that a significant cause of the 1857 uprising (known also as the Mutiny), was the annexation by the East India Company of the kingdom of Awadh the previous year. Many of the men who mutinied in the Company's Bengal Army came from Awadh and the assumption of power in their homeland by the Company was too outrageous for them to overlook. Another grievance was the shabby treatment of the last King of Awadh, Wajid Ali Shah, who was deposed and pensioned off by the British, as we shall see in a later chapter. The annexation, which took place in February 1856, was not a sudden Imperial whim. There had long been threats from Calcutta that the Company would move in, if the hedonistic Nawabs did not reform firstly themselves and secondly their kingdom. In 1831 Lord William Bentinck, the Governor General, visited Awadh and issued a stern warning that unless 'the existing disorder and misrule' was remedied 'it would then become the bounden duty of the British Government to assume direct management of the Oudh Dominions'.[1] Promises of better behaviour were made by the King, Nasir-ud-din Haider, but ultimately there was no visible improvement in British eyes. In fact, if anything, things seemed to get worse.

Eighteen years later Colonel William Sleeman in his investigative *Journey through the Kingdom of Oude* reported lawlessness and a general breakdown in rule, though he advised against direct annexation, warning presciently that it 'would inevitably lead to a mutiny of the sepoys'.[2] A further report by James Outram, appointed British Resident at the Lucknow Court in 1854, painted the same picture and added 'the lamentable condition of this kingdom has been caused by the very culpable apathy and gross misrule of the Sovereign and his Durbar'.[3] When Outram's report reached the Governor General, Lord Dalhousie, known for his aggressive forward policy, it seemed almost inevitable that Awadh, too, would become part of the Company's possessions.

As rumours of the proposed takeover spread, and arguments for and against were aired, a short book was published entitled *The Private Life of an Eastern King,* written by William Knighton, Professor of History and Logic at the Hindu College, Calcutta.[4] The author had met an Englishman who had worked as librarian for Nasir-ud-din Haider in Lucknow in the mid 1830s. Dismissed by the King, Edward Cropley had become an indigo planter, but a bad season in 1840 had left him almost bankrupt. He was still full of bile about his dismissal, and attributed it mainly to the machinations of another Englishman at Court, George Harris Derusett, known as the Barber of Lucknow. Derusett, claimed Cropley, was the real power behind the Awadh throne, the intimate companion of the King, not only his barber, but his food taster, his wine-supplier, his companion in bawdy palace evenings, and in short 'the king's agent in all his evil practices'. His baneful influence was the main theme of Knighton's book, based on Cropley's sour reminiscences.[5]

If doubts were voiced by those opposed to annexation, then Knighton's book was the perfect answer. It was an immediate success for it told people what they wanted to believe. The book opened a window into the mysterious world of the Lucknow palace and the harem. The first edition was ready by May 1855, a second followed the same month, it was translated into French the following year, and was mentioned in British Parliamentary debates on Awadh. It was praised by the influential *Calcutta Review,* under the heading 'The Age of Conquest—Is It Past?' to which the answer was clearly 'no', followed by a stirring plea for annexation.[6] Knighton showed, through anecdotes, that even as Nasir-ud-din Haider was promising reforms to Bentinck, he was continuing on his giddy round of pleasure and debauchery, orchestrated by the English barber. Why should the Company imagine that his relative, Wajid Ali Shah, would behave any better? It was but one more example, Knighton argued, of the duplicitous conduct of Indians who were unfit to rule themselves, let alone their subjects.

The book was also, had Knighton realised it, an indictment of lax Company policy, which allowed men like Derusett to leave British India and travel up country to a native kingdom in the first place. Derusett was by no means the only unsuitable person to have slipped through the net and installed himself at Court. Much of the Resident's time was taken up by petty disputes among such people. But now the Company was faced with a paradox. The King had admitted quite frankly that he loved the English, and wanted as many English people around him as possible. He had taken at least one Anglo-Indian woman into his harem, and he appeared frequently, like his grandfather Saadat Ali Khan, in English clothes. But the Company chose not to capitalise on the King's anglophilia. Instead they declared that his attachments were to the 'wrong kind' of English person, a view that seemed to them fully borne out by subsequent events.

The barber quickly became notorious. His ill-fame spread beyond Awadh and he was satirised by the Press. Colonel John Low, the British Resident, reported as his 'painful duty' that at palace suppers, guests 'have several times seen His Majesty dancing Country dances as the partner of Mr Derusett! the latter dressed after some grotesque masquerade fashion, and His Majesty attired in the dress of an European Lady!!' There were, Low hinted darkly 'still more gross, indeed most shocking indecencies'.[7] In August 1836 the *Agra Ukhbar* reported 'The barber, Derusett, has retired from the service of the King taking with him his Majesty's deep regret, and several lacs of rupees. The rest of the reptile tribe, the jeweller, the coachman etc. will migrate when they have nothing left to consume.'[8] Derusett disappeared, a mythic figure, but he had played his part. The justification for annexation, if the British needed one, was now clear.

No one ever attempted to put Derusett's side of the story, though there was an odd little postscript in 1857, when he met the Magistrate of Fatehpur, Mr Sherer, and 'declared that [Knighton's] book was a pure romance, but he [Derusett] was too interested a party to be received as an impartial critic'.[9]

Early in 1994 I learnt that relatives of George Derusett were living in England and Canada, with some precious family possessions, including the barber's Cash Book for the crucial years of 1835–36 when he was at the height of his powers.[10] There was also an exquisite Court suit of canary yellow silk, brocaded with silver work, made for his young son.[11] Suddenly George stepped out of the pages of history and became a real person, a man who had returned to England with the money got in Lucknow, who speculated unwisely in a distillery and the new railway companies, and who was declared bankrupt in 1854. A flattering contemporary portrait of him exists with his second family, in which he is playing an accordion. His ginger curls frame a well-rounded, shrewd face, and he wears a waistcoat of Indian fabric over his ample stomach.[12]

A sepia photograph, taken in the early 1850s, shows a plump, tired looking man, still fashionably dressed, but with a mournful expression, perhaps due to illness or drink.[13]

10. The Barber of Lucknow

The Cash Book, which was generously loaned to me, noted every
anna disbursed by George and every rupee received, as well as letters and
receipts from 1834 to 1837. It showed that Knighton had not exaggerated the extent of his influence at Court, even if his interpretation was
open to question. There was also, tucked into the book, a six-page pencil-
written refutation of Knighton's story. 'I have most carefully perused
this book', wrote George, 'and most solemnly declare that the principle
[*sic*] part of the scenes described never did take place, and those scenes
described of a minor character are grossly exagerated [*sic*] and moreover
had the scenes described actually have occurred the author from sheer
debility alone could never have witnessed them even had he been permitted by His Majesty to accompany him in his sporting excursions or
other amusements.'

Had this rebuttal been made in 1855, as soon as Knighton's book
came out, and had George been able to win over public opinion, the
annexation debate may have taken a different turn and Dalhousie might,
possibly, have stayed his hand for a little longer. The Lucknow Court,
shown in a more rational light, may have looked a little less like Sodom

and Gomorrha (to which it had once been compared), and a lot more like a potential market for British goods. Trade could have preceded the flag, for Wajid Ali Shah was as keen as his predecessors on European goods for his palaces. Whether the disastrous decision to move into Awadh would ultimately have been delayed for long is doubtful, but I believe George's voice deserves to be heard after all these years.

By the time he arrived in Calcutta in the late 1820s, George was a trained hairdresser, who, like many coiffeurs, felt a French name would suit him better, and he became Derusett. He worked at his trade, but business was not good and he was reported as 'a Barber and Hair dresser who was glad to cut any persons' hair for one Rupee'.[14] He tried to diversify by setting up a shop in partnership with a Mr Boaz as provision merchant. But this venture did not prove profitable either, and he decided to travel up country to Lucknow, some time during the winter of 1830–31 'to look for any sort of employment that he could obtain'. Dr William Stevenson, the Company doctor in Lucknow at the time, later described how George's luck suddenly changed. The King had often asked the Resident 'to procure European servants for him, and among others a Hair Dresser . . . [George] happened one day to cut the Resident's hair—that the King heard of this, and immediately asked the Resident whether Mr Derussett was an expert hairdresser and that upon being told that he was so, HM [His Majesty] immediately applied to have him in his own service.'[15]

By July 1831, George was already an established favourite with the King, so much so that when he fell ill the King grumbled that his absence 'creates much inconvenience in the performance of the Household business'.[16] A solution was found. George's brother William was also a hairdresser, and also in Calcutta. (The two brothers may have travelled out together.) To William's delight 'some time in July [1831], I received an offer of employ to serve His Majesty the King of Oude and enjoined by my brother to leave Calcutta as early as possible by Dak'.[17] William arrived in Lucknow in such a hurry that he forgot to obtain a licence to reside in Awadh, and this had to be back-dated and provided.[18]

William soon found himself a young Anglo-Indian wife, Sarah Duboist, daughter of a band-master in the King's service, and the couple hired the Dilaram Kothi, a tall, English-looking house on the north bank of the Gomti, conveniently opposite the King's palace of Farhat Baksh, and joined to it by a bridge of boats. Two years later, in 1834, William was dead, and his baby son fatherless.[19] George promptly asked, and got, the King to pay the sea passages from England for a third brother, Charles, and 'Master George', the barber's own son. The Resident when asked later by the Company how so many Europeans came to be employed at Court, explained that George had recommended his brother to the King and that after William's death, he was 'succeeded in the same way by another Brother Charles Derusett'.[20] George now moved himself and his son into the Dilaram Kothi together with a woman mentioned in the Cash Book only as 'Mrs D'. Where she came from and where she went is a mystery, but it seems likely that she was Indian, for there are references to a 'silver mouth piece' for her hookah (rarely smoked by English or Anglo-Indian women), and the fee for her medical expenses paid to Hakim Yakub Ali Beg, not Dr Stevenson who normally attended Europeans.

The entries in the Cash Book begin on 25 November 1835, and show how deeply George was by then involved in the King's affairs. There can have been little time left for hairdressing, and in fact two Indian barbers from Calcutta were now employed by him as assistant hairdressers. George's many purchases and commissions for the King show a wealthy, if extravagant monarch, and also confirm contemporary descriptions of Lucknow as one of India's richest cities, indeed a panorama of pomp, luxury and frequent celebration. The barber was firstly, in charge of 'all His Majesty's pleasure Boats, Budjerows, pinnaces etc all most beautifully fitted up some with richly coloured silken sails etc. [and] all the Bridges crossing the River'. A major project was the conversion of a very large two-masted pinnace, purchased in Calcutta from John and James Beaumont and renamed the *Sultan of Oude* in honour of the King. It was brought up to Lucknow with a sixteen-man crew and docked in front of the Farhat Baksh, even grander than any of the royal ships on the waters of the Gomti.[21] George explained that 'The King ordered me to convert her into a three masted vessel, and to give her as much the appearance of a ship (sails and all) as possible, to have 16 or 18 Guns, to spare no expense in fitting her up in the handsomest manner . . . She had a beautiful carved and Gilt figure head with an elaborately carved and Gilt stern the interior was arranged so as to have a light appearance and the beautiful looking glasses were so arranged so as to reflect many fold the splendid . . . pillars which supported the deck above this part was fitted up for the accommodation of the zenanah the Queen and her Court or Ladies . . .'

How, one wonders, did a hairdresser set about converting and fitting up a pinnace? George was clearly a born organiser as well as a creative designer. He engaged William Trickett, a British engineer who had come out to Lucknow twenty years earlier with the iron bridge and steam engine ordered by Saadat Ali Khan. Under George's direction, Trickett supervised work on the pinnace, until 'he unfortunately fell sick, but I had the benefit of his advice, and the use of his professional books with which and the co-operation of a very clever Native workman or Mistry [carpenter] and the Serang [skipper] of the vessel together with my own application I managed to turn the Sultan of Oude out of hand to the satisfaction of all'.

Elaborate and costly fittings for the *Sultan of Oude* are noted, like lengths of orange-coloured velvet, pieces of shisham wood for the hatchway, 78 feet of teak for the deck and shower bath, mahogany for the window sashes, and 'a ships rig complete with mast, sail and 6 oars'. Since it was to be a pleasure boat four dozen bottles of brandy, a pair of decanters, and 54 'Brandy fruits' were included, for the King was determined to be as English as possible. A splendid awning with a gold fringe covered a throne, which was itself embroidered with 104 tolas of gold thread. 'At the Mast Head was floating the Royal silken banner with the Royal arms painted upon it by Muntz' [Charles Mantz, the German artist and Court painter].'

The King, George continued, 'had been very anxious for some time to see the juhaz or ship from the reports he had heard of its progress, and according a day was fixed for hauling or floating her out of the dock. Her crew had been increased to 30 men, all newly dressed for the grand occasion.' On board, musicians, nautch girls, and mimics waited 'and when His Majesty made his appearance it was the signal for general rejoicing. The Boatswain piped his whistle, as if by magic the yards were manned, a new sight entirely, and with which sight HM was delighted.'

'Manning the yards' involved the crew members climbing the rigging and treading along the cross beams, preparatory to letting out the sails. The scene was so novel that 'the king was [so] astonished at the agility displayd [*sic*] by the crew . . . that he had them piped up and down till they could scarcely move and the Boatswains piping pleased mightily, when the crew were lined up manning the yards he made the mimics ascend into the Tops and to see them shivering & shaking amused him much . . .' Brass guns with the royal arms cast on the breech fired a salute, which was echoed by the guns of the Arsenal on the shore. 'His Majesty inspected every part of the ship and expressed his delight & admiration I came in for my share of wah wahs.' George was rewarded with a *khilat*, the title of Surafranz Khan and an official seal, or *mohur*.[22]

Only one photograph is known of the *Sultan of Oude*, far removed from her prime as the King saw her that day. She appears, listing badly, her sails gone, but with the three masts and cross beams still identifiable, in 1858. She lies partially submerged in the Gomti, in front of the Farhat Baksh, itself ravaged by the British re-occupation of Lucknow. In the foreground, beached on the bank, is one of the steam-powered 'fish-boats' with wicker fins, which has previously been wrongly named as the 'state barge'. With George's detailed description, we can now identify the *Sultan of Oude* in the background, still at her moorings. She was already rundown by 1845 when a visitor found her with the King's apartments 'fitted up in the most costly manner; but which, as well as the vessel itself, is now in a very dirty and neglected state'.

Another appointment held by George was 'Master of the Royal Robes (European)'. On first examining the Poshak-khana or Wardrobe, it was found that several of the King's coats had been sporting, unwittingly, the crested gilt buttons of the East India Company. 'I soon altered this state of things,' he wrote. Working from diagrams supplied by Mr Nuthall, 'Tailor Habit & Pelisse Maker' of Calcutta, George sent him the King's measurements and got a number of European suits made up. His Majesty 'was so delighted with his new style of dress that he would not allow any person else to measure him'. George noted the King's measurements on a scrap of paper—he was a man of medium height, 5'6" tall, though of slight build with a 32½" chest and slender waist of 27½". George subsequently employed two Europeans, Mr Garztein (or Garstein) and then a Mr Powers, to superintend the fourteen Bengali tailors and chiken-work embroiderers brought up from Calcutta 'at a heavy cost for transit to Lucknow Being more experienced in making European costumes than up country tailors I spared no expense . . .' Clothes were made for the royal women too, from Europe Green satin, for the King 'saw in the wide Indian pyjamas, which are called *gharara*, a resemblance to a British lady's evening gown, and liked them so much that he made the Begams of the palace wear them'.[23]

A 'Tailor's Shop' was established, in or near the Dilaram Kothi, providing among other items 'Embroidery Bows and Buttons for a figured silk coat and a pair ditto Breeches for HM', 'a pair of Cuffs and Collar for Shirt', 'a Blue Velvet Robe Contg 4019 [tolas] of Gold' and '22 Large Splendid Gold Tassels for two Embroidery Coronation Robes 909 tolas'. As we have seen, the Kings of Awadh were recrowned annually by the Residents 'thus demonstrating the ruler's source of authority', as well as providing an irritating reminder that the East India Company were always at hand.[24] Insulting as this may have seemed to a quasi-independent monarch, the King chose to ignore the political implications and instead used the occasion for celebration and a new set of Coronation robes every year. For everyday wear the King appeared in the fashionable cutaway jackets of a Regency dandy but wore a lightweight crown instead of a hat. George made several purchases of 'Steel Wire and Silk for repairing H.M. Crowns'. Although wigs were going out of fashion in England at this time, money was 'paid to Women for dressing Tale [*sic*] Wigs for HM'. Sometimes temporary staff had to be hired for the tailor's shop, in order to meet deadlines, and twenty-seven tailors worked through one night to finish a special order for which they were paid overtime.

Costumes and ornaments for the King's retinue were provided from the shop for ceremonial occasions, like coronations. These were truly glittering events, that brought back something of the splendour of the old Mughal Court. There were the hookah bearers with gold leaf gilding their silver crowns, the palace bearers with silver fishes decorating their embroidered turbans, the coachmen, trumpeters and bass drummers in new gowns, the *chattarberdar* with his cape of dyed feathers, holding the ceremonial parasol of yellow silk with a silver handle, and the bodyguards with their gold-tasselled silver walking sticks.

Inside the palace a rare picture of domestic life emerges, where George was employed as Superintendent. The public rooms were clearly English in appearance, with their chintz tablecloths, chintz furnishings, tasselled silk cushions, silk-covered couches, artificial bouquets, and engraved silver breakfast dishes. Glassware and porcelain decorated the tables and an exotic touch was given by silver chairs. Because the King was fearful of being poisoned by supporters of a putative heir (a fear which seems fully justified by later events), George checked and sealed up with wax and kid leather the bottles of wine, champagne and spirits sent up from Calcutta for the royal table. He oversaw the King's French chef, Francis Ribeaut, and purchased food in bulk for the kitchens. Many entries record cash payments for 'HM Tiffin and Supper expenses' which were remitted to him through John Rose Brandon, another Englishman working at Court, with whom George was to become closely involved, and who we shall meet again in a later chapter.

By 1835 much domestic expenditure in the royal household was being channelled through George's hands, from the re-tinning of cooking pots, the purchase of '2 pairs of Jockey Boots for HM Coachman, and hides for the kettle drums' to 'pitterahs and numdahs' (felt covered pots for transporting ice). Outside the palace one or more of the royal stables was nominally under George's care too, though here his duties were

delegated to Raja Bakhtawar Singh, one of the King's officials who, together with Darshan Singh, superintended building works for the King.
Another nominal appointment was that of Head of the King's Menagerie
across the Gomti, 'a sort of park-ranger, in fact' as Knighton described
it, as well as the superintendence of the palace gardens and the building
of an ice-house. George also supervised the royal hunting parties which
now lasted for days rather than weeks, as they had done fifty years earlier.
But the most elaborate preparations still had to be made including the
provision of tent pieces, bamboo, twine, curtains, food and wine, as well
as the hire of temporary porters and carts to move all this equipment,
new thatching on the covered carriages and inspections and repairs to
bridges and roads that the royal party would cross.

Like other employees, George had to lay out his own money for
goods required by the King, and to pay the wages of the tailors, carpenters,
ship-fitters, gardeners, and other workers under his charge. He presented
his monthly bills to the King, which were reimbursed from the Treasury.
The actual bills were long scrolls of paper, joined as necessary, and rolled
up like maps. Knighton describes one of George's bills which, when un-
rolled, measured four and a half feet long, and totalled Rs 90,000
(£9,000).[25] Many people had found it curiously difficult to extract money
from the royal purse for wages or items bought, but George had discovered a way around this, as John Low reported. 'Mr Derusett and the natives
who execute commissions for the King, generally take the opportunity
of getting their accounts or their applications for advances of money,
signed by the King, when His Majesty is in a state of intoxication.'[26]

Indeed the King's drunkenness and wild supper parties were a cause
of frequent complaints by the Resident, acting on the Governor General's
instructions to monitor closely Nasir-ud-din Haider's behaviour. On
several occasions Low had had to rebuke the King for the 'extraordinary
liberties which he allowed Mr G. Derusett to take with him'. 'All the
community knew that Mr Derusett was a man of dissipated and disreput-
able character . . . [he] has been from first to last the prime mover of
these supper parties . . . [he] invites the other guests . . . they are virtually
his servants.'[27] Like a true courtier, reflecting his master's temperament
'the barber was always in the same mood as the king'.[28] Then there was
the shameful occasion when the King, in his cups, had insisted on going
to the Chandganj fair, across the river and a known rendezvous of prostitutes and 'a vile tribe of dancing Eunuchs' (hijra). After this last episode
the Resident took the King aside and told him privately to reform his

drunken habits. Low wanted to spare him the embarrassment of being told off in front of his courtiers, but the well-meaning gesture was wasted when the King promptly related the private conversation to eager listeners and added that 'happen what may he will continue to amuse himself . . . and that he would drink Hip Hip Hoora'.[29]

Rebuffed, the Resident then complained to the Governor General that the King 'wishes to go on with his childish desire to be surrounded with European servants about his Court in preference to having his own countrymen and subjects'. He wished 'to imitate the English in everything' although Low noted that 'His Majesty unfortunately never imitates the better portions of European customs or conduct, but selects only the vices or follies or the trifling customs of Europeans as fit subjects for imitation, such as drinking wine or spirits to excess, giving public toasts at his table in a noisy manner, dressing at all times in the English costume, which he does completely, excepting that he wears a Crown instead of a hat—eating his meals after the European manner, and having English furniture and English books (which he cannot read!) in his rooms etc.' 'His most intimate associates both European and Native are menials in his own service, amongst the first class his principal favourite for a considerable time past had been a Mr Derusett who holds the situation of Barber . . . there is a Mr Brandon, a Gardener and Mr Munz a musician.' The King has 'an inveterate predilection for low Company, addiction to drinking and frequent intoxication', having spent 66 lakhs a year on pleasure since his accession in 1827.

The supper parties continued 'and Mr Derusett is going on accumulating immense sums of money (he has already several lacs of rupees) by taking advantage of the King's habits, to obtain from His Majesty, when in a state of inebrity orders for the payment of accounts for Commission for buildings for the Keep of Horses etc'.[30] All Low's annoyance at the King's behaviour became focussed on George, a working-class man in class-ridden English society. It would be unfair to call it snobbery, because it was simply perceived as the natural order of things at the time. People like George and his friend John Rose Brandon were not gentlemen, in the nineteenth-century sense. It was inevitable that a Colonel and Resident of the East India Company like John Low was not going to see eye to eye with a London hairdresser. George was guilty on several counts. He was projecting the wrong kind of image for an Englishman in India. There were certainly a number of decent, respectable, family men in Lucknow engaged in trade and manual occupations, but George was not one of them. He clearly exerted that amount of influence over the King which the Resident felt should have been his. Moreover, he was creaming off large sums of money which the Company thought could have been better spent, or indeed have been put towards their own long-standing debt with the King.[31] There were also a number of complaints about him by other Europeans, which went up to the Resident for action.

Although a favourite with the King, who called him his 'dearest friend and brother, often drinking to excess with him, and sometimes hugging and embracing him in the presence of the servants of the Palace', George was not popular among many of his English contemporaries in Lucknow. He seemed to fall out with nearly everyone, except John Rose Brandon, although he was apparently always the wronged party. For example, the fourteen Bengali tailors for the shop had been selected by Mr Powers, himself a tailor, who travelled with them to Lucknow. George agreed to pay Powers Rs 150 per month, and provided his board and lodging. Soon after his arrival, however, Powers got into bad company 'with a Society that completely estranged his mind from my business . . . repeatedly being absent at Night, and returning at day break in such a state of intoxication and insensibility, totally unfitting him for any kind of business, untill [sic] he had a sufficient rest to Sleep off the effects, which occupied the greater part of the day'. Clearly George himself suffered no ill effects from his own drunken evenings with the King. Powers was dismissed after several warnings, complaining that the fourteen Bengalis were being held 'by force' in the tailor's shop, though this accusation was not followed up by the Resident. George had called Powers 'an ungrateful scoundrel' but it was noted that Powers' predecessor, a Mr Garztein had had to leave too, after an 'unfortunate misunderstanding'

A more serious complaint came from James Beaumont, who came to Lucknow to fit up the *Sultan of Oude*. George, he said, had not only initially promised him a job working for the King, but had talked of a shop 'for the manufacture of furniture, for which Mr Derusett was to have found funds independent of any risk to Mr Beaumont and Mr Beaumont was to keep the accounts of the shop and profits to be divided equally'. Neither job came to fruition, and Beaumont, having 'incurred debts to a considerable amount to articles supplied in the fitting up of the Pinnace, the workmen being clamourous for payment', submitted his account to George, who then refused to pay, saying Beaumont had broken his engagement. The case went to arbitration under the chairmanship of the Resident. Both parties chose their own arbitrators, who jointly decided against

George, and ruled that he should pay Beaumont Rs 1,180.12. Strangely George's memory played him false, for he claimed later that Beaumont 'conducted himself so very unsatisfactorily and even dishonestly that we parted, after which he made a false charge to the Resident against me, in which I beat him'. The person that George had chosen to act for him as arbitrator was Edward Cropley.

In spite of local difficulties, as news of George's influence at Court spread, he began to receive letters of solicitation for jobs in Lucknow. This was the usual approach to powerful men at a time when most appointments were secured by personal recommendation, or payment, or both. Some of his correspondents wanted jobs for themselves, others sought jobs for friends, whom they themselves could vouch for. Dr Colquhoun, for example, recommended Mr Campagnac as an officer to a new brigade of the King's, then wondered whether there might be a job for him too, organising a proper body of subordinate medical officers. News of possible openings at Court travelled quickly. Early in September 1836 George received a letter from Mr Grant of Tank Square, Calcutta, who had been supplying him with English books for the King. Grant had just met a friend of George, Yusuf Khan Kamalposh, adjutant in one of the King's brigades, who was about to set out on a voyage to England. 'Eusuph Khan, to whom you lately did me the pleasure of an introduction has very kindly communicated to me that the situation of Librarian to His Majesty the King of Oude had just prior to the dispatch of your last letter to him, become vacant.' (This was Cropley's former post.) Mr Grant felt he would be just the person, as he had been for eight years the Managing Proprietor of the Library known as 'The Calcutta Depository'. A reference would be sent to George 'on whom I am led to suppose the appointment will in a great measure, depend'.

Others, less subtle, simply offered money. Captain Leslie told him, 'You will not repent by coming to my terms of assisting me. You are well aware that I am up to the custom of the Natives and can at this present Moment push few Thousands in your pockets if we become on a friendly footing and all in an honourable way.' Another writer, asking for an introduction to the King, promised Rs 3,000 through a chit or *rooka* drawn on 'one of the greatest Men of Money in his Trade in Lucknow when you are sure of the dibs then do the needful for me'.

Apart from such opportunities, how did George amass his substantial fortune? It was the difference between the actual cost of goods bought for the King and the bills submitted that gave George his profit. Because

there was normally a delay between purchase and refund, it is difficult
to calculate exact figures from the Cash Book, especially as there was another set of accounts kept in Persian (as was customary), and 'other
English books' kept by Brandon. But the fact that George was able to
bear very substantial outlays, which were, in effect, loans to the King,
confirms John Low's statement of his assets. On most pages in the double-
entry accounts outgoings exceeded incomings, although the latter could
be enormous too. In January 1836, for example, George got £17,805
which included part payment for the *Sultan of Oude* and the coronation
robes for the year before.

Money came in regularly through John Rose Brandon and Raja
Bakhtawar Singh for the expenses of the royal stable. Small but costly
items were sold to wealthy Indians. Roshan-ud-daula, the Prime Minister, was in George's debt for some gold jewellery and watches he had
purchased. It was the Minister who brought George £6,008 from the
King for the Wardrobe expenses, having received his own 5 per cent
commission on the bill. Punctilious in recording his own outgoings,
we know less about the money George received. £1,400 arrived in January 1836, but someone has cut out with sharp scissors the name of the
sender. Bags of rupees arrived, carried by bearers (whom George tipped),
from Captain Fateh Ali Khan, Commander-in-Chief of the King's forces
and royal treasurer, but it is not clear in which capacity the captain was
sending the money. Was it a sweetener from the King's troops, or George's
wages from the treasury? There were generous gifts from the King too,
with Christmas presents of Rs 500 each for George, his brother Charles
and his son Master George, as well as *khilats* on special occasions.

The large sums accruing to George do not, of course, reflect the real
cost of living in Awadh during the 1830s, but say much about his financial
acumen. He was one of the very last of the old fashioned 'nabobs' more
often found sixty or seventy years earlier. The Lucknow Court, after the
East India Company's seizure of Delhi thirty years earlier, was now the
richest in India. This is why the impoverished Company was so interested
in it, and why Lucknow had attracted so many foreigners in the past. But
after George's departure there were no more official complaints about
Europeans exploiting gullible rulers. Outside the rarefied atmosphere of
the Court, services and goods were still cheap enough for Westerners to
live comfortably and save money for their return to Europe, but the opportunities to make a fortune had mostly gone. George's personal expenditure showed a modest lifestyle with ordinary household items like
candles, lamp oil, charcoal, writing paper, ink, postage, bazaar expenses,

food for the family's sheep, and 'Victuals for the Bull dog', all at a few annas or rupees each. His most expensive purchase for himself during 1835–36 was a new buggy from Messrs Cornish and Greig, which cost Rs 500. Total expenses for a journey to Cawnpore, including the bridge toll for five palkees, buggy and horses, the chowkidars on guard at night (for this was at the height of the thuggee terror), horse fodder, and coolie hire, amounted to Rs 19.9 annas (less than £2.00).

Small gifts of money to servants were important to oil the wheels of daily life. The palace *chobdar* who brought a dinner from the King to the Derusett brothers in the Dilaram Kothi got a Rs 5 tip. In fact any gift received from the King had to be properly acknowledged, like the two *khilats* which were worth a Rs 100 tip to the *chobdar* and *durwan*. At Christmas the Dilaram Kothi servants and the King's servants got Christmas presents from George. Occasionally people who worked for him received gifts in kind like Moti Mistri (possibly a silversmith, in spite of his name) who got eight yards of nainsook for a *chupkun* and *dupatta* and three yards *charkhanah* for an *angurka*. There were other small expenses including the monthly subscription of two rupees to the Lucknow library, run by Mr Archer and a Rs 200 donation to the Reverend Dawson towards a new church room. A modest two rupees went as 'charity to a poor Christian by order of Mrs D' and one day George bought 'three chances in a Raffle for a Buggy and Horse Rs 30' from Mrs Trickett, widow of the engineer who had worked on the pinnace. But sensibly George put some of his profits into East India Company bonds, payable in England, and some into Government Promissory notes, transactions that went through the British Residency without query, despite the Resident's criticisms of him.

At the time of his departure from Lucknow, just after Christmas 1836, George was in charge of the King's boats and bridges, his stables, his wardrobe, his kitchen and cellar, his palace, his crowns, his gardens, his menagerie and his elaborate hunting parties in Awadh. 'I secured the best available talent to superintend the various appointments of which I had charge one appointment led to another and by dint of application & tact, I succeeded in all,' he wrote later. So why did he suddenly leave, officially to execute some commissions for the King, although privately he told his friend John Rose Brandon that he had a problem with his mouth and needed to consult a dentist in Calcutta?

We need to go back to the previous summer when George had been on an extended buying trip to Calcutta, for the King. According to Cropley's story, the other Europeans at Court took advantage of his absence by trying to turn the King against him. They further urged him to reform by stopping the drunken evenings and debauches, which the Resident had already tried to do. On George's return in August 1836, after an absence of four months, he took the King in to dinner as before. But this time the King's tutor, Mr Wright, refused to sit at the same table with him, in spite of the King's pleas. Wright and Cropley subsequently fled the Court under the Resident's protection and made their way to Calcutta. The King, thus deprived of his friends, turned on George and reproached him for their loss, which marked the beginning of the end of the barber's reign.

But this was not how George saw it. In the pencilled account written after Knighton's book was published, he describes how he first employed Cropley, who was a jeweller by trade. George put him in charge of the goldsmith's shop in December 1833, lending him money to purchase materials and allowing him half the net profits. Meanwhile, 'His Majesty having a very extensive and valuable Library both Oriental & European and being desired to procure some English works to place in the vessel Sultan of Oude and also in his Library which was under the superintendence of Natives unacquainted with the English language I thought it a grand opening for Mr Cropley as Librarian. Not that he was competent according to ideas of such a post at home . . . he merely had to arrange the Books, and keep them so. I proposed Cropley to H.M. for the appointment, which he was graciously pleased to confirm at a monthly salary of Rs 500—without deduction although I am accused of [?] Bribery . . . all went on smooth until I had occasion to proceed to Calcutta . . .'

Unfortunately the following pages are torn away, and the narrative does not recommence until George is back in Lucknow to find the King accusing Wright and Cropley of an unnamed 'offence' against the barber. Loyal to his 'dearest friend' His Majesty said 'that for his part he could never place confidence in men who could act with such base ingratitude as they had been guilty of towards me . . . he observed that I was very unfortunate in the selection of my friends alluding to Mr W & Mr C and others in my own employ complaining falsely to the Resident, but I beat them all . . .' The King, just like the hero in a fairy story, then gave George 'some beautiful cashmere shawls', a *khilat* and *pugri*. Turning to Wright and Cropley, who had witnessed the presentation, His Majesty pointed to the barber saying 'there stands the Honored Surafranz Khan while you are dismissed with disgrace. Leave Oude within 24 hours.'

But the relationship between George and the King deteriorated during the remaining four months that they spent together. Cropley later claimed that George had intended to 'defect' during the summer trip to Calcutta, and that he had been transferring his cash into Company stocks, which was certainly true. Another friend, Mr Last (or possibly Fast), who had been in Lucknow during George's absence told him that 'a report then prevailed that you intended to proceed to Europe'. The King was not prepared to discuss the matter and told the Resident that he had dismissed Wright and Cropley, who received large salaries 'with a view to economy', an obvious falsehood when we know that Cropley's Rs 500 per month was a trifle.[32]

Some time in December 1836 George really did leave Lucknow for good. The last entry in his Cash Book is for 25 November, when the King sent some fireworks for Master George. Leaving behind his brother and son, but accompanied by the mysterious 'Mrs D', George travelled unexpectedly one night to Cawnpore, and was in Benares by the beginning of January, claiming toothache. Three letters in quick succession from John Rose Brandon, gave him news of the King's reaction, and advice on how to proceed. At first, on 3 January, Brandon requested him 'to write out a Persian petition and send it for us to give [the King] stating of course how your mouth is and the Number of Months you require with a Doctor's certificate'. The certificate was obtained immediately from the Civil Surgeon at Benares who strongly recommended George proceeding to Calcutta 'and putting himself under a Dentist's care'.

Three days later Brandon reassures George that all seems well at Court, and money continues to come in. 'I believe the Minister [Roshan-ud-daula] will behave well to us—he paid me the 15,000 and I now want the 20,000 in advance, which I asked him for today.' 'How is the 20,000 Rs advanced to you to be accounted for as I wish to make it out as soon as possible in case of accidents but I rather think H.M. will behave better to Charles now he gave him a plain ring yesterday. As soon as the boats arrive let us have some champayne [sic] and English claret if you can manage it.' The reason Brandon wanted to know 'how to make out the 20,000 bill is because I thought the Old Moonshee knew but he says he only knows what you said about the Palenkeens and Boachers [chair palanquins]. I rather think Mr Ord the new chap that attends table will be turned out—one less—you are well aware that we have plenty of Brass to stand out anything H.M. may say about you and I am so determined that I do not care but we may be able to manage 6 months I think

very easy. I have nothing more to say with the exception of the Minister
always asking how you are and desiring to be remembered to you, but
I am awake to the old rascal.'

However, two days later, Brandon was less sanguine about brazening
it out at Court for long. It was, he claimed, impossible to give the King
George's Persian petition and the doctor's certificate. 'I am afraid it will
be most injurious to our Interest and I can assure you the Minister has
news from Benares daily of what you do . . .' '. . . when he finds you have
left [Lucknow] without his sanction we shall suffer as he told me only
today to write to you and tell you to send him some of the best Beer . . . and
asked when you would come back.' 'I would not willingly keep you but
I am afraid it will play the devil with us.'

Commenting on George's final departure, John Low reported that
the Minister had told him George saw 'Some symptoms of his power
being on the decline, and that he himself solicited the mission to Calcutta,
with the Secret View of safely carrying off his fortune, and with the settled plan of not returning at all . . .' and that the King had suspected this
and was already looking for a new hairdresser.[33] Six months earlier the
uninhibited *Agra Ukhbar* had claimed that 'society is anxiously expecting
"the Barber of Lucknow", with his investment. The "prime minister's"
dak has long been laid for his escape when his time comes; and it is said
that all his women, horses, jewels and furniture have already been
despatched. Enough has been kept to keep up appearances.'[34] With George
gone, the real Prime Minister, Roshan-ud-daula could breathe more
easily. His influence had been compromised by the barber's powerful
hold on the King. The Resident also reported that Roshan-ud-daula had
been afraid of Ganga Khawass, a low-caste gardener and drinking companion of the King 'and of Mr Derusett the Barber'. Now, with George
gone, the King had dismissed the aggressive gardener.

On the evening of 10 February 1837 John Rose Brandon and Charles
Derusett unwisely got into a drunken argument with the King and tried
to persuade him to re-instate Ganga Khawass. Nasir-ud-din Haider, in
a lucid moment, recalled his position and told the pair not to interfere.
Inflamed by drink Charles then 'lost his temper and swore in a very
violent and vulgar manner'. The King took offence and summoned his
Bodyguard, who rushed into the supper chamber. Charles lashed out
and hit a sepoy in the face, but the two Englishmen were overpowered,
dismissed from their jobs on the spot by the King, and confined as prisoners in their own houses, until they had accounted for money already

advanced to them for repairs to the Garden Houses and for the garden-ers' pay.[35]

George was back in England by the summer of 1837, without 'Mrs D' but with a sum estimated at £90,000.[36] Charles Derusett and John Rose Brandon, released from house imprisonment, joined him, bringing Master George with them.[37] Brandon was later to marry the barber's daughter Mary Ann, thus becoming George's son-in-law. Only six months after George's flight Nasir-ud-din Haider, the fun-loving King was dead, aged only thirty-five. He was generally thought to have been poisoned by one of his father's many wives, who then attempted to put her own son on the *masnad* in a dramatic move, as we shall see. One wonders whether the King would not have survived if George had still been there to check the wine bottles and supervise the kitchens.

Though a rogue in British eyes, this is not necessarily how Nasir-ud-din Haider, or other Indians, might have seen him. Was he a hero or a villain? George was certainly no better nor worse than many other Eng-lishmen who had exploited Awadh, including former Residents and Warren Hastings himself. Indeed, his haul was modest compared to that of earlier Company officers. But it was George's bad luck that he fell out with Edward Cropley, who then related the story to Knighton at an opportune moment twenty years later. Whatever his faults, George had looked after the King well, and had kept him entertained for five years. He had translated Nasir-ud-din Haider's anglophilia into practical channels. If he had had the backing of the Resident, instead of the surly opposition encountered, he might have brought the King into the fold of the East India Company, as a useful ally. After all, George had proved a surprisingly able manager of the royal estates for a man who had started life as a humble barber.[38]

NOTES AND REFERENCES

1. Edwardes, Michael, *The Orchid House*, Cassell, London 1960, p. 38.
2. Ibid., p. 152.
3. Ibid., p. 183.
4. Knighton, William, *The Private Life of an Eastern King*, London 1855. In 1921 it was republished with an introduction by S.B. Smith and my references are to this edition. It was also translated into Urdu and published in India in 1885.
5. Although Knighton does not specifically name Edward Cropley as his source, George Derusett was in no doubt that Cropley was his informant.

6. *The Calcutta Review,* Calcutta, July–December 1855, p. 117. 'Conquest—Is It Past?'

7. 6 March 1837, nos 92–5, India Political Consultations, Colonel John Low, Resident at Lucknow to the Political Secretary to the Government of India at Fort William, OIOC.

8. *The Asiatic Journal,* New Series, Calcutta, January–April 1837, p. 94, quoting the *Agra Ukhbar* of 6 August 1836.

9. Edwardes, op. cit., p. 56.

10. George Derusett's Cash Book, 25 November 1835 to 25 November 1836 and miscellaneous papers from 1835 to post 1855, now in the possession of Janet Dewan, formerly with Basil de Rusett.

11. See Christie's auction catalogue for 23 February 1993, sale of 'Fine Costume, Needlework and Textiles', item no. 149, p. 15. Suit now in the possession of Janet Dewan.

12. Oil painting in the possession of Janet Dewan.

13. Photograph in the possession of Basil de Rusett.

14. Op. cit., ref. 7.

15. 27 February 1837, no. 31, India Political Consultations, Colonel John Low to Secretary to the Government of India, Fort William, Calcutta, OIOC.

16. 2 September 1831, no. 95, Bengal Political Consultations, Nasir-ud-din Haider to John Paton, Assistant Resident, Lucknow, OIOC.

17. 16 September 1831, no. 51, Bengal Political Consultations, William Derusett to John Paton, OIOC.

18. 2 April 1832, no. 71, India Political Consultations, OIOC.

19. William Derusett's son, Charles, was sent to 'Mr Mackinnon's School' in Mussoorie. This was the newly opened Mussoorie Seminary, on the site of the old brewery (see *Mussoorie and Landour: Days of Wine and Roses,* by Ruskin Bond, pub. Lustre Press, New Delhi 1992, p. 21). Charles later became a photographer and hotel keeper in Simla. It was Charles's son who became known as the 'White Sadhu of Jakko'. Born in 1859, and named Charles William Francis, he was educated at Bishop Cotton School, Simla, and subsequently worked as a spy for the British Government, visiting Tibet. He was later described as residing in the Monkey Temple at Jakko, Simla, wearing a red quilted cap crowned with a peacock's feather and a gold caste mark. *The Mystics, Ascetics and Saints of India,* John Campbell Oman, London 1905, pp. 222–3.

20. See ref. 15 above.

21. There were royal steam boats and barges with oarsmen on the Gomti, but the *Sultan of Oude* seems to have been the first royal sailing ship.

22. Probably *sur-i-faraz,* exalted, honoured.

23. Sharar, Abdul Halim, *Lucknow: The Last Phase of an Oriental Culture,* trans. E.S. Harcourt and Fakhir Hussain, London 1975, p. 177.

24. Fisher, Michael, *A Clash of Cultures: Awadh, the British and the Mughals,* New Delhi 1987, p. 161.

25. Knighton, op. cit., p. 71.
26. See ref. 7 above.
27. Ibid.
28. Knighton, op. cit., p. 71.
29. See ref. 7 above.
30. Ibid.
31. See Llewellyn-Jones, *A Fatal Friendship: The Nawabs, the British and the City of Lucknow*, OUP, Delhi 1985, p. 4, for the origins of the Nawab's debt.
32. 27 February 1837, no. 32, India Political Consultations, the King to Colonel Low, OIOC.
33. See ref. 7 above.
34. *Agra Ukhbar*, 18 June 1836.
35 See ref. 7 above.
36. *Agra Ukhbar*, op. cit., p. 34.
37. 'Master George' grew up to become an engineer and returned to Lucknow in 1849 on a salary of Rs 150 per month. He died in the uprising of 1857. John Rose Brandon returned too, this time as a 'horticulturist' on Rs 200 a month.
38. George Harris Derusett died in Sydney, Australia, in 1861, aged 60. Death Register No. 1017 in the NSW Pioneers Index. Information kindly provided by Catherine Keelan-Parsons, of Hampton, Australia.

CHAPTER FOUR

Indian Visitors to England

The cantonment at Cawnpore was established in 1770 as a base for East India Company troops who had been sent up-country to guard the ford across the river Ganges. Cawnpore then lay within the territory of the Nawab of Awadh, Shuja-ud-daula, and the troops were stationed there, at the Nawab's expense, to defend his borders against the Mahratta and Rohilla incursions. It was a convenient arrangement, particularly for the Company, giving it a legitimate excuse to establish a strategic foothold in foreign territory during the early years of expansion into northern India. In the next three decades the cantonment grew rapidly to become the largest military encampment outside the Presidency towns of Calcutta, Bombay and Madras. In 1801 Shuja-ud-daula's son Saadat Ali Khan was forced to secede Cawnpore, together with other parts of Awadh, to the Company, who then moved in another army, this time of officials, administrators, revenue collectors, engineers, lawyers and chaplains. A town had already grown up around the original cantonment to service the needs of the troops, but now Cawnpore developed into a sophisticated inland city to serve and entertain the new civilians as well. There were the Assembly Rooms, a theatre, a racecourse, European shops, and later, hotels.[1] It became a convenient and comfortable halt for European travellers to and from the new Nawabi capital of Lucknow, sixty miles distant.

These Europeans would have arrived in India through Calcutta, and then turned westwards again. A journey up-country from the western port of Bombay was not feasible when few *pukka* roads existed, and the Company had no authority or allies across western India. River transport was generally safer, faster and easier until the mid-nineteenth century,

and travellers could come all the way up to Cawnpore from Calcutta
along the Ganges, which was navigable all the year round. There had
been an attempt to cut a canal between the Gomti and the Ganges in
1831, to facilitate waterborne traffic but it was unsuccessful. When the
Grand Trunk Road from Calcutta to Peshawar, via Delhi, was surfaced
in the 1830s it went through Cawnpore, making it still easier to reach,
but Lucknow remained isolated. The traditional *kutcha* road between
Cawnpore and Lucknow which meandered through villages and baza-
ars was not supplemented by a metalled road until 1842. So travellers began their journey into Awadh by crossing the bridge of boats over the
Ganges, and continued with various difficulties through pleasant, well-
wooded plains until they reached the Chowk, the main artery of old
Lucknow.

Along the road to Lucknow were to come an increasing number of
Company officials, troops and traders, but there were sightseers and
artists too, impelled by curiosity. Many of the latter, men like Thomas
Twining, George Forster, the Comte de Modave, Lord Valentia and Prince
Saltuikov, left accounts of their visits. William and Thomas Daniell,
William Hodges, and others, sketched and painted for armchair travellers
at home, eager to learn more of the dazzling new buildings of the city,
richly endowed by the wealthy Nawabs. But there was a small trickle of
people going the other way too, flowing against the tide, a handful of
Indians from Lucknow travelling to England, whose adventures are little
known, even today.

The number from Lucknow (or indeed, from the rest of India), who
made the journey to Britain during the late eighteenth and early nineteenth centuries, was understandably small. Of the people who came to
Britain as sailors (lascars) on passenger and merchant ships, or as servants
to Britons who had worked in India, we know little. Their voices remain
largely silent.[2] None came as traders in their own right, for the East India
Company guarded its prerogatives jealously, though there may have been
a small amount of unofficial business. Few distinguished Indians published accounts of their visits, in sharp contrast to the garrulous English travellers. Diaries or letters which may still be in private hands in India have
not been made known. Against the mass of European travellers' accounts,
there is little to work on when the picture is reversed. In most cases we
can only guess at the reactions of these enterprising people, for whom
there was no helpful *vade mecum* on what to expect in England.

The reasons which took people from Lucknow to England were as
varied as the people themselves, and some are intimately connected with

the brief history of the Nawabi capital. One woman, Halima, went for love, and was cruelly disillusioned. Mirza Abu Talib Khan Isfahani, the 'Persian Prince' went to escape a deep depression following the loss of his young son. The soldier Yusuf Khan Kamalposh went purely out of curiosity, as a tourist. The Nawab Iqbal-ud-daula went, unsuccessfully, to redress a grievance, as did the Queen Mother, Janab Alia Begam, mother of the last King, Wajid Ali Shah. There were others too, including Mir Hussein Ali Londoni, who had been employed at the East India Company College at Haileybury in Hertfordshire for many years, and who, on his return home, brought an English wife with him, better known as Mrs Meer Hassan Ali, author of the often quoted book *Observations on the Musulmans of India.* Londoni, whose name reflects his sojourn in England, at a time when 'London' was sometimes used to represent 'England' was then employed in the British Residency as a *daroga*, or superintendent. All these travellers were Muslims, people not bound by religious prohibitions against sea-journeys, like their fellow Hindus. Some were never to return home.

Halima is known to us today as Helena Bennett, the anglicised name that she took after her marriage to General Benoit de Boigne, Claude Martin's friend. She was born in Lucknow in 1772, the daughter of a Persian cavalry officer in the service of the Emperor Shah Alam I, and a local noblewoman.[3] Halima was married at an early age to the Nawab of Pundri, just west of Delhi, but her husband died before the marriage could be consummated and she was left a widow before she was fifteen years old. During a visit to Delhi in 1788, Halima met de Boigne who had been placed in charge of the Red Fort after its capture by the Muslim chief Rana Khan, for the Mahratta leader Mahadaji Scindia. De Boigne was present when Shah Alam I, shamefully blinded by the Rohilla chieftain Ghulam Kadir, was re-installed on the Mughal throne. The Frenchman had played a decisive part in the recent battle of Agra, which marked the successful conclusion of Scindia's plan to reconquer northern India, with a coalition, in the name of the Emperor. De Boigne and his battalions had saved Scindia's life a year earlier in one of the battles that led to the Mahratta entry into Delhi. He was at the height of his success, a handsome 'man of the world' as Claude Martin described him, twenty years older than Halima. Within a short time he had married the young widow 'according to the ways and customs of the country', presumably a Muslim marriage, and a daughter was born in Lucknow to the couple at the end of 1789.[4] The child was given two names, one Indian, Banoo, and the other English, Anne. On her marriage, de Boigne's wife became Hélène Benoit, 'Hélène' after de Boigne's mother, Hélène Gabet, and 'Benoit', from the General's first name. Both names were anglicised on her arrival in England in 1797, and she became Helena Bennett.

More is known about Helena's older sister, Faiz-un-Nissa, who also married a foreigner, William Palmer (later Lieutenant-General), about 1780. Palmer fathered six children, though not all of them by Faiz-un-Nissa. The eldest boy, William, Helena's nephew, grew up to found the Hyderabad banking firm of Palmer & Co. A portrait of the Palmer family, painted by Francesco Renaldi about 1786 shows Helena's sister as a pretty, fair-skinned woman, and we can imagine that Helena too, was an attractive person.[5] Helena's second child, a son, was born in Delhi at the beginning of 1792. She may have been staying in her father's household at the time, for de Boigne was then commanding his battalions on Scindia's behalf in Rajasthan. The boy was named Ali Baksh, but baptised (nine years later, in London), as Charles Alexander Benoit de Boigne.

Like his brother-in-law, de Boigne took a second Indian wife, named Mehr-un-Nissa, from a fortress town near Bikaner. De Boigne had successfully besieged the fort in a series of minor, punitive campaigns in western India. On its fall he was 'given' Mehr-un-Nissa in gratitude for his chivalrous behaviour during the siege and he married her shortly afterwards. But it seems to have been a marriage in name only, and de Boigne later wrote to Joseph Quieros that 'It was intended when I got this girl she would live with me rather in an inferior condition . . . but she was far from being handsome, and of a most violent disposition and temper as well as bad condition . . .'[6]

During the early 1790s de Boigne's health began to deteriorate, due to recurring malarial attacks, and he started to take opium to relieve the symptoms. After the death of Mahadaji Scindia in 1794 he had been made an unprecedented offer by Shah Alam II to become his Wazir and 'to restore the Mughal Empire'. This was a flattering acknowledgment of his success in training Indian soldiers on European lines to become a skilled fighting force.[7] But wisely de Boigne declined, as he did another grandiose offer the same year from Shah Zaman, the King of Afghanistan, to enter the latter's service. He decided to return to Europe to restore his health and he spent 1795 and most of 1796 tying up his affairs. He entrusted the payment of pensions for Mehr-un-Nissa and Zeenat, another Indian wife he had acquired, to Joseph Quieros. Although no children were born from either of these marriages, de Boigne did leave at least one illegitimate daughter in India, apparently with little or no financial support.[8] The General embarked with Helena, Anne and Charles Alexander for the English port of Deal, in Kent, at the end of 1796.

Why de Boigne chose to arrive in England, rather than his native town of Chambery, in Savoy, is explained by his biographer, Desmond Young.[9] At that period Savoy was still suffering from the aftermath of the French Revolution, and a wealthy man with no revolutionary sympathies would have found life there difficult, if not dangerous. Secondly, many of the friends made during his time in India had by now retired to England, including the former Governor General Warren Hastings, the Assistant Resident at the Lucknow Court, Richard Johnson, the artist Johann Zoffani and Anthony Tremamondo, former Riding Master to the Bengal Army. De Boigne took a house in Great Portland Street, London, for his wife and children, and he became a naturalised British subject on 1 January 1798.

Whether his naturalisation gave Helena British citizenship too is an arcane point of law, depending on whether a Muslim marriage between a European and a Muslim was recognised as valid in a British court of law. It was never put to the test. Only a few weeks later de Boigne was introduced in a London drawing-room to Adèle, the beautiful seventeen-year-old daughter of the Marquis d'Osmond, a French nobleman. Now nearing fifty, de Boigne immediately fell in love with the young woman, and proposed marriage, through a friend, in days. Within a couple of months he had persuaded Helena to accept a settlement that released him from any financial or moral obligations towards her. She is said to have refused to take him to court to obtain justice (which strengthens the argument that her marriage was valid), and to have accepted her lot with resignation. In return she got a house at Enfield, in Surrey, a capital sum that produced £300 per annum, school fees and the custody of her two children. John Walker, Geographer to the India Office and Helena's trustee wrote: 'An eminent lawyer at the time offered to take up her case and bring an action against the General, but she declined it on account of the children. She afterwards retired to Enfield, a pleasant village near London, where she lived quietly and respectably and was received in every company, being considered his legitimate wife.'[10]

De Boigne, on the other hand, wrote of her: 'She is a respectable woman in every regard and it would be fortunate for me if my legitimate wife [Adéle d'Osmond] should have the refined sentiments and principles of this Indian lady.'[11] Either he believed that the ceremony which had taken place in Delhi eleven years earlier was not binding on a naturalised

Briton now living in England, or more interestingly, he had divorced Helena in London according to Muslim law. Possibly de Boigne had conveniently adopted Islam for his first three marriages and abandoned it for his fourth. Certainly he wrote to Helena, custodian of the two children, 'I will not recommend you, my dear Begum to give your earnest care and attention to their principles, yours having always been those of a good and well-behaved woman. They could never be under a better guardian than you, so I am perfectly easy in regard to it when at home, as also in regard to their health, as you have always been to them a good mother. They will, when of age, be sensible of it and prove in return to be dutiful children to you, in being the comforts and supports of your old days . . . I have seen you a good daughter to your mother, an affectionate wife to me and tender mother to your two offspring. God will reward you . . . believe me with most sincere affection for ever, your friend.'[12] Helena was not entirely without other friends, including some who had known her in Lucknow, like Dr William Blane, surgeon to the Nawab Asaf-ud-daula. There is no hint that she ever considered returning to India to live with her sister and brother-in-law, for this would have meant leaving the children. Her eldest daughter, Anne, was now at school in Hammersmith, London.

Claude Martin, to whom de Boigne had written twice in May 1798 with news of his engagement and a painting of Adèle, responded enthusiastically about the 'young and beautiful girl . . . and pretty as an angel, eighteen years old . . . Oh, my good friend! The painting is so beautiful that I envy your luck and am even jealous.'[13] Not a word or question about Helena, his best friend's wife who would certainly have known Martin's own favourite mistress, Boulone.

Within a year of his marriage, in May 1798, de Boigne had separated from Adèle, although there were to be a number of reconciliations and further separations. He kept in touch with Helena and wrote to her in 1801 that he was 'a little more happy than I have been for these three years past' but was 'afraid it will never turn out a lasting happiness'. De Boigne subsequently returned to Chambery, where he bought the chateau of Buisson Rond, and another house near Paris, where Adèle joined him. He then proposed, rather impractically, that Helena and the children should join him too. In the event only Anne, then aged fifteen, travelled to Paris and here, tragically, she died from a fever shortly after her arrival. Describing Anne's many good qualities, her grieving father wrote that she was 'of an extremely agreeable colour to the eye, although born to an Indian mother, who mourns her no less than I'.[14] Among the private archives of the de Boigne family is the letter, in English, from Helena on learning of her daughter's untimely death. 'I think you ought to give thanks to God for having many relations, friends and acquaintances where poor I had but very few or next to none.'[15] Some time before Anne's death Helena had abandoned her Muslim faith and become a Catholic.

Her son, Charles, was educated at St Edmund's College in Hertfordshire, and kept in touch with de Bogine, who, like many a divorced father, sent messages to his former wife through the boy. He clearly remained fond of Helena, his fondness for an earlier, happier relationship undoubtedly fuelled by the aberrant behaviour of his second wife. In 1815 Charles joined his father in Chambery and succeeded him as heir on his death fifteen years later. The present de Boigne family are descended from Charles.

After her daughter's death Helena moved to the hamlet of Lower Beeding, near Horsham in Sussex, into a small house paid for by de Boigne. Understandably the presence of a noble Indian lady in an English village made an impact. Oral tradition says she became known as 'The Black Princess', not because she was particularly dark-skinned, but because she was of a different race, and a different class, from a foreign country. The term 'black' did not then have the pejorative meaning it does today. There is good evidence that Helena was the Indian lady that the poet Shelley mentioned as wandering about in the neighbouring St Leonard's Forest. Local historians have established that she used the Horsham firm of solicitors Pilfold Medwin, who were Shelley's uncles, and the poet was thirteen years old when she settled in his neighbourhood. It may, then, be no coincidence that he became so absorbed later in Persian mysticism and Islamic lore. Moreover, he has left some fragments of an unfinished drama, written in 1822, the year of his death, in which an Indian speaks with a lady who has been abandoned by her lover in a strange land. The fictional deserted lady says at one point:

> I offer only
> That which I seek, some human sympathy
> In this mysterious island . . .

a sentiment that Helena might well have felt, if not expressed.[16]

Towards the end of her life, she moved into lodgings in North Street, Horsham, and it was here that she died on 27 December 1853, aged eighty-one. Half a century after her death Helena's former maidservant Mrs Caroline Budgen, herself then an old woman of eighty-two, was questioned about her former employer. A vivid picture emerges of the old Indian woman in exile. 'Sallow in complexion with strange dark eyes, she would sometimes stay in bed until noon and often kept on her night-cap when at last she got up. She took no trouble at all about her dress but wore magnificent rings. She smoked long pipes (presumably a hookah), lost her temper very easily and could not bear to be bothered about anything.' She attended Mass at the Catholic Church in nearby Horsham on Sundays, being driven over in a pony cart. She was 'exceedingly good to the poor and often sent to Horsham for bread to distribute among them. She was also very fond of animals and bought numbers of all kinds.'[17] There is no evidence that she enjoyed any kind of social life in her later years. No accounts exist of her in local memory, other than as 'The Black Princess' who was a generous benefactor to the poor. Although a Catholic she was buried in the Protestant cemetery of St Mary's Parish Church at Horsham on 4 January 1854. Her grave is the only one aligned north to south, which has led to speculation that she wanted to make her separation from Islam painfully clear. The inscription on the flat stone reads 'Requiescat in pace. Helena Bennett vidua defuncta obitt 27 Decembris 1853 aet. suae LXXXI. Beati qui lugent quia illi consolabuntur.' (Rest in peace. Helena Bennett, widow died 27 December 1853, aged 81. Blessed are they that mourn for they shall be comforted.)[18]

It was the death of another child that prompted Mirza Abu Talib Khan Isfahani to visit England two years after the de Boigne family's arrival there. Abu Talib was, like Helena, of Persian descent, his father having fled Isfahan when Nadir Shah overthrew the ruling Safavid dynasty in 1736 and seized the Persian throne. The family settled in Lucknow where Abu Talib's father, Haji Muhammed Beg Khan was befriended by the second Nawab of Awadh, Safdar Jang, whose own family had come from the Persian town of Nishapur. Abu Talib was born in Lucknow in 1752, and his mother received a grant from the third Nawab, Shuja-ud-daula to pay for his education. But there was bad feeling between Haji Muhammed Beg Khan and the Nawab that led Abu Talib to leave Lucknow when he reached sixteen years of age. He settled in Calcutta, which not only led him to take a more objective view of Awadh politics, but exposed him to English society and ideas. On Shuja-ud-daula's death he returned to Lucknow where the new Nawab Asaf-ud-daula was establishing his headquarters. There were opportunities for bright young men like Abu Talib and an early appointment was as Amaldar at Etawah, collecting land revenues in the countryside. Later he worked as collector to Colonel Alexander Hannay and he was to write that during this period he spent nearly three years 'in tents or temporary houses composed of mats or bamboos'. This gave Abu Talib a valuable insight into peasant life and he was subsequently seconded to work for the British Resident Nathaniel Middleton, on the recommendation of Warren Hastings. His specific task was to curb a peasant revolt, which he did, but with much criticism of the Lucknow government and the behaviour of its corrupt officials.[19]

He was an outspoken critic of the Nawab's own extravagance too, as Asaf-ud-daula's 'building mania' embellished the banks of the Gomti with costly palaces. He was remarkably sympathetic towards the poor of Lucknow, especially those who lost their houses in the Nawab's mad rush to demolish everything that stood in his way. His radical views, though shared by some British commentators, were unusual at the time for an Indian, and he made some powerful enemies. He seemed to be without fear and criticised the Chief Minister Haider Beg Khan, who had been put in charge of revenue collection in 1782 for 'throwing the Nawab's affairs into confusion'.[20] The Minister promptly got Abu Talib's annual salary of Rs 6,000 stopped. He then lost the patronage of his English employer Middleton, when the corrupt Resident was recalled to Calcutta by Warren Hastings. Abu Talib himself retreated to Calcutta and spent the next five years collecting and publishing Persian poetry, which included the *Diwan-i-Hafiz*. He also began a history of Asaf-ud-daula's reign, which was published in Persian and translated into Urdu as *Tareek-i-Asafi*.[21] He combined his intellectual interests of literature and history with the practical duties of a government official, not unlike later district officers with their collections of folk songs and translations of obscure manuscripts. At the same time he seems to have been something of an irritant both to the Nawabi Court, and the British Residency. Although the Governor General, Lord Cornwallis was aware of his many good qualities and recommended him to a further Resident at Lucknow, he was not offered another appointment there. Although unemployed, he was not a poor man and he remained in Calcutta, living comfortably with his wife and children.

By the end of the decade however, he was suffering from a deep depression, following the death of his four-year-old son, a victim of the unhealthy climate. An English friend of his, Captain David Richardson suggested that he accompany him to England to dispel the gloom that hung about him after his bereavement. The pair left Calcutta to board the Danish ship *Christiana* which set sail for Cape Town in February 1799. From there they took the *Britannia* to Ireland and Abu Talib began to make regular, detailed notes. The manuscript of his travels was finished by 1804, and *The Travels of Mirza Abu Taleb Khan in Asia, Africa & Europe During the Years 1799, 1800, 1801, 1802 & 1803* was published in London in 1810. It was translated from the Persian by Charles Stewart, Professor of Oriental Languages at the East India Company's College at Haileybury and went into a second edition four years later. The translator introduced it as 'The first time the genuine opinions of an Asiatic, respecting the institutions of Europe, have appeared in the English language'.[22] This was factually correct, for although the first book written in English by an Indian author, Dean Mahomed, had been published in 1794 in Ireland, it related his travels in India only. Abu Talib was the first published Indian writer to comment on the English in their native habitat.[23]

His *Travels* is an entertaining book, not only for its objective view of early nineteenth-century England, but for what the author unconsciously reveals about himself. He comes across as a pompous, self-opinionated man, quick to name drop, and something of a snob, but with an undeniable amount of charm, energy and enthusiasm. If his translator chose to call him 'the Persian Prince', then he was not going to argue. Possibly his father *was* a minor member of the deposed Safavid family, if not, then his family certainly *knew* a number of princes in India and he himself had married well. Abu Talib was, according to his own account, lionised by English society and immediately accepted into the best circles, due to his exotic and cultured personality and his many connections with members of the East India Company now returned home. He was a wealthy man, and travelled with a large retinue of servants, one of whom, a negro, he had been obliged to sell at the Cape, finding himself temporarily short of cash there after a longer stay than he had anticipated.

One sentence gives the flavour of the man: 'I may perhaps be accused of personal vanity by saying that my society was courted, and that my wit and repartees, with some impromptu applications of Oriental poetry, were the subject of conversation in the politest circles.' One of the 'Oriental poems' is appended as a 'Translation of an Elegy on Tufuzzil Hussein Khan, Envoy from the Nabob of Oude to the Governor General of India' which he wrote on 2 May 1802 and presented to Lady Elford. It paints an eloquent picture of the gifted Lucknow philosopher and diplomat who had died in 1800:

> Alas, The zest of Learning's cup is gone
> For he, their sage belov'd, is dead; who first
> To Islam's followers explained their laws,
> Their distances, their orbits and their times.
> As great Copernicus once half divin'd,
> And greater Newton, proved: but, useless now,
> Their works we turn with idle hand and scan
> With vacant eye, our own first master gone.[24]

Another original poem was entitled 'Ode to London' although Abu Talib seemed unable to decide whether he liked England or not. On the one hand he found the English irreligious, arrogant, greedy, lazy, vain and selfish. He was surprised at the amount of liberty which the women had and thought the many prostitutes he saw on the streets implied 'a want of chastity' on the part of the men. He had however, chosen to live in Rathbone Place, off Charlotte Street, just north of London's Soho, where half the street was then inhabited by courtesans. He drew no analogy between it and Lucknow's red-light district, the Chowk, which contemporary English people found just as shocking.

Due to bad weather, the *Britannia* could not put into the English Channel and was forced to dock at Cork, in Ireland. Here he had a chance meeting with fellow Muslim Dean Mahomed, and noted the latter's book 'containing some account of himself and some about the customs of India' which may have given him the idea of doing something similar himself, but setting it in Europe.[25] The poverty of the Irish scene, even before the potato famine, shocked him. 'The peasants of India are rich when compared to them,' he observed, though he found plenty of grandeur too in Dublin's fine houses with their coloured chandeliers that reminded him of those in the Great Imambara at home. While in Dublin he renewed his acquaintanceship with his former patron Lord Cornwallis, now Viceroy of Ireland. In spite of his reservations about the English character, on his arrival in London, via Holyhead and Chester, on 21 January 1800, he found that curiously, 'From my first setting out on this journey, till my arrival in England I ascended the pinnacle of magnificence and luxury; the several degrees or stages of which were Calcutta, the Cape, Cork, Dublin and London: the beauty and grandeur of each city effacing that of the former. On my return towards India everything was reversed, the last place being always inferior to that I had quitted. Thus, after a long residence in London, Paris appeared to me much inferior.'[26] He was one of few foreigners, perhaps the only one, to find English cuisine more appealing than French.

He was an assiduous tourist, visiting London's attractions including the Bank of England, the Royal Exchange, the Vauxhall Gardens (which he must have found strangely familiar after living in Lucknow), Woolwich Arsenal, the Tower of London, the Law Courts, Greenwich and the British Museum in Great Russell Street, which then stood on the periphery of the city. From one of its many windows Abu Talib could look north to the 'beautiful villages of Hampstead and Highgate' glimpsed across rich meadows and verdant fields. In the King's Library at Buckingham House (the future Buckingham Palace), he inspected the Padshahnama of Shah Jehan, which had been given by Asaf-ud-daula to the Governor General Sir John Shore during the latter's first visit to Lucknow in the spring of 1797.[27]

His observations of mundane things are perhaps more interesting to us. He found that English roads were very good, wide and formed of stone or gravel with good, substantial bridges (in sharp contrast to the *kutcha* path between Lucknow and Cawnpore). He noted the neat eighteenth-century town houses of brick and stone, often four storeys high, with regular rows of glazed windows and roofs 'sloped like a tent, and covered with tiles or thin stones called slates'. 'The streets and shops are lighted all night,' he marvelled. He had described the extravagant marriage of Asaf-ud-daula's heir, Wazir Ali, in Lucknow but this spectacle paled into insignificance compared with the illuminations of London. He found numerous garden squares with iron gates and railings around them which the key-holders could enjoy without being molested. He described the proposed tunnel under the Thames (which Yusuf Khan Kamalposh was to visit nearly forty years later), a brewery, steam engines and the hydraulic machines for supplying London with water, which was raised to a reservoir and conducted by conduits and leaden pipes. He saw early spinning engines, where as many as a thousand threads could be spun and woven at the same time, though he thought that the finished product was not as good as Indian cloth. Mechanisation was being introduced in many areas following the Industrial Revolution and 'In short, the English carry their passion for mechanics to such an extent, that machinery is introduced into their kitchens and a very complete engine is used even to roast a chicken.' Daily newspapers, coffee houses and Clubs, including the Indian Club for 'gentlemen who have resided for some years in the East' were pleasant ways of spending time. He wrote perceptively about the English upper classes that 'Like the Arab tribes, they forsake the cities during the summer season, and seek, in the fresh and wholesome air of the country, a supply of health and vigour for the ensuing winter.'

In Oxford he noted that 'All the public buildings are constructed of hewn stone, and much resemble in form some of the Hindoo temples,' an interesting counterpoint to Bishop Heber's remark that Hazratganj, the main street of new Lucknow, reminded *him* of Oxford High Street 'in the colour of its buildings and the general form and Gothic style of the greater part of them'.[28] He visited the anatomy department and saw the dissection of a corpse in progress, no doubt viewing it with the rational

eye of the eighteenth-century man of reason. He proposed a Public
Academy to be patronised by the Government which would teach
Hindustani, Persian and Arabic to Company men destined for India. 'I
met with no encouragement,' he reported, although he later claimed to
have been offered £750 per annum to set up and superintend such an
institution himself, either in Oxford or London.

Socially Abu Talib was a great success. He was presented at Court to
George III and Queen Charlotte and subsequently met them on several
occasions. 'Prinny', the Prince Regent, entertained him to dinners at
Carlton House and treated him with 'the greatest kindness and con-
descension'. He met Mr Christie, the auctioneer, and Josiah Wedgwood
'the manufacturer of China ware'. Many English people with Indian
connections wanted to meet him, men like Sir Charles Cockerell, a wealthy
Nabob of the East India Company and member of the trading house of
Paxton, Cockerell and Trail (de Boigne's London agents). Sir Charles
had commissioned his country house Sezincote in Gloucestershire, on
the pattern of a Mughal building, one of the earliest in England to feature
the Saracenic style. Designs for Sezincote had been vetted by the artists
William and Thomas Daniell, whom Abu Talib also visited. He was pleased
to see their portraits and paintings of Indian scenes, having heard that
some English people claimed there were no buildings worth painting in
India. He stayed for a week with Warren Hastings, now retired to Dayles-
ford in Gloucestershire, his new house stuffed full of Indian treasures.
In London he was invited to attend meetings of the Royal Society of Arts
and Sciences, founded by Sir Joseph Banks, and was introduced to the
Sanskrit scholar Charles Wilkins. It is possible, as Raymond Head, has
suggested, that Abu Talib's eighteen months in England acted as a catalyst,
renewing interest at home in Indian architecture, art and language.[29]
Perhaps the Prince Regent's inspiration for the oriental Pavilion at Brighton
may have been born during those dinners with the 'Persian Prince'. (Similarly Abu Talib's fruitful meetings at the Royal Society may have inspired
his later treatise on astronomy.)

Abu Talib also looked up Nathaniel Middleton and Richard Johnson
'now my London Bankers' and numerous other old East India Company
hands and their families, but no meeting can have been so poignant as
that with Helena and her two children, whom he visited at her house in
Enfield. She was dressed 'in the English fashion' and was overjoyed to
see him. She gave him a letter for her mother, which he promised to deli-
ver on his return to Lucknow. He left England in 1802 and wandered

through France, visiting Lyons where he found adjoining the Hotel de Milan 'the house in which my old acquaintance the famous General Martin of Lucknow was born. It is still occupied by his nephew; and the General bequeathed a large sum of 'money to build a college on the spot.'[30]

He returned to India overland, passing through the Middle East, and the Arabian peninsula, where he made his pilgrimage to Mecca. He arrived at Bombay by ship on 4 August 1803, in the company of Captain Thomas Williamson, who later published *The East India Vade Mecum*, a comprehensive guide to which Abu Talib may well have contributed from his own observations. He had been absent for four and half years. He settled again in Calcutta, where he entertained his English friends there at dinner parties with the same charm he had exercised in London. He was later appointed Collector of Bundelkhand and died there in 1806, his family subsequently receiving a pension from the East India Company.

Yusuf Khan Kamalposh's entertaining account of his visit to England was written in Urdu, and does not seem to have been translated into English. It was first published in Delhi in 1847, under the title *Safer-e-Yusuf* (The Travels of Yusuf), a decade after his journey, though it may have been circulating in manuscript form on his return. A paragraph in the *Asiatic Journal* for 1838 notes that 'Eusoph Khan, soubedar of Lucknow had visited England and had concluded that Englishmen in his country [India] and Englishmen at home are totally different in point of character', a theme he was to enlarge upon.[31] After the Delhi edition was published, Kamalposh was approached by the owner of a printing press in Lucknow, and was encouraged by Mr Joseph Johannes 'who thought highly of his excellent souvenir' and supported its re-publication. Johannes was from an Armenian family, long resident in Lucknow, who had worked for successive Nawabs. He had successfully made the transition from painter to photographer when the camera was introduced into India, and had a photographic studio in Lucknow.[32] Kamalposh agreed to a reprinting and the first Lucknow edition was published in 1873, when the author was probably in his mid-sixties, with the new title *Ajaibat-i-Farang* (The Wonders of Europe). It was reprinted again in January 1898 by Munshi Nawal Kishore at the Mission Printing Press, Lucknow, with the same title and pagination as the 1873 edition. If Kamalposh was still alive when it came out he would have been nearly a centenarian.

Kamalposh left his native city of Hyderabad in June 1828 (we do not know when he was born) and travelled through Dacca, Delhi and into

Nepal before arriving in Lucknow. 'Here, thanks to Fortune and the friendship of Captain Mumtaz Khan Bangash, I got the honour of working for King Nasir-ud-din Haider.'[33] He was given a post in the prestigious Suleimani Corps, and was for a time adjutant to Captain Magness, one of the longest serving officers in the King's army. He was also, as we have seen, a friend of George Derusett. He writes: 'Suddenly I was seized with a desire to find out all I could about the English language, and in a few days, after great labour, I learnt it. After that I read many history books, and learning about different customs and the conditions of other cities and lands, awoke my enthusiasm for them. All at once in the year 1836 I wanted to see the world, and especially the country of England.' This early paragraph typifies the style of the book and the man—straight to the point, slightly exaggerated, fast-moving and infectiously readable. Perhaps because he was a soldier, rather than a court official like Abu Talib, Kamalposh's memoirs are constantly more engaging and more intimate.

Receiving permission to absent himself from the Suleimani Corps for two years, he set out for Calcutta, 'seat of [British] Government', where he spent six months before embarking on the *Isabella* on 30 March 1837. During this period he had a miniature portrait painted of himself, almost certainly by the artist and author Colesworthy Grant, which was later given to George Derusett. Grant subsequently included a drawing of Kamalposh in his *Sketches of Oriental Heads* published in 1850, where he is described as 'Eusuph Khan Soobadar. A Pathan. Native of Hyderabad, Dekhun'.[34] It is this portrait that is included in the 1898 edition, showing a handsome, bearded man, with a dagger stuck in his *kummerbund*.

The *Isabella* was a Europe ship, one that made the journey regularly between India and England, averaging about five months for a single run. The Captain on this voyage was David Brown, travelling with his wife. Kamalposh was accompanied by a single servant, whose name we never learn, but who was obviously in the worldwide tradition of providing comic relief for their masters. The voyage was uneventful, apart from a storm that swept overboard twelve sheep and several hens and ducks which would have provided fresh meat *en route*. The *Isabella* put in at the Cape and after being checked by the medical officer there for infectious diseases, the passengers were allowed to explore. After weeks at sea the wooded mountains refreshed the eye and 'my senses were gladdened and my heart stirred. The trees and flowering shrubs moved gently in the breeze and their sighs drew one's heart towards them.' But even in this Garden of Eden, Kamalposh detected snakes, in the form of negroes

11. Yusuf Khan Kamalposh

'black as the ink on my pen' and he parrots the already well-worn stereotype of the African as 'caught up in gambling and drinking wine' and squandering his wages. He was not to know that only two decades later, it would be African mercenaries who fought to the last, alongside Indian soldiers, against the British in Lucknow during the Great Uprising of 1857.[35]

By the end of August, the *Isabella* had reached a port somewhere on the south coast of England, unfortunately unidentified by the author. The majority of India ships put in at Southampton, but if this was the case with the *Isabella*, then Kamalposh seems to have gone somewhat out of his way to reach London by the stage coach, for he describes what can only be Stonehenge, on Salisbury Plain in Wiltshire. He was told, correctly, that the giant megaliths had been constructed 'by a race of people, before the English language and religion had been established, who came and stood underneath these stones and worshipped the sun'. In the same paragraph he writes that the coach journey was at first rather spoilt for him, because the driver sat 'a very ugly woman next to me—she was the size of a mountain—I loathed her appearance. I drew myself away from her as much as possible, but even then her grossness offended me. God was good to me—she got off halfway!' This juxtaposition of the sublime and the petty is very characteristic of the author. Not only did his quick eyes take in every detail, he recorded it too, so that his prose jumps from elegant description to noting the crudities, as he judged them, of early nineteenth-century England. He also had a great appreciation of female beauty, revelling in descriptions of fairy-faced Englishwomen, so the fat lady must have been particularly offensive to his nice taste.

The first thing that struck Kamalposh on reaching London was its pavements. Not that they were paved with gold, as many provincial Britons believed them to be, but that they existed at all. (The idea of separating pedestrians and animal traffic had clearly not yet been introduced into Indian cities.) He noted a wonderful road 'made out of stones, in the middle was a path for animals and there men were not allowed to go. Here and there, for three or four yards, was a road for people, and accordingly it was extremely clean. On two sides lamps were hung on iron branches, that worked on gas. Their brilliance put the stars to shame. On both sides were the most splendidly constructed houses, standing there like two rows of soldiers. They were all equal in height and tallness.' This was at a time when rapid municipal improvements were taking place in England, which were not to reach India for decades. Glazed shopping arcades had appeared, another wonder for Kamalposh, and he learnt it was possible to travel by train from London Bridge to Deptford on Britain's first passenger line, opened only a few months earlier.[36] (The earliest passenger service in India, from Bombay to Thana, began in 1853.) His first sight of the railway is described in minute detail. 'We saw a road which seemed to be made out of fish scales and on both sides, level with the ground, iron was placed so that the carriages would not go up and down and stones would not strike them. There were seven or eight carriages standing there and one large carriage right at the front—men were sitting in it burning coal. Each coach was attached to the other by a chain, and the big coach was fastened by a chain too. When everybody was seated, the machine of the large coach started to turn. Immediately, like an arrow, an enormous roar was let out and each chained coach started to move together. I had never seen anything like it and I was extremely startled and asked the coach-driver "Where are you going?" He replied "Eight kos further on." "Let me come too," I said. He replied "It's better if you sit and ride in the rear coach." He turned the machine in the coach and it immediately set off—my spirits rose. I stuck my head out once as we went along and the speed of the coach nearly snatched the turban away from my head. I quickly drew my head back inside.'

Kamalposh had found lodgings in central London at 30 Seymour Place, off Oxford Street and here was another surprise in the form of piped water, then being introduced into homes, replacing the old communal pumps at street corners. The new lodger, inspecting his rooms, found 'a little sink in a room, with a tap coiled above it. Your humble servant, being entirely innocent of the customs and habits of that country, thought that [this] was the bath place and started to wash himself. And having opened the twisting tap, my servant began to soap me all over. In a short time the room was filled with water.' A serious flood was only prevented when the housekeeper rushed in and started laughing, explaining between guffaws that he was washing in the kitchen, not the bathroom. 'When I heard this I felt ashamed and I didn't know how to answer her.' Kamalposh would have felt less ashamed had he known how recent was the idea of the English taking a bath even weekly, much less daily.

Apart from domestic innovations, Victorian engineering had produced by 1837 Isambard Kingdom Brunel's tunnel under the Thames, first proposed at the time of Abu Talib's visit. When Kamalposh saw it, the tunnel was still being constructed, as a pedestrian footpath under the river Thames. (It is now part of a railway line.) He was greatly impressed by the skill of the excavators, who were often in danger as cracks appeared in the fabric and water began to penetrate. As a soldier he was fascinated by the Arsenal at Woolwich, where he was allowed to wander around. He was especially attracted by the neighbouring home for retired soldiers, and commended the humanity of the English for providing them with a good pension and comfortable living quarters. 'If only', he mused, 'a master would show such kindness to his servants—then how gladly would the servant regard his master's interest as his own.' Ever eager for new sensations, he visited the Diorama and the Colosseum in Regent's Park. In the former he saw an elaborate magic lantern show illustrating paintings of architectural and romantic subjects.[37] In the Colosseum, with its huge painted panorama of London he had the terrifying experience of being shot to the top of the building in London's first passenger lift, known grandly as the 'Ascending Room', which according to him 'flew up into the air like the throne of Lord Solomon'. Skating on the frozen pond in Regent's Park with 'iron shoes' was a more pleasant curiosity.

Kamalposh experienced the seamier side of London life too. One dark evening, when he was returning to Seymour Place, he found a tearful

young woman in the clutches of a villainous-looking man. It was obvious
she was being abducted against her will. Kamalposh looked around for
a policeman (a regular police force had been introduced ten years earlier
by the Home Secretary, Sir Robert Peel), but he decided by the time he
found one, the young woman would have been carried off. Summoning
up his courage, he knocked the bully to the ground and tied his legs together with his *kummerbund*. The villain immediately repented, begged
for release and concluded a pretty speech by saying to Kamalposh, 'May
God bless you, that in spite of being a foreigner and a stranger, you restrained me from this evil act.' The episode ended happily with the penitent
man released and the young girl taking Kamalposh to her home in triumph,
where his bravery earned him the gratitude of her anxious family. This
incident, which could have come straight from the pages of Dickens,
shows Kamalposh at his best. The fact that he is aware of it does not de-
tract from his engaging narrative.

He could certainly be gullible, repeating glibly that St Paul's Cathedral, which he visited, was built a thousand years ago, but he never hesitated to seek out a wide range of experiences. He visited a synagogue at
his own request, and engaged in theological discussion with the rabbi,
Mr Liebson. He explained, pragmatically, that the reason cows and trees
were held in such esteem in India was purely practical. If they were not,
he argued, cows would be slaughtered, depriving people of their many
uses, and India would soon be deforested, leaving the landscape bare and
desolate.

Unlike Abu Talib, Kamalposh was never presented at Court, for he
did not have the right connections. But he stood at the upper window of
a house hired specially for the occasion, watching the Lord Mayor's Parade
pass below on 9 November 1837 and saw the young Queen Victoria in
her jewelled coach. He found her rather stolid features 'radiant—an example of the divine, worthy of magical respect. I prayed "Oh Allah! let the
intoxicating carriage pass near me and let the goddess tarry for a moment." ' He was nearly as enchanted by the horses of the Lord Mayor
('the highest Vizier'), all of 'excellent pedigree and nimble-footed'. But
the Queen's horses, drawing her coach 'embellished with unblinking
jewels' were even more magnificent so that 'one forgot hunger and thirst
in looking at them'. The spectacle reminded Kamalposh of pictures of
ancient Rome, with its occidental splendour and pageantry.

Kamalposh had a group of friends, whom he met frequently during
his four-month stay, including John Rose Brandon, then living near
Rotherhithe, who met him 'with great warmth of friendship [and] took

me to his home and entertained me for a long time . . .' Although George
Derusett had returned to England that summer, Kamalposh does not
appear to have met him in London. After an interesting visit to France,
Kamalposh decided to return to India by the overland route, and left
London on 18 January 1838, taking a sad farewell from his friends 'Butcher
Sahib' and 'Roger Sahib'. On his return to Lucknow he learnt that Nasir-
ud-din Haider had died the previous summer, and he visited his tomb
north of the Gomti. He had some harsh things to say about his home
town, sounding remarkably like the sahibs he had left behind. 'Lucknow
is blessed that here there are some novelties and handicrafts but the
power of invention, the arts and skilled workmanship that this humble
one [faqir] saw in the country of England, well, even the smallest part is
not found here.' People were too heavily taxed and the Nawabs were ruining the country. 'The nobles of Hindustan are lying in a doze. They
waste their whole lives in playing with pigeons, doves and kites.' He
found no zest for learning, and no culture of hard work like there was,
at that time, in England. The women of India were 'imprisoned' in their
houses and ignorant of the world. Kamalposh must have found the absence
of women hard, after constantly falling in love with 'fairy faces' in the
West, but he never visited England again.

Both Abu Talib and Kamalposh had been well received in England, by
old English friends returned from India, and by new acquaintances. The
authors' views on the East India Company's management, or mismanagement of their own country are seldom mentioned, although there
must have been some lively political discussions when they met at friends'
houses for dinner. Abu Talib, for example, would have been intrigued to
hear Warren Hastings' views on the Lucknow Residency, twenty years
after Nathaniel Middleton had been recalled in disgrace by the Governor
General. And if Kamalposh had moved in similarly exalted circles, his
own views on his fellow soldiers in the Suleimani battalion would have
given British policy-makers a valuable insight into the loyalty of the
Nawab's army. Both men, separated by nearly four decades, remarked on
the tolerance and lack of restrictions they found in British society.
Kamalposh reported with astonishment how he was allowed to enter St
Paul's Cathedral, even though he was wearing a turban and was clearly
a foreigner. 'In Muslim mosques and Hindu temples [in India], apart
from their own creed, they will not allow others to go in.'

But then neither man had a quarrel with the Company, or its Directors,
as the families of the Nawabs had. On two occasions, when they could
get no redress in Calcutta for their grievances, Nawabi relatives travelled

to England, where they imagined they would get a fairer hearing. Company policy in Awadh was to block direct communication between the ruling Nawabs, and the British royal family. Similar restrictions had been placed on the Mughal Emperors in Delhi.[38] The Company insisted on channelling all such correspondence through the Governor General in Calcutta, who decided whether it would be forwarded to London or returned with no explanation. These controls were also applied to gifts, which led to embarrassing situations where the Nawabs had to 'smuggle out' presents for the British royal family to evade the Company's clutches. Ghazi-ud-din Haider managed to get some presents to London for the King, including a pair of 'embroidered Lucknavi slippers', but Nasir-ud-din Haider was not so lucky. His carefully chosen presents for William IV and Queen Adelaide, sent with permission from both the Lucknow Resident and the Governor General himself, and accompanied by Mr Friell and Colonel Dubois were confiscated by Company officials on their arrival in England. Of the vast number of gifts, the shawls, horse saddles, chairs, books including an illustrated *Gulistan* and *Ajeb-ul-Nucklau*, a gold bedstead and many jewels, the royal couple were only allowed to accept two horses, two elephants and the rhinoceros, which all went to London Zoo. The Queen was said to have been mortified at not receiving a valuable diamond necklace which mysteriously 'disappeared' on its way back to Lucknow, with the remainder of the confiscated gifts.[39]

The Nawabs were also deliberately isolated within India, from fellow Indian notables. Prince Mirza Ali Kaddar (Qadr) of Benares wrote formally to the Governor General in 1837 requesting a letter of introduction to Nawab Nasir-ud-din Haider, but was told that his request 'cannot be complied with'.[40] Not only did the Company forbid overt communication between certain Indians in their own country, it also introduced the notorious 'Black Act' of 1836 which placed restrictions on their movements outside India. 'No native of India "lascars" (that is, mariners) excepted, shall quit the territories under British rule, without an order from Government.'[41] Understandably this caused protests, particularly from Calcutta. Clearly it took courage and persistence to seek a higher ruling from London, and only a burning sense of injustice, coupled with sufficient funds, led a few people to England. It was less easy to restrict the movements of Indians once they managed to get to England, for the Company had no jurisdiction over them there. They were made welcome, as we have seen, and found, perhaps to their surprise, that the Company was by no means popular, nor even powerful, in its own country.

In 1814 the death of Saadat Ali Khan, the sixth Nawab of Awadh, had deprived the state of one of its ablest rulers. The Nawab had three recognised sons, the eldest of whom, Ghazi-ud-din Haider, succeeded him in 1814. In turn, Ghazi-ud-din Haider was succeeded by his own son, Nasir-ud-din Haider. Well before the latter's sudden death, probably by poison, in July 1837, questions had arisen over the next legitimate heir. There were two immediate contenders, the crown prince Kaiwan Jah (?–1838) and his step-brother Munna Jan (1825–46). Both boys had been repudiated by Nasir-ud-din Haider when he fell out with their mothers, the Nawab declaring that neither were sons of his. This was probably unfair to Munna Jan, who was supposed to resemble the Nawab closely, but intrigues, feuds and unexplained deaths were an integral part of Nawabi family life.

Munna Jan, although described as 'a little monster' had become a favourite of the queen-mother, the Padshah Begam, who rightly or wrongly regarded him as her grandson. Immediately on Nasir-ud-din Haider's death she attempted to put Munna Jan on the throne of Awadh, quite literally, by seizing the throne in the Lal Baradari and seating the twelve-year old boy on it. A dreadful scene followed, as the British Resident intervened and was struck down. Rioting had broken out in the city, and forty or so people lost their lives. The Company's troops were cantoned at Mariaon, four miles north of the city and it took them several hours to arrive and to restore order. They opened fire in the Lal Baradari as Munna Jan and the Padshah Begam were hurried under guard to the Residency. An eyewitness reported that the Company's sepoys then took the opportunity to plunder the rooms, and that the throne itself 'was entirely stripped of its valuable gems', no doubt winkled out on the point of a bayonet.[42] The Padshah Begam, Munna Jan and the crown prince Kaiwan Jah (who had taken no part in the affray) were exiled to the fort of Chunar, on a small Company pension.

The Padshah Begam had acted swiftly on the Nawab's death, but the British Resident, Colonel John Low, had moved even faster. Muhammad Ali Shah, third son of Saadat Ali Khan, and now a feeble old man in his sixties, was brought from his sick bed to meet the Resident in the middle of the night. A document was thrust under his nose for signature which read 'I hereby declare that in the event of my being placed on the throne I will agree to sign any new treaty that the Governor-General may dictate.'[43] Many questions were later asked about the legality of this document, and the subsequent treaty put to the new King, but for the present the Company congratulated itself that it had, once again, got a compliant monarch on the bloodstained throne of Awadh.

While all this was going on, the man who considered he should be king was preparing to take his case to London. Iqbal-ud-daula was Saadat Ali Khan's grandson, through the late Nawab's second, and favourite, son Shams-ud-daula. During his father's reign Shams-ud-daula had been appointed to act as his deputy and he served as Chief Minister of Awadh for sixteen years, from 1798 to 1814. It was due to his careful management that the Nawab had been able to increase the collection of land revenue to meet the Company's demands. In a dignified letter to the Governor General, Shams-ud-daula laid out these facts as the basis for his claim to the throne, on his father's death, adding that Lord Moira (later the Marquess of Hastings) had 'promised' it to him on receiving a crore of rupees, as a long-term loan.[44] His elder brother, Ghazi-ud-din Haider, was not at first considered suitable to succeed to the *masnad*, in fact Saadat Ali Khan had described his first born as 'deranged in his mind' and odd stories about him continued to circulate. But the Company predicted, correctly, that the malleable Ghazi-ud-din Haider would prove a more lucrative ally than Shams-ud-daula, and he was duly installed on the *masnad*, claiming it 'as my just and hereditary right, through the favour and support of the British Government'.[45] Shams-ud-daula was hurried into exile at Benares, 'on the grounds of public expediency' with a Company pension recommended by the Governor General. He died there in 1827.

There is no doubt that the former Chief Minister's claim to the throne was a good one, especially in view of his elder brother's erratic behaviour. So one might imagine that Shams-ud-daula's son would have an equally good claim when the throne became vacant again in 1837. Certainly he would have proved a fitter king than the enfeebled old man whom Colonel Low dragged from his bed and thrust onto the throne that July night. Twenty years later, in discussing the 'Awadh question' which had by then developed into the Awadh problem, Benjamin Disraeli, the British Prime Minister, described Iqbal-ud-daula as 'the prince, who by custom and by law ought to have succeeded. Of that prince I have some knowledge by the information I received some years ago from men most competent to speak of him. He lives in a distant eastern city upon a pension allotted to him by the Indian Government, and he was commended to me long before the question of Oude interested public attention as a man of spotless character, enlightened and amiable, and more competent, perhaps to become a benevolent and judicious prince than, perhaps, any other that ever existed in the East.'[46]

Even William Sleeman, later Resident at Lucknow, and generally no

critic of Company policy, hesitated. Writing of Muhammad Ali Shah's
unexpected elevation, he said 'his right to the throne could be disputed,
not only by Moona Jan [Munna Jan] the supposed son of the late King
but by the undoubted sons of Shums-od-Dowlah, the elder brother of
the present King, whose rights were barred only by the peculiar feature
of the Mahommedan law'.[47] The 'peculiar feature' known as *mahjub*
(literally 'excluded') generally barred a claimant's son from inheritance
if the claimant died before he himself could inherit. In this case it excluded
Iqbal-ud-daula or his brothers from succeeding to the throne because
their father had died shortly before his elder brother, Ghazi-ud-din Haider.
It was a convenient excuse for the Company to dismiss Iqbal-ud-daula's
claim, and it was widely broadcast, because in so doing the Company
could be seen, for once, to be upholding native law.

Nevertheless Iqbal-ud-daula set out for London, in the belief that his
case would, at the very least, be fairly considered by the Board of Control
which had been established in 1784 to oversee, and if necessary, over-rule
the Court of Directors of the East India Company. He also intended to
collect the interest on his father's loan, made in 1814 to the Company.
The crore of rupees had been invested in a Company trust fund, and interest was computed at £25,000 per annum. The Nawab was apparently
encouraged in his resolution by an unnamed British officer, who told
him to 'Present yourself in Parliament as being entitled to the throne and
tell them your father was in charge of the royal treasury.'[48] On reaching
Calcutta, he met the Governor General, with a petition, and subsequently
produced a book for him and the Council members, outlining the situation
in Awadh. This was translated into English and sent to the Court of
Directors in London in advance of his arrival. Accompanied by his son
Mirza Jalal-ud-din Haider, some attendants, and the unidentified 'Major
Sahib', Iqbal-ud-daula arrived in London in 1838 and took up residence
in a London hotel.

There is a curious little memento of his visit, a small, now very rare,
booklet of sketches of the royal party, drawn by an anonymous Englishwoman, entitled 'The King of Oude, his brother, and some of their
attendants, sketched while on their visit to England'.[49] The short introduction reads succinctly: 'The Princes of Oude are very wealthy, and are
under British protection. The succession having gone to an uncle, by the
native rule of descent, the elder Prince, The Nawab Ukbal ul Dowlah,
considering himself entitled to the Throne, visited England in 1838,
hoping to influence the East India Company in favour of his claims. That
body refused to interfere, having no right to disturb the national law, and

His Highness was not acknowledged otherwise than as a Prince of the Royal blood. In consequence he did not attend the coronation [of Queen Victoria], for which occasion he had brought the frame-work of a carriage formed of solid silver, and his presents of most costly value were rejected. The sketches were made by a lady, then an invalid, while staying in the same hotel in London in which the Prince had taken his residence. She endeavoured to draw the different costumes with as much accuracy as the transient glances she could obtain of the individuals when passing up and down stairs, or moving to or from their apartments, would permit.' Although the sketches are by no means professional they convey a good impression of these exotic visitors on their fruitless mission.

When Iqbal-ud-daula visited the imposing East India Company House in Leadenhall Street, he sent in his card for an interview, but officials there refused to see him. They directed him to Lord Hobhouse, President of the Board of Control, but Hobhouse too refused to see him, telling the Nawab to 'write in to him'. When his claim was finally laid before the Board it was dismissed on the grounds that Iqbal-ul-daula had claimed to be the eldest son of Shams-ud-daula, when in truth he was the third son. Although Iqbal-ud-daula was unsuccessful both in obtaining the interest due to his father, and in having his claim to the throne recognised, he attracted a good deal of sympathy for his situation, fuelled by the indignation of the Calcutta newspapers on his behalf. When Lord Auckland queried why Iqbal-ud-daula had been granted permission by the Indian Government to visit England, he was told that a refusal would have led to 'serious consequences' in India, and that the family of the late Shams-ud-daula were venerated in Awadh as 'fallen martyrs to British ambition'. Although snubbed by the Board of Control and the Palace, there was clearly much goodwill for the Nawab in England. He became a useful rallying point for Members of Parliament opposed to the high-handed treatment of the old man who now sat on the throne of Awadh. In particular they castigated Lord Auckland who as Governor General had coached Colonel Low into getting the blank cheque signed by Muhammad Ali Shah before he was enthroned.

The Nawab did not return to India immediately after the failure of his mission. He decided to tour the newly industrialised Midlands, and found many novelties there. *The Manchester Guardian* reported in September 1838: 'His Highness is a great man, otherwise than by birth; for though only three months turned thirty years of age, his stature is upwards of six foot and he is an exceedingly large and heavy person. To save the inconvenience of ascending and descending the various flights of stairs at a manufactory, His Highness was conveyed to and fro in the hoist, which seemed to give him great satisfaction and he exclaimed "Ah! you English do all by steam." ' Passing a weighing machine and learning its use he 'wanted to be weighed. 23 stone!' He was astonished at the rapidity of transactions, commenting 'Ah! here everybody busy . . . all in hurry.' On his arrival in Liverpool he was welcomed by the Mayor in the Town Hall and taken on a tour of the city and the docks. He spent some time in Dublin where he was also warmly received, particularly in the Mendicity Institution where he distributed to 400 'aged and infirm' inmates a piece of silver each, from his own hand. 'Similar munificence has been repeatedly shown by His Highness on visiting public and private institutions.'

After a further expensive stay in London he travelled with his party to Paris and then home to India, via Egypt, Syria and Iraq. It was at Baghdad that the Nawab's son contracted smallpox and died there, his funeral procession being conducted 'with very great splendour' according to the historian Kamal-ud-din Haider. Iqbal-ud-daula became a changed man after the death of his heir. After another fruitless petition to London, he was awarded a Government pension of Rs 2,000 and thenceforth 'led an exemplary life, but what advantage did he gain from it, as the throne of his ancestors remained lost to him'.

One of Iqbal-ud-daula's British supporters had been Captain William White, formerly of the East India Company's Army, who had served in Lucknow. White had, unusually, resigned from the Army in protest over an incident in which a British officer had shot three Indian officers. In 1838 he published a booklet entitled 'The Prince of Oude or the Claim of the Nawab Ekbal ood-dowlah Behador to the Throne of Oude' and addressed it 'To the British Nation'. White used much of the book to air his personal grievances against the Company, especially the incident which had led to his resignation, and his booklet did little or nothing to further Iqbal-ud-daula's cause. But it is worth noting for White's prescient forecast of the eventual demise of British rule: 'The day of retribution, however, is not far off; nearer, probably, than what some persons may imagine. One hundred and twenty millions of people, differing in manners, habits and religion, who look upon us as intruders, and feel our presence as a nuisance, will not much longer put up with our company . . . We are aliens, and the soil sooner or later must return into the hands of the natives.'[50]

There are certain parallels between the unsuccessful mission to England of Iqbal-ud-daula in 1837 and that of Janab Alia Begam nearly twenty years later. In both cases the throne of Awadh was the goal, in neither case was it achieved. Both royal parties were courteously treated in the social milieu, but brushed aside by officials when they attempted to put forward the cases which had brought them to London. Both suffered unexpected deaths abroad on the journey home to India, with suitably grand funerals. Both made a considerable impression on Victorian society, amply fulfilling its notions of Eastern splendour with their exotic dress and seemingly unlimited funds.

On annexation in 1856 Wajid Ali Shah had sent his mother, brother and son to plead his cause before Queen Victoria in 1856, when illness prevented the deposed King from going himself. The royal party left Calcutta in June, on the *ss Bengal*, making for the little transit port of Suez at the mouth of the Red Sea. From there they made the short journey in closed carriages north to the Mediterranean. The journey time between India and England had been almost halved, to less than three months when the overland route between Suez and Alexandria was developed in the 1840s. Steamships run by the Peninsula and Oriental Company travelled regularly between Alexandria and Southampton and the Queen Mother's party arrived at Southampton on the *ss Indus* on 21 August 1856.

The group that stepped ashore on that late summer's day presented a picture of oriental grandeur that fully matched the expectations of the vast crowds who filled the dock to watch them disembark. The Queen Mother, widow of the Nawab Amjad Ali Shah, whose full name was Malika Kishwar Bahadur Fakr-ul-Zamani Nawab Tajara Begam (Janab Alia Begam) was carried in a sedan chair, 'closely veiled' and attended, according to *The Times*, by nine ladies. Other members of the party included her son General Mirza Mahomed Jawad Ali Sikander Hashmat Bahadur (younger brother to Wajid Ali Shah), her grandson, the heir apparent Mirza Mohammad Hamid Ali Bahadur, the King's legal representative Maulvi Masih-ud-din Khan, the Maulvi's deputy Munshi Qamar-ud-din, and the interpreter Haider Jung Bahadur. To serve this distinguished group were 110 attendants including the Queen Mother's medical officer, General Mirza's aide-de-camp, several soldiers acting as bodyguards, and seven eunuchs, one of them a Nubian 'well nigh seven foot tall'. The entire party went straight to Mr White's Royal York Hotel in Southampton, which had been taken over for ten days at a cost of £100.[51]

Two slightly less exotic figures accompanied the group, the ubiquitous John Rose Brandon and Major Robert Bird, former Assistant Resident and keen race-goer. Both men had left Lucknow five months earlier with the King and his party, for Calcutta. In spite of his banishment from Court in 1836, Brandon had wormed his way back in favour in 1847, only to be expelled again, this time by the Resident, in 1852.[52] He had managed to return to Lucknow yet again in the upheaval of annexation, where he met his old friend Major Robert Bird, who had also returned after being transferred to Ajmer, primarily to keep him away from William Sleeman, his superior officer. Neither Brandon nor Bird had any reason to support the Company, both were implacably opposed to Sleeman, and whatever their past misdemeanours, they were to prove useful companions on the journey to England.

The royal family was furnished with 'an immense sum of money', despite the unfortunate loss of jewels worth £50,000 in the Red Sea, which had been intended as a gift for Queen Victoria. This early misfortune was the first of several to dog the ill-fated mission. According to Maulvi Masih-ud-din Khan, the jewels had been entrusted to the heir apparent by Wajid Ali Shah. The eighteen-year old boy had in turn handed them over for safe-keeping to one of the eunuchs who somehow managed to let them slip into the Red Sea while the party was disembarking at Suez.[53] The maulvi had had a low opinion of the majority of his fellow travellers from the start, describing them as 'men of no character and position . . . *do paise ke log*', whose presence and behaviour in England ruined any chance he may have had of presenting the King's case with dignity. He felt justified in his opinion when the Chairman of the Board of Directors reportedly told him, 'Moulvi Sahib, you have done well to bring these depraved swindlers with you, whose mere presence here is enough to prove our charges against the Awadh king.'

The Times, torn between xenophobia and snobbery, reported almost daily on the sojourn in Southampton.[54] There was a steady procession of worthies paying their respects to the royal visitors, the Earl and Countess of Hardwicke, Sir George Wombwell, the Mayor of Southampton Mr Andrews, Sir George Pollock, Admiral Aysough and 'several parties of ladies'. The Queen Mother, in purdah, shook hands with the Mayor through a curtain. But there was, at the same time, 'mere vulgar curiosity on the part of the multitude who design only to see the dresses and appointments of the servants and followers and greedily drink in the absurd tales of the fabulous wealth and jewels of the royal party which have been industriously circulated'. While the royal family kept to the upper rooms of the hotel, where the Queen Mother's ladies could be glimpsed peeping round the curtains at the crowd on the pavement below, the servants had colonised the basement. They were described as 'unusually filthy', squatting before charcoal fires and smoking 'dirty opium pipes'. Clothes were strewn all over the floor, so that their quarters looked like a rag merchant's premises and there were complaints from passersby of 'smells'. Whenever the servants went out to look at the shops, they were followed by crowds of idlers.

Disagreements arose between Brandon and Bird, both jockeying for power, in an echo of earlier European behaviour at the Lucknow Court. Major Bird had been put in charge of all the arrangements for the party, but it was Brandon who was sent off to London to rent suitable accommodation, which took nearly two weeks to find. At the end of August the whole group travelled to London, having hired a special train for the journey. Cabs were ordered to take everyone to the railway station, the servants cheerfully piling on top with the luggage and waving farewell to the crowds lining the streets. The stationmaster had refused to close the station to the general public, but the eunuchs kept them at bay. The problem of how to get the Queen Mother from her closed carriage across the platform and into the train was neatly solved by a human corridor of servants holding up calico sheets behind them, between which Janab Alia Begam passed.

More crowds greeted the travellers on their arrival in London, as they drove to Harley House, on the north side of Marylebone Road. The detached residence, rented by Brandon for a year for £550 was surrounded by a high brick wall, but had a convenient side entrance into Regent's Park. Harley House was let unfurnished and Brandon had had no time to organise furniture so a number of upholsterers were called in, while groups of servants went out on shopping expeditions. The royal party was to stay here for thirteen months.

Was their mission to England doomed from the start? Or did news of the 'Munity' that broke out next year harden English hearts against the Awadh family? Iqbal-ud-daula had become a focus for English people opposed to the East India Company's highhanded policy of king-making, but there is little evidence that Janab Alia Begam attracted much anti-annexation sympathy in Britain. Although there were individuals 'who have identified themselves with the interests of the Royal family', like Brandon and Bird, there was certainly no visible public opposition to the takeover. The publication of William Knighton's *Private Life of an Eastern King* in 1855 was immensely damaging to the Awadh royal family, and as we have shown, was a popular and widely read book. An editorial in *The*

Times just after the royal party's arrival at Southampton conceded that it was 'a daring conception to bring the late Court of Oude bodily before the British public' and attributed this to Major Bird who 'artfully treated his theme'. But, it continued, 'Oude was virtually a part of British India' and suggested a public reading of Knighton's book if there were any doubters among the crowds of sightseers on Marylebone Road.

The *Illustrated London News* commented more sympathetically that 'A dethroned monarch is always an object of commiseration, even when his conduct has merited animadversion' and that 'the reception of the ex-Queen [*sic*] in this country should be marked by delicacy and consideration'.[55] But not restoration. In answer to Wajid Ali Shah's petition to the Court of Directors, sent from Harley House on 10 December 1856, the Court ruled that an annual pension of Rs 12 lakhs should be offered to him but no titular sovereignty. The title of 'king' would cease on his death. In a curiously chilling sentence reminiscent of twentieth-century Communist ideas of 're-education' the Directors recommended that 'The young princes are to be trained and educated so as to become "useful citizens" so as to prevent them from sinking into degraded habits of life.' It was suggested that the royal family should become *jagirdars* and that the Rs 12 lakhs would descend as an hereditary grant.[56] How much the hopes of the royal family had been falsely encouraged by Robert Bird and John Rose Brandon in Calcutta, one cannot say. Did the two mavericks genuinely believe that a personal appeal from one Queen to another would reverse a political decision in India? Almost certainly not, but one should not cynically condemn their motives, anymore than one should censure those few Europeans who fought against the British during 1857. After all, the wheel of history has often turned yesterday's dissidents into today's freedom fighters.

Two short books and a pamphlet supporting the Awadh royal family were published in London during 1857, the latter by Major Bird, entitled *The Spoliation of Oudh*. Samuel Lucas, about whom little is known, published *Dacoitee in Excelsis or The Spoliation of Oude by the East India Company*, and Maulvi Masih-ud-din Khan wrote *Oude: Its Princes and Its Government Vindicated*.[57] Khan's book, written in English but probably translated from the original Urdu, was suppressed shortly after its publication, only a few copies surviving. It is impossible to say how widely these three works became known, but safe to say that none, despite their passionately felt convictions, stood any chance against *Private Life of an Eastern King*.

On 16 January 1857, while Wajid Ali Shah's petition was still before the Court of Directors, General Mirza Hashmat and the heir apparent were entertained by those same Directors at East India House, in a cere-monial visit. Attended by Major Bird and a Colonel Rawlinson, the two princes in their magnificent costumes of crimson velvet and jewels attracted the usual crowds. They were formally received, introduced to the Directors, shown around the Company's museum and entertained to a 'dejeuner' in the Finance Committee room, perhaps in ironic acknow-ledgment of the substantial contributions made by their forefathers to the Company's coffers. The meal was served 'in a style of great elegance under the personal superintendence of Mr Bathe of the London Tavern' and broke up at 3.30 p.m. when the princes returned to Harley House.[58]

The uprising of 1857 is generally reckoned to have started on 10 May at Meerut, although there were earlier indications of trouble. When news of the outbreak reached the royal family at Marylebone they sent a petition to the House of Commons, making it clear that Wajid Ali Shah had no hand in the troubles. His sole concern, and the reason for the prolonged stay in England by his relatives, was to get the decision on his dethronement reversed. His Majesty, the petition stated, 'relies only on the justice of his cause, appeals only to Her Majesty's throne and to the Parliament of Great Britain, and disdains to use the arm of the rebel and the traitor to maintain the right he seeks to vindicate'.[59] Indeed, it would have been madness for Wajid Ali Shah to have aligned himself with the rebels while his mother, brother and son were in London pleading for his re-instate-ment as a loyal, if wronged, friend to the British Government and Crown.

Despite the worrying news from India, arrangements went ahead for a meeting between the royal party and the woman they had come to see, Queen Victoria. There are two accounts of what took place on the afternoon of 4 July 1857 at Buckingham Palace, the first by Queen Victoria herself, who kept a daily journal. 'After luncheon received the Queen of Oude. Much trouble in arranging that no man should look at her. She was placed in the "Closet" (next the White Drawing-room) where my ladies remained with her & her son & grandson. We entered behind her with our 7 children, Mr V. Smith and Sir G. Clark (who acted as inter-preter). She threw back her veil and kissed my hand, which the grandson also did. She was much weighed down by her heavy dress, her crown & jewels, being very small. She has fine eyes, painted, as is customary. The grandson also wore a sort of crown & both the Princes had long loose robes, like dressing gowns, on. A few words were exchanged, when the Queen & I were seated. Albert, with 2 eldest Boys and Gentleman stood behind her. She gave me a letter & a handsome ornament of pearls & precious stones, to which is appended an ornament with sweet smelling

Monday ### COURT CIRCULAR.. *July 6*

The Queen of Oude and the Princes of Oude were presented to Her Majesty on Saturday, at an audience, by the Right Hon. R. Vernon Smith, President of the Board of Control.

Lord Byron and Sir Frederick Stovin were the Lord and Groom in Waiting.

His Majesty the King of the Belgians, the Prince Consort, the Count of Flanders, and Prince William of Prussia visited the Exhibition of the Royal Academy on Saturday morning. Captain Burnell and Captain the Hon. D. de Ros were in attendance.

The Queen, accompanied by the Princess Royal, the Princess Charlotte of Belgium, and the Prince of Wales, took a drive in an open carriage and four in the afternoon. Lord Alfred Paget and Major-General the Hon. C. Grey attended on horseback. His Royal Highness the Prince Consort, with Prince Frederick William of Prussia and the Count of Flanders, rode out on horseback, attended by Captain the Hon. Dudley de Ros and Count Moltke.

His Serene Highness the Prince of Hohenzollern dined with Her Majesty on Saturday.

Her Majesty and the Prince Consort, accompanied by His Majesty the King of the Belgians, the Princess Royal, Princess Alice, Princess Charlotte of Belgium, the Prince of Wales, Prince Alfred, Prince Frederick William of Prussia, the Count of Flanders, and the Prince of Hohenzollern Sigmaringen, honoured the amateur performance, under the management of Mr. Charles Dickens, of Mr. Wilkie Collins's drama of *The Frozen Deep*, at the Gallery of Illustration in Regent-street, with their presence on Saturday evening.

In attendance were the Viscountess Jocelyn, the Countess d'Yve, the Hon. Eleanor Stanley, the Hon. Louisa Gordon, Sir Frederick Stovin, Count de Moerkerke, Captain Burnell, Baron Moltke, Major-General the Hon. C. Grey, Captain the Hon. D. de Ros, Dr. Koepl, and Baron Alvensleben.

Yesterday the Queen, the Prince Consort, the Prince of Wales, Prince Alfred, the Princess Royal, the Princess Alice, Princess Helena, Prince Frederick William of Prussia, the ladies and gentlemen of the Court, and the domestic household attended Divine service in the chapel in Buckingham Palace.

The sermon was preached by the Rev. Dr. Jeremie.

His Majesty the King of the Belgians, attended by Major-General Sir Edward Cust and Her Royal Highness the Duchess of Kent, also attended the service.

Their Royal Highnesses the Duke and Duchess de Montpensier, attended by Colonel Mon and Countess de Sala, were at Her Majesty's Concert on Friday night.

His Majesty the King of the Belgians visited her Royal Highness the Duchess of Kent on Saturday at Clarence House, St. James's.

Her Royal Highness the Duchess of Kent visited the Duke and Duchess de Montpensier at Grillion's Hotel on Saturday, and in the evening, attended by Lady Anna Maria Dawson, Lady Augusta Bruce, and Colonel Stephens, honoured the Royal Italian Opera with her presence.

Lady Anna Maria Dawson has succeeded Lady Augusta Bruce as Lady in Waiting to the Duchess of Kent.

12. Court Circular, Monday, 6 July 1857

perfume,—very curious. We then retired, but missed the interesting sight of her departure in state . . .'[60]

The second, more detailed account is given by the historian Kamal-ud-din Haider, and must have come from one of the Awadh people who were present. Janab Alia Begam was escorted from her carriage by several female attendants, who spoke Hindustani, and taken into the small room to await Victoria's arrival. It had been agreed that there would be no men present apart from the two attendants, and of course the Prince Consort. The Queen came in wearing a simple 'circular' dress (a crinoline) and after 'respectful salutations' from both sides, accepted a *nazr* of gold mohurs from the Indian Queen. Her son, and grandson offered their own *nazr* and made to kiss the back of Queen Victoria's hand, but she preferred to shake hands with them. Whatever the Queen Mother may have expected from this meeting, it could not have been a discussion on boating. 'Do you sometimes go sailing?' asked Victoria. 'Janab Alia Begam replied humbly "In our city there is a very small river, the Gomti, but we have never sailed on it." ' A gloomy discussion on boating accidents and the miseries of the sea voyage to England followed.

The Queen enquired whether Janab Alia Begam had seen many English mansions, and offered to arrange visits to some of them for her. She then asked if the young Prince of Wales could enter the chamber and be presented. (One imagines him waiting eagerly in an antechamber to be called in, if the Queen Mother agreed.) Janab Alia Begam is said to have taken Edward on her lap affectionately and to have spoken to him with great fondness. The Prince of Wales was then sixteen years of age and no stranger to Indian royalty, having photographed the exiled Maharaja Duleep Singh the previous year. The Queen Mother took off her necklace, from which hung a jewelled *itrdan* or perfume flask and put it around the boy's neck. She explained that it was their custom to fill the flask with perfume when a guest departs, to leave something sweet in the memory.[61] At any rate, the audience came to a graceful conclusion, the fissures of mutual incomprehension having been neatly smoothed over by the veneer of polite conversation.

We know what the princes looked like during their meeting at Buckingham Palace, because shortly afterwards they visited the photographer Mr Mayall of Regent Street for a studio portrait in 'full Court costumes, which present a blaze of diamonds, and are only worn on State occasions, such as the recent presentation to the Queen of England. They each wear the same sort of high coronet cap of gold and jewels, but ornamented with a few small feathers, and without the silver

13. The 'Prince of Oude' and his suite

ornaments peculiar to the crown of the Queen. The young prince is magnificently decorated with jewels, the dress itself being composed of cloth of gold. The young prince, or as he is more ceremoniously styled, His Royal Highness Mirza Hammid Ally Valee Ahud Behadoor, is the son and as the Oudians still delight to call him, the heir apparent to the deposed King of Oude. The second crowned head is that of his uncle and military adviser, His Royal Highness the General Mirza Mohamed Jowad Ally Sekonder Hushmat Behadoor.'[62] Also in the group were the Maulvi, the aide-de-camp and the interpreter.

News of the arrest of Wajid Ali Shah with two of his Ministers, which had taken place on 15 June, did not reach the royal party for nearly four weeks. As soon as they learnt of the arrest, Masih-ud-din Khan, the spokesman, issued a public appeal that the King should not be condemned and that there had been no conspiracy on his part, as Company officials claimed. The Queen Mother and the princes composed a paper for the House of Lords stating, 'Your petitioners have sustained their own peculiar cause of pain and sorrow' on learning of the King's detention. They asked to know what he was charged with, by whose authority he had been charged, and that he should be permitted to correspond freely with his family. The arrest marked the end of a mission that had been hopeless from the start. 'The position of the unfortunate queen-mother of Oude, and the two princes her relatives, in this country, had now become one of extreme embarrassment both to themselves and the government . . . the alleged conspiracy and imprisonment of the king in Fort William, naturally surrounded them with difficulties that, for a time at least, were insurmountable, and in the end were destined to be fatal. The object of the mission of the queen and her relatives had already been long before the government and the court of directors, but no step appears to have been taken by either towards a satisfactory termination of the question between the king of Oude and the East India Company, when the revolt broke out.'[63]

The petition to the House of Lords was presented by Lord Campbell on 6 August and pettily rejected on a minor technicality. 'Their Lordships declined to receive [it] on account of an objection having been taken to it by Lord Redesdale, because it did not style itself the "humble petition".' It was subsequently placed before the House of Commons, who declined to discuss it and ordered it to 'lie on the table'.

As a horrified British public learnt of the scale of the Indian uprising during the autumn of 1857, the royal party remained quietly in

Marylebone. Towards the end of year Janab Alia Begam sought and received permission from the Court of Directors to leave England and proceed to Mecca on the journey home. None of the fanfare of publicity that had accompanied her arrival marked the departure. There were no curious crowds outside Harley House as the group departed for Paris in January 1858 on the first stage of their return to India.

The party settled into a hotel in the rue Laffitte, and it was here on 23 January that the Queen Mother died, aged fifty-three. Her elaborate funeral procession to the newly opened Muslim portion of Père Lachaise cemetery included thirteen carriages for the mourners, among whom were the Turkish and Persian Ambassadors. Her son and grandson followed the hearse which was drawn by six horses. At the burial ground prayers were read over the pall-draped coffin, and a temporary canopy erected over the grave.[64] Illustrations show General Mirza weeping and deeply affected, surrounded by a solemn crowd of Frenchmen and women in mourning. Some time after the funeral, arguments broke out between the two Princes and Maulvi Masih-ud-din Khan, not helped by contradictory messages from Wajid Ali Shah in Calcutta. The heir apparent decided to stay on in Paris, while his uncle and the Maulvi returned to London. General Mirza himself died shortly afterwards, and his body was taken back to Paris, to lie next to that of his mother, both exiled forever. Theirs was, perhaps, the saddest story of all the visitors to England.

NOTES AND REFERENCES

1. See, *Traders and Nabobs: The British in Cawnpore 1765–1857*, by Zoe Yalland for the best account of early Cawnpore. Michael Russell Publishers, Salisbury 1987.
2. Visram, Rozina, *Ayahs, Lascars and Princes: Indians in Britain 1700–1947*, Pluto Press, London 1986. Chapters 2 and 3.
3. Young, Desmond, *Fountain of the Elephants*, Collins, London 1959, pp. 99–101.
4. *L'Extraordinaire Aventure de Benoit de Boigne aux Indes*, ed. Jérôme Boyé, Echanges Culturels et Actions de Dévelopment, Paris 1996, 'Chronological Essay', by Jean-Marie Lafont, p. 149.
5. Archer, Mildred, 'Renaldi and India: A Romantic Encounter', *Apollo Magazine*, London 1976, pp. 98–105.
6. Young, op. cit., p. 146.
7. Boyé, op. cit., p. 150.
8. There are references to a daughter of de Boigne in Claude Martin's letters

from Lucknow. After the General's return to Europe, Martin wrote to him 'I am paying Rs 500 to the mother of your daughter according to your order, this good widow is keeping well and often asks me for news of you.' (Letter dated 22 April 1798). On 30 November 1799 however he told de Boigne that 'the Mother of your daughter to whom I gave Rs 500, this poor woman said to me she is dying of hunger, and you haven't given me any [further] order to pay her anything, and she torments me daily.' Claude Martin's letters from the Private Archives of the Comte de Boigne, Paris.

9. Young, op. cit., p. 193.
10. Young, op. cit., pp. 213–14.
11. De Saint Venant, Marie-Gabrielle, *Benoît de Boigne (1751–1830) Du général au particulier*, Société Savoisienne d'Histoire et d'Archélogie, Chambery 1996, p. 87.
12. Young, op. cit., p. 293.
13. Claude Martin to General de Boigne, 30 November 1799, op. cit., ref. 8.
14. De Saint Venant, op. cit., p. 96.
15. Young, op. cit., pp. 242–3.
16. Baldwin, Marjorie, *The Story of the Forest*, St Saviour's Church, Colgate, Sussex, 2nd edition 1985, pp. 19–22.
17. Young, op. cit., pp. 294–5.
18. LaBourchardière, Basil, letter of 18 August 1984, in the Horsham Local History File, Horsham Library, Sussex.
19. Kabir, Professor Humayun, *Mirza Abu Taleb Khan* (The Russell lecture at Patna College delivered 16 April 1961), Patna 1961, OIOC P/V 2538.
20. Stewart, Charles, trans., *The Travels of Mirza Abu Taleb Khan in Asia, Africa and Europe During the Years 1799, 1800, 1801, 1802 & 1803, Translated from the Persian*, London 1814, p. 14.
21. The Persian history was called *Tafzihu'l Ghafilin* and was translated into English by William Hoey, and published at Allahabad in 1885, as *The History of Asaf-ud-Daula, Nawab Wazir of Oudh*.
22. Stewart, op. cit., vol. 1, Introduction, p. x.
23. Fisher, Michael, *The First Indian Author in English: Dean Mahomed (1759–1851) in India, Ireland, and England*, OUP, Delhi 1996.
24. Stewart, op. cit., vol. 2, p. 249.
25. Fisher, op. cit., p. 240.
26. Stewart, op. cit., vol. 1, pp. 64–5.
27. Beach, Milo & Koch, Ebba, *King of the World: The Padshahnama* (Exhibition catalogue), Azimuth Editions Ltd 1997, p. 13.
28. Llewellyn-Jones, Rosie, *A Fatal Friendship: The Nawabs, the British and the City of Lucknow*, OUP, Delhi 1985, p. 57.
29. Head, Raymond, *The Indian Style*, Allen & Unwin, London 1986, pp. 30–2.
30. Stewart, op. cit., vol. 2, p. 269.
31. *The Asiatic Journal*, vol. 27, London 1838.
32. The title page reads in part: 'The book was printed at Delhi in 1847 and

because its author was a resident of Lucknow and the owner of the printing-press having met him and thought highly of this excellent souvenir by an inhabitant of this subah, Mr Joseph Johannes, unequalled in good qualities and kindness, and unparalleled in the photographic arts, etc. encouraged it.'

33. All translations by Rosie Llewellyn-Jones from the 1898 Lucknow edition.

34. A miniature in the possession of Janet Dewan shows Yusuf Khan full face. A note on the back is inscribed C. Grant to Eusuph Khan, Calcutta, 23 November 1836. The miniature also carries the signatures of three members of the Grant family, one of whom was probably the Mr Grant of Tank Square, Calcutta, who at Kamalposh's suggestion applied for the job of librarian to Nasir-ud-din Haider.

35. See Taylor, P.J.O., *A Companion to the 'Indian Mutiny' of 1857*, OUP, Delhi 1996, p. 56. An African eunuch, nicknamed 'Bob the Nailer' shot many British defendants during the siege of the Residency before being killed. Coincidentally the African was positioned in the house of Jacob Johannes, father to Kamalposh's photographer.

36. Information supplied by the National Railway Museum, York. London Bridge was the first railway passenger terminus, opened in December 1836. The line ran to Deptford, about five miles east.

37. Hobhouse, Hermione, *History of Regent Street*, Macdonald & Jane's Ltd, London 1975, p. 39.

38. Fisher, Michael, *A Clash of Cultures: Awadh, The British and the Mughals*, Manohar, New Delhi 1987, p. 143.

39. Fisher, ibid., p. 164.

40. Bengal Political Consultations. Index for 1837, entry dated 24 January, OIOC.

41. White, William, *Mirza Kaiwan Jah or the Dethroned King of Oude in Chains! A Letter to Lord Viscount Melbourne by Capt. White, Late of the East India Company's Service*, London 1838, p. 21, OIOC.

42. Edwardes, Michael, *The Orchid House: Splendours and Miseries of the Kingdom of Oudh 1827–1857*, Cassell, London 1960, pp. 106–10.

43. Pemble, John, *The Raj, the Indian Mutiny and the Kingdom of Oudh 1801–1859*, Harvester Press, Sussex, p. 82.

44. White, William, *The Prince of Oude or the Claim of the Nawab Ekbal ood-dowlah Behador to the Throne of Oude*, 1838, OIOC.

45. Fisher, *A Clash of Cultures*, op. cit., p. 116.

46. Azhar Mirza Ali, *King Wajid Ali Shah of Awadh*, Royal Book Company, Karachi 1982, p. 177. (Azhar wrongly states that Disraeli's eulogy described Munna Jan.)

47. Sleeman, William, *A Journey Through the Kingdom of Oude in 1849–1850*, London 1858, vol. 2, p. 136.

48. Haider Kamal-ud-din, *Qaysar al-Tawarikh*, vol. 1, Nawal Kishore Press, Lucknow 1879, p. 273.

49. *The King of Oude, His Brother, and Attendants. Sketched While on Their Visit to England, by a Lady*, Ackermann & Co, London c. 1838.

50. White, op. cit., p. 93.

51. *The Times* (London), reported extensively on the arrival of the Queen Mother's party at Southampton, and the subsequent journey to London, but seemed to lose interest thereafter. See reports for 19 August, 22 August, 27 August, 28 August, 30 August, 1 September, 2 September 1856.

52. For more on John Rose Brandon, see *Our Bones are Scattered: The Cawnpore Massacres and the Indian Mutiny of 1857*, by Andrew Ward, John Murray, London 1996, pp. 62, 132.

53. Bahadur, Maulvi Mohammad Masih Uddin Khan, *Oude; Its Princes and Its Government Vindicated*, John Davy & Sons, London 1857. Reprinted as *British Aggression in Awadh*, ed. Safi Ahmad, with foreword by Professor Mohammad Habib, Meerut 1969, p. 3.

54. *The Times*, op. cit.

55. *Illustrated London News*, London, 18 July 1857.

56. *The Times*, 11 February 1857.

57. *The Spoliation of Oudh*, by Major Robert Bird, published in London in 1857 is a 24-page pamphlet [BL 8023cc49(1)]. *Dacoitee in Excelsis or The Spoliation of Oude by the East India Company*, also published in London in 1857 is a book of 214 pages (BL 9056.f.14). It is sometimes attributed to Bird as well, but the British Library catalogue attributes it to one Samuel Lucas. The contents of pamphlet and book are different.

58. *The Times*, 17 January 1857.

59. Ball, Charles, *The History of the Indian Mutiny*, vol. 1, London 1858, p. 631.

60. The Royal Archives, Windsor. The gracious permission of Her Majesty The Queen to quote material from the Royal Archives is most gratefully acknowledged.

61. Haider, op. cit., pp. 413–15.

62. *Illustrated London News*, 1 August 1857.

63. Ball, op. cit., p. 163.

64. *Narrative of the Indian Revolt from the Outbreak to the Capture of Lucknow*, London 1858, p. 324, OIOC.

CHAPTER FIVE

Before the Storm

Lucknow was the epicentre of the 1857 uprising, almost the first city to rise up against the British, and almost the last to be recaptured by them in March 1858. The six-month long siege of the Residency quickly took on a mythological status in Victorian England, as we shall see. So did the triumphant British march back into Lucknow and the subsequent 'punishment' of the former Nawabi city. But that curious interregnum between the annexation of Awadh by the East India Company on 7 February 1856 and the firing of the Mariaon cantonment on 30 May 1857 has never really been examined in detail. People often imagine that the annexation, which began with the forced abdication of the last King of Awadh, Wajid Ali Shah, immediately preceded the siege of Lucknow. In reality there was a period of more than a year, when the Company, oblivious of the gathering storm, had, at last, the prize of Awadh in its hands. 'Annexation' is a common enough word in imperial history, but what did it actually mean in practical terms? What were the signs and changes that people first noticed as they came under British rule? These questions, and the way in which the Company tried to create a model British colony in Awadh are the subjects of this chapter.[1]

Awadh in February 1856 was certainly not, as we have seen, an untouched example of a post-Mughal state. The Nawabs had connived at, even in some cases welcomed, a superficial 'westernisation', which was most evident in their buildings, although the majority of their institutions were still those of a medieval Muslim monarch. Surrounded by elaborate courtly protocol, the last King was not however totally inaccessible to the common man. Wajid Ali Shah had 'complaints boxes' placed in the streets, and silver petition boxes carried in procession when he drove outside the Qaisarbagh. He dealt personally with the contents of the boxes, passing orders as necessary to his staff. A chance encounter during a royal progress might result in a talented man's sudden elevation to Court, or, more frequently, a pretty woman's entry into the royal zenana.

By the 1850s Lucknow was 'the largest and most prosperous existing pre-colonial city in the sub-continent. In contrast Delhi, Lahore, and Agra, the once great Mughal capitals, were . . . not quite equal to half the population or the commerce of Lucknow.'[2] It was the fourth most populous city in India after the Presidency towns of Calcutta, Bombay and Madras. Awadh was indeed a prize, and a potentially rich one too, once the land revenue collection had been purged of corruption, and the extravagance of the King finally restrained. The Company had already done very well out of Awadh even before the take-over. The Nawabs had been debtors to the Company since the mid-eighteenth century and the days of Shuja-ud-daula. In addition, they had also been cajoled into making very substantial loans to the Calcutta Government, which amounted to nearly £5 million pounds, and which would not now have to be paid back.

Quite apart from financial considerations of course, the Company had convinced itself that annexation could only benefit the people of Awadh, who would welcome their release from what seemed like capricious Nawabi rule, or misrule. 'No great class in Oude is our enemy,' wrote a Calcutta councillor. 'For one bad subject who feels our administration as a check, we have there got a hundred who hail it as a blessing.'[3] This belief, which was soon to be so shaken, that Awadh was in fact being annexed *for its own good,* has to be seen in the context of the times. It was tempered by many events beyond India, of which the last Kings were mainly kept in ignorance, discouraged by the Company from travelling outside Awadh, and with their postal service halted on Company orders. It included the wave of revolutionary unrest in Europe in the 1840s, the liberal reforms which had been pushed through Parliament, the growth of industrialisation in Britain, the rapid improvements in communications and technology, and the beginning of public health reforms. What is relevant here is how these mid-Victorian concerns directly influenced Company administrators in Awadh, once it was theirs, and how they implemented these new ideas in a new province. Over the centuries British colonialism has taken many forms, some cruel, some benevolent, with a broad spectrum in between. During that first year in Awadh, there was something very domestic about the annexation. It was as though a great estate had been taken over by a group of businessmen, which indeed is what the Company still was at heart. An audit had to be made of the attached land, the surplus livestock sold off, the old servants pensioned off, the armed retainers reduced, the account books scrutinized, the old storerooms cleared out, the public rooms refurbished, and modern gadgets introduced to make life easier. The fact that the former owners had been acquired with the estate, and were still brooding in their rooms was an inconvenience, but one that was soon resolved by the departure of the head of the family.

By November of 1855 the Governor General, the Marquis of Dalhousie, had got from the Court of Directors in London, a qualified agreement to proceed with annexation. In anticipation of trouble, but also to act as a lever, additional British troops were moved up to Cawnpore, the nearest British cantonment, on the border of Awadh. Early in the New Year Colonel James Outram, the British Resident, paid a visit to Calcutta, ostensibly to say goodbye to the outgoing Governor General, but secretly to collect his instructions for the take-over. Outram returned to Lucknow on 30 January 1856, carrying with him four documents. There was a letter from the Governor General to the King, saying that the British Government could no longer 'lend its countenance and support' to the Awadh regime, and a draft Treaty in which the King was to sign away his rights to the revenues of the kingdom and to agree 'that the sole and exclusive administration of the Civil and Military Government of the territories of Oude shall be henceforth vested *for ever*, in the Honourable East India Company'. There were also two Proclamations. The first, Proclamation A, was to be read if the King agreed to sign the Treaty, announcing that he had relinquished his kingdom. The second, Proclamation B, in case the King did *not* sign the Treaty, announced that the Company was taking Awadh over anyway.[4] Alarmed by speculative newspaper reports, the Chief Minister, Ali Naki Khan, approached the Resident immediately on his return, and asked whether the kingdom was indeed to be annexed. Outram indignantly denied this, saying speciously that he could not account for the presence of the British troops at Cawnpore, unless they were there to quell a disturbance which had broken out on the Nepalese frontier.[5]

As Major General Sir Hugh Wheeler led the troops towards Lucknow, a number of interviews took place between the Resident and the King, and, at her own request, between the Queen Mother, Janab Alia Begam, and the Resident. The last meeting was on 4 February, by which time the advance guard was on the outskirts of Lucknow. Outram made a final demand from the King for his response to Dalhousie's letter and the draft Treaty. In an outburst of grief, which is recorded both by Outram, and the palace officials, Wajid Ali Shah said, 'Treaties are necessary between equals only' and explained that since he appeared to have been *already* stripped of his title, rank and honour, he was unable to sign anything. He then took his turban off his head and placed it in the Resident's hands, a poignant and futile gesture.[6] Outram, no doubt embarrassed, but unmoved by Oriental emotion, then gave the King three days to change his mind. When no word came from the Palace, the Resident formally deposed the King and annexed the province on 7 February at noon.

It was a bloodless coup, for the King had ordered that his own troops, including the palace guard at Qaisarbagh, should be disarmed. They were, however, to remain at their posts in case there was trouble in the city. Wajid Ali Shah may have thought there was the possibility of an armed uprising on his behalf, which would clearly have been put down with much bloodshed, but it is more likely, given his subsequent behaviour, that he still believed the matter was open to negotiation, and that annexation could be 'reversed' if only he could appeal in person to Dalhousie.

British plans for annexation had been well laid over the past year. Town-criers, preceded by drummers, were sent out into the streets, proclaiming the news. Hand-bills from the Residency printing press were posted up. Rumour and gossip had already led to a general understanding of what was going on, although no more than a handful of British officials and military officers were present when Outram, in his last act as Resident, convened a meeting with the newly appointed Judicial and Financial Commissioners, Manaton Collingwood Ommaney and Martin Gubbins, who had arrived the day before, in readiness. He placed the city in the hands of Major John Sherbrooke Banks, Commissioner for Lucknow, who began work immediately with the city's Chief Magistrate, the Kotwal, Mirza Ali Raza. At noon that day, Chief Minister Ali Naki Khan and the chief revenue and police officers were summoned to a conference, and told to hand over their records, the treasury, and other public offices of the city to Ommaney and Gubbins. Outram himself became the first Chief Commissioner, for the post of Resident no longer existed, now that there was no Royal Court. The former kingdom was split into four Divisions, each under a Commissioner. The Divisions were further subdivided into three Districts each, with Deputy Commissioners, making a total of sixteen major British administrators. Outram concluded a long day's work by dictating a detailed report to Calcutta, writing that the 'city is in a state of tranquility, and that everything bids fair for the quiet introduction of our rule'.[7]

The following day, 8 February 1856, Captain Weston took over the Baradari Hazur Alam, recently constructed by Ali Naki Khan, and established the Court of Justice there. He next visited the Kotwali, the city's main police station in the Chowk, where the kotwali staff politely offered him *nazr* (ceremonial gifts) as a mark of their respect and acknowledgment, then began on the task of re-organising the city's 52 *thanas* or sub police stations. The Chief Magistrate had already offered his resignation, because of his close connection with the former regime, but Outram would not accept it. He later described the Kotwal as 'an officer of much reputation and whose experience and aid was useful on taking possession of the Province'.[8] The Kotwal's salary was increased by Rs 200 per month and he was asked to superintend the city's sanitary arrangements. Annexation had begun in earnest.

The new Chief Commissioner had been extensively briefed, during his January visit to Calcutta, on how Awadh should be administered once the immediate take-over had been completed. He was to 'take the system of management which has been pursued in the Punjab for his model, and to enable him to do this, he was supplied with copies of all the Circulars, Revenue and Judicial' issued by the Punjab government.[9] Whenever questions of procedure arose in Awadh, from the disarming of the King's troops, to the introduction of English education in the province, British officials were referred to precedents in the Punjab. One of Dalhousie's first acts on his appointment as Governor General, had been the annexation of the Punjab following the defeat of the Sikh army at Gujrat in 1849. In retrospect, it was folly to imagine that because the Punjab had been successfully amalgamated into British India, Awadh would follow suit. Although on the surface the situation in Awadh seemed promising, with its superficial westernisation, the friendly attitude of its rulers to the Company, and the very lack of armed protest for nearly a century, the Company made the fatal mistake of treating the two provinces in exactly the same way. There was a world of difference between the young Sikh Maharaja of the Punjab, Duleep Singh, who was pensioned off and settled in England as a kind of royal lap-dog to Queen Victoria, and Wajid Ali Shah, hereditary monarch and guardian of the old Mughal traditions. The Punjab had been annexed after a military victory by the Company, a fact which was comprehensible to all. But Awadh had been taken by stealth, with British documents that its King refused to sign, and without the chance of diplomatic or military protest.

The deposed King withdrew into Qaisarbagh to consider his next move. Even though he had refused to sign the Treaty, Dalhousie had privately written to Outram that the King would receive Rs 1 lakh (£10,000) per month as pension. But within three weeks of his deposition the King informed Outram that he intended to go to Calcutta to petition the outgoing Governor General, and attempt to get the annexation reversed. If Dalhousie would not listen, then the King would travel to London himself, to petition Queen Victoria in person. The King was supported in this by his relatives and Court officials, but not surprisingly the Government opposed the plan, although it could not physically prevent him from travelling.

Not since the days of Saadat Ali Khan, fifty years earlier, had a ruler of Awadh stepped outside the kingdom, and Wajid Ali Shah's proposed journey raised delicate questions of etiquette, which were made all the more difficult by his new status as a king without a kingdom, but not in exile. Outram had initially requested, on the King's behalf, that the district authorities throughout Bengal should 'pay His Majesty every mark of respect; and provide him with everything he may require in the shape of supplies for himself and his attendants'. But once the scale of the royal journey became clear, Dalhousie advised Outram to tell the King that no more than 500 attendants could expect transport and accommodation 'on the road'. Once he arrived in Calcutta, the King and his retinue would have to fend for themselves as they were not the invited guests of the Government.[10] Messages were sent out through the electric telegraph from Fort William to the commanding officers along the King's proposed route of Cawnpore, Allahabad and Benares. They were ordered to provide a 21-gun salute, 'but to pay him no other honours'.

On the evening of 13 March the King left Lucknow with John Rose Brandon, the one-time partner, and son-in-law, of George Derusett. (It is possible that the Englishwoman noted as being in charge of the King's sons in the early 1850s was Mary Ann Brandon.) Brandon was now a successful businessman in Cawnpore, where he owned the 'Central Star' newspaper and the North Western Company mail coaches, which made the regular run of eight hours to Lucknow and back. Outram reported that 'The King has been encouraged and sustained in his resolution to adopt a course of negative opposition and passive resistance by the advice, I am told and believe, of Mr Brandon, a merchant at Cawnpore, whose antecedents of meddling mischievousness are well known . . . This individual assures His Majesty that, if deputed to England as his Agent, he will, without doubt, obtain his restoration.'[11]

The King travelled in one of the Cawnpore mail coaches, accompanied by Brandon, who sat on the coachbox with the driver. He was followed by three of his wives, his younger brother General Mirza Mahomed Jawad Ali Sikander Hashmat Bahadur, the Queen Mother, Janab Alia Begam, and the heir-apparent. Also in the royal party was a second Englishman, Major Robert Bird, the former Assistant Resident at Lucknow and one of the few, perhaps the only, Company men to champion the King. There were no crowds at his departure, as the coaches set out from Qaisarbagh, for few people believed he was leaving forever. Outram himself thought the first (and last) stop would be the new country house at Alambagh, five miles south of the city. He confidently forecast that the King would 'thence return to his palace appalled by the discomfort of his undertaking'.[12] But although the King was alarmed at the heat of the journey, for the hot weather had now set in, the royal party arrived the next morning in Cawnpore. The King spent his first night on British soil in Brandon's bungalow, and rented accommodation for his retinue was taken in adjoining houses.[13]

Here the news that a new Governor General, Lord Canning, had been appointed, raised the King's spirits. He sent Canning a letter of congratulation and added that he was 'confident that through your kind assistance I may yet be restored to my territory'. But this was shortly followed up by a second letter, complaining that the King was being held up in Cawnpore because Outram had detained the Chief Minister in Lucknow. 'His personal attendance on me is absolutely necessary,' wrote the King. He requested the new Governor to reply immediately, through the electric telegraph, and even sent him a prepaid reply form. But Ali Naki Khan was being held back by the Chief Commissioner to assist in sorting out the arrears of payment for the palace staff.

Other palace officials and servants who tried to follow the King got as far as the Ganges but were then hauled back on Outram's orders. They included seven of the King's personal attendants, the Chief Eunuch, his doctor, his Chamberlain, his chef, the 'Master of the Wardrobe' and the 'Provider of the Lights'. Having allowed the King to leave Lucknow, Wajid Ali Shah now encountered 'a passive opposition which meets me at every step'. He complained again to the Governor General that Outram continued 'to throw obstacles in my way . . . demanding bail from every person in my retinue likely to be useful to me on my journey with the view no doubt of arresting my progress'.[14] He said that although coaches for the next stage of the journey had been standing by in Cawnpore for several days, incurring heavy costs, he felt unable to leave without so many members of his staff. There followed an involuntary stay of three weeks, during which time the King met Cawnpore's Indian and British dignitaries, though not, as far as we know, the Nana Sahib, residing in his palace at Bithur twelve miles away. The Indian officers and sepoys of the regiments stationed at Cawnpore were reported to be particularly indignant at the King's deposition and the enforced delays, and harrassment of his staff created a resentment that was not to be assuaged for another year. The depleted royal party finally moved on, reaching Calcutta on 13 May 1856.

The majority of the King's household, including his second wife Begam Hazrat Mahal, his relatives and servants had been left behind in the Qaisarbagh and Dilkusha palaces. Even before his departure, awkward questions had arisen about the status of the palace inhabitants. The government's response had clearly not been worked out in advance and here there was no Punjab precedent which could be used. Wajid Ali Shah was to keep the title of King, given in perpetuity to Ghazi-ud-din Haider by the British Government in 1819. Whatever their private opinions, British officials were punctilious in all correspondence, in referring to him as 'Your Majesty' and in Urdu as 'Hazrat'. Then, in an odd reminder of the tussles over the British Resident's authority in Lucknow before annexation, an attempt was made to establish the extent of the King's remaining powers and privileges. Outram had pointed out to the Governor General 'the necessity that exists for defining the authority of the King, to what places it is to extend and whether the King's relatives, or other dependents are to be made amenable to our Courts'. Canning ruled that the deposed King was 'to remain undisturbed in Qaisarbagh and Dilkusha and the park' and beyond the reach of the new government's judicial system. 'The process of our courts will not run [there].' Only if the King abused his power, or if Canning *felt* he was abusing it, would this privilege be withdrawn.[15]

No other buildings belonging to the King 'shall be exempt from legal process', and claims to several other palaces in the city by him and other members of the royal family were to be investigated by the Judicial Commissioner. This meant that Martin Gubbins' judicial officers could demand entry anywhere else apart from Qaisarbagh and the Dilkusha. Lucknow was full of huge palaces, from the old Macchi Bhawan to the Daulat Khana and the Chattar Manzil, in addition to many smaller palaces like the Khurshid Manzil and Barowen. There were plenty of people to occupy them too, for royal protection and pensions (*wasiqa*) extended to many former wives and descendants of previous Nawabs, as far back as

Saadat Khan, founder of the dynasty in the early eighteenth century. The King was asked to provide a list of residents in the two palaces still under his control, and no one who was not registered, would subsequently be able to claim legal immunity. Anyone who sought refuge there could be extradited and subjected to Company jurisdiction. All these decisions were taken within a month of annexation, but on learning that the King had left Lucknow, these privileges were abruptly withdrawn. The Governor General now ruled that 'during the absence of the King . . . the ordinary civil and Criminal Courts are to exercise jurisdiction within the palaces above mentioned [Qaisarbagh and Dilkusha] . . . as in any other part of the Territory which has been brought under our administration'.[16] This effectively removed the element of protection from all remaining members and dependants of the royal family.

British concern with extraditing people from the palaces may seem initially like another example of aggressive colonial policy, but in this case it was primarily to assist Indians pursuing claims against the royal family who might have to be brought to court. One of the first to take advantage of this was Ali Mohamed, a merchant of Bholagunj. He petitioned the new Judicial Commissioner's Court, in April, against a widow of the late Nawab Nasir-ud-din Haider, claiming that she owed him Rs 14,695. This was not the first time she had run up debts with the trader either, because Ali Mohamed said he had previously served a summons on her through the King's law court. However, in making out the summons against her, the new Assistant Commissioner used the familiar Urdu forms of address *tum* and *tumhare* instead of 'the usual deferential equivalents'.[17] Not surprisingly the summons was returned unanswered. Although the Assistant Commissioner blustered that 'there is but one form of legal summons, for all persons of whatever rank', he was over-ruled both by Ommaney and the Governor General. 'It would be better . . .' the latter admitted, 'if there were no exception to an uniform administration of the law in Oudh', but egalitarianism could go too far. If members of the royal family *had* to attend the new Court of Justice, they should receive a *rubakari* (warrant) instead of an ordinary summons, and it should be delivered by Captain Fletcher Hayes, the Military Secretary. Hayes had been appointed to the difficult role of go-between to the royal family and the Governor General. He was also responsible for ensuring that the royal pensions were paid, and the inevitable complaints channelled to Company officials.

Out in the countryside the Divisional Commissioners set up their own law courts in new or existing *kutcheri* buildings. They had been given the seemingly irreconcilable task of following the existing Islamic code of law, but modifying it with British regulations. (A standardised Indian penal code was not introduced until 1860.) A request went to Calcutta for law books, including the 'Printed Decisions of the Sudder Dewanee and Nizamut Adawluts' (the High Court for civil suits and the Supreme Court of Criminal Justice). These 'Printed Decisions' gave precedents for judicial rulings, particularly for cases dealing with mortgages and disputed property ownership. One unexpected bonus of annexation was a general amnesty for petty criminals. The Governor General, who was later nicknamed 'Clemency' Canning, ruled that only serious offences committed before 7 February 1856 were to be brought to trial. Although murder was the only crime under Islamic law which carried the death penalty, Canning suspected that 'crimes against property [had been] visited with punishments so severe as generally to result in the death of the culprits'.[18]

However, by the end of May, the hard-line Judicial Commissioner, Ommaney, sought to extend capital punishment to crimes below murder, saying he believed 'the punishment of death in a few such instances would be in the end the most merciful course by the terror it would occasion among [the] community'. He then wildly over-exaggerated his case by adding that 'lawlessness and insecurity of life, and property have prevailed [in Awadh] to an extent perhaps unprecedented in the history of any nation or principality'.[19] Canning asked the Chief Commissioner to produce comparative crime figures in Awadh for 1855 and 1856, and these certainly showed that murders had diminished from 202 to 37, and woundings from 239 to 57, since the take-over. Part of this reduction might have been in response to a new and cruel punishment—that of transportation for life. Transportation had already been used for convicted criminals in British India, particularly during the dacoit and thuggee crackdowns of the early 1850s. Men were shipped to British penal colonies in Singapore, Penang and Malacca which were known then as the Straits Settlement, and a number had already died in futile escape attempts. A petition from the mother of Jagan Nath Doobaty of Faizabad, one of the first men in Awadh to be convicted and sentenced to transportation in May 1856, was rejected by Ommaney. Horrible as the Nawab's jails were before annexation, at least their inmates had still been in their own country, with the possibility of release or intercession by relatives.

Although the British had been preparing for annexation for over a year, they were unable to estimate how much it would actually cost them. Money had been put aside for the purpose, but it was only when officials began dismantling the trappings of royalty after the King's departure that they became aware of the scale of his liabilities. His huge debts had to be offset against the land revenue collection, itself an unknown factor in February, before officials could get out into the fields and start assessing the spring crops. The immediate task was to pay the arrears of the King's army and then disband it. Ordered by Wajid Ali Shah not to cause a disturbance, the troops had, for the moment, obeyed him, but with his departure it would have been imprudent, not to mention expensive, to keep all the men on. The King's troops had not fought a serious campaign since the Rohilla war at the end of the eighteenth century, but they were useful for helping with the land revenue collection, which sometimes had to be brought in by force. Now an army committee was set up and all the troops assembled and interviewed at four stations in Awadh. These interviews were to establish if the men wanted to be enrolled in the new British-led Oude Irregular Force or the Military Police. They were also to find out when the men had last been paid. It was discovered that most of the King's 52 regiments were in arrears for the whole of the previous year and many individuals for much longer than that. Only after these interviews was it possible to draw up a correct muster roll, and the total number of men was put at 60,349. They were made up of regular and irregular troops, horse troops and artillery.[20]

Among the King's regimental officers were a number of Europeans and Anglo-Indians, many of whom had served successive Nawabs over long periods. They included Captain R.J.H. Magness, whose one-time adjutant had been Yusuf Khan Kamalposh. Magness had served for twenty-seven years, only six months longer than Henry Duboist, an uncle of Sarah Derusett. The oldest serving officer was Joseph Johannes, the Armenian who had joined up in 1814, when Saadat Ali Khan was still Nawab. Johannes' son had himself served for eighteen years. The Rottons were there too, James who could not speak English, in Captain Bunbury's Corps, and Felix, Commandant of the King's Artillery, who had served for twenty years and who was to fight with his Indian comrades against the British next year. All of these officers took the opportunity offered to retire on pensions, leaving their men to join the new Force. Captain Magness' own unit, known as 'Magness ke Pultun' now became part of the 7th Oude Irregular Infantry.[21]

But of the 60,000 odd Indian soldiers, only half could be accommodated in the new Oude Force and the Police, leaving a total of 31,097 to be paid off and dismissed. With the advantage of being able to assess the day-to-day situation, Outram believed that the payment of all arrears was a

priority, and he promised the men, on his own authority, that this would
be done. The Governor General initially refused to backdate pay before
the Muslim year 1263H (AD 1856) and he rebuked Outram for his
promise, pointing out that Rs 12 lakhs had already been set aside for the
troops. At Outram's insistence a compromise was hammered out and
arrears for the last 16 months agreed, but he was defeated on his proposal
that room should be found for another 2,000 men in the new regiments.
Clearly a greater number of men than expected had agreed to transfer
their loyalty, and the Chief Commissioner was embarrassed that they
could not all be taken on. Paying off the unwanted men began on 2 April
at the palace of Barowen which had been requisitioned for the headquarters of the new Oude Irregular Force. Conveniently the old lines
and barracks vacated by the King's regiments in Lucknow and other
places, could, with some adaptation, now be used as permanent quarters for the new Force. Men from the Company's 32nd Regiment were
moved into the Chaupar Stables on Hazratganj, now emptied of animals,
and the officers commandeered the Khurshid Manzil palace, the miniature castle with its little moat and drawbridge.

Not all the ex-soldiers were prepared to be bought off without protest. The Chief Commissioner was becoming increasingly alarmed by
the behaviour of the unwanted irregular troops, armed with their own
matchlocks and swords. When offered financial compensation if they
would surrender these old-fashioned, but still effective, weapons, 'they
moreover openly display their sympathy for the late King and are ready
to a man to join any standard which would hold out a prospect of restoring
them to their former life of rapine'. Some men had refused to attend the
District Committees to collect their money, and others had actually
imprisoned their former officers. 'The spirit of disatisfaction evinced by
this large body of armed men, now let loose upon the country to the
number of 30,000 is a very serious consideration,' Outram warned. To
add to his unease, he was aware that within a short time 'there will be
thousands of retainers of the principal zemindars turned adrift, and many
hundreds of idle followers of the Court and Stables who have heretofore
fattened at the Capital on the plunder of the country [who] have already
been discharged, and it can hardly be hoped that such vast numbers of
men, hitherto supported by rapine and plunder will at once settle down
to peaceable pursuits . . . very strict vigilance and an imposing force alone
can ensure tranquility'. He foresaw that the King's artillery, of whom
nearly 6,000 were dismissed 'will be the most dangerous of all the troops
should any of the zamindars hold their forts against us'.[22]

His concerns on disarmament were slightly eased when an unexpected proposal came in from some of the zamindars themselves. To the
Financial Commissioner's surprise, land revenue collectors were being
offered cannon and guns in lieu of cash from the spring harvest. Outram
seized on this as a 'politic' step and 'the least ambiguous mode of reducing
the armaments of many zamindars'. A sliding scale of payment was quickly
worked out. Brass guns were accepted at Rs 30 per maund, and iron guns
for the value of the metal only. Forty-one guns came in, under escort,
from Sitapur District, and Mahmudabad District sent in six, some of
which were re-used for the new Force. The number of arms traded in
was, however, small, compared to the amount of weaponry still in private
hands, whether the hands were those of the landowner or the disgruntled
ex-soldier.

Nothing was said about the men who may have deserted when the
King's regiments were disbanded, though there is a discrepancy of nearly
17,000 between the Company's muster roll, and the figure given by a
contemporary Indian historian.[23] Certainly the disbandment had led to
a substantial number of civilians being thrown out of work too, because
the Company now brought in their own contractors to supply food, uniforms, animal transport and weapons. The old civilian contractors and
other people who had serviced the King's troops were estimated to
number about 14,000. They had no reason to welcome the British, either.

The King had been told, on annexation, that the royal establishments
would be abolished. This was part of the penalty of deposition. All those
things which had entertained former Nawabs and so annoyed the British
were to be cleared away in the name of economy. The King's animals
were the first to go, auctioned early in March. Not only were the ceremonial elephants, camels and horses, used in state processions sold off,
but the cavalry horses from the disbanded regiments, the King's animals
in the Chaupar Stables behind Hazratganj, and all the inhabitants of the
royal menagerie and aviary, established eighty years ago by Asaf-ud-daula,
had to go. No provision had been made for feeding the animals after annexation, and the new Government, to its credit, took on the responsibility. It was found that the cost of food alone amounted to Rs 1,000 per
day and an urgent request went to the King asking him to choose what
animals he wanted, before the remainder were sold. This he refused to
do, explaining quite reasonably that since he had not been consulted
over *any* of the arrangements for the disposal of his belongings, it was
unnecessary for the Chief Commissioner to begin negotiations now.
Outram was therefore instructed by the Governor General to auction all

the animals, with the proviso that the King could be later recompensed for any he considered his personal property.

It was a heartbreaking and chaotic event that took place in front of the Dilaram Kothi, the old Derusett home. Auction notices had been posted up throughout the province, and buyers came from as far afield as Delhi and Lahore. The scene was sympathetically described forty years later by the English writer Flora Annie Steel in a novel entitled *On the Face of the Water*.

' "Going! Going! Gone!" The Western phrase echoed over the Eastern scene without a trace of doubt in its calm assumption of finality. It was followed by a pause, during which, despite the crowd thronging the wide plain the only recognisable sound was the vexed yawning purr of a tiger impatient for its prey. It shuddered through the sunshine, strangely out of keeping with the multitude of men gathered together in silent security; but on that March evening of the year 1856, when the long shadows of the surrounding trees had begun to invade the sunlit levels of grass by the river, the lately deposed King of Oude's menagerie was being auctioned. It had followed all his other property to the hammer, and a perfect Noah's Ark of wild beasts was waiting, doubtfully, for a change of masters. "Going! Going! Gone!" '[24]

Many valuable animals and birds were knocked down at bargain prices. Local people were accused by outsiders of trickery and deceit, and the Lucknow butchers, who had been expected to buy the cows and bulls, refused to trade, possibly because they had already struck a deal with the auctioneer. The Kotwal of Lucknow bought several hundred of the royal pigeons, to give back to the King as a gift. Ex-army officers whose own horses were auctioned, were able to buy them back for a song. Nawab Muftah-ud-daula made a handsome profit by buying horses at Rs 250 each and re-selling them in Cawnpore for Rs 1,000. Even buyers who came along without enough cash were allowed to take their purchases away, if they left their home address and a deposit with the auctioneer. Saddest of all were the royal elephants, with their personal attendants. Once they had carried the Nawabs and now 'they stood frequently throwing dust over their heads and people saw tears in their eyes'. One attendant, also in tears, said he had cared for the animals for thirty years and now both beast and man were homeless. 'The Dilaram Kothi became a place of admonition,' wrote Kamal-ud-din Haider, who witnessed the scene.[25] 7,000 animals were estimated to have been sold in one day, including 200 elephants, over 100,000 pigeons, 107 lions, cheetahs, antelopes, parrots and a rhinoceros. The Government found the daily food bill had dropped to Rs 90 for the few animals left unsold.

On 22 April James Outram stepped down on medical grounds, and an Acting Chief Commissioner, Coverley Jackson, took over. Almost at once he was at loggerheads with the two men who should have been his closest allies, Ommaney and Gubbins. Quarrels arose over the most petty matters, but the real conflict was about who exercised ultimate control in Awadh. As Chief Commissioner, Jackson naturally believed it was him, although both the Financial and the Judicial Commissioners maintained they had been given total jurisdiction over their own respective areas. Unlike Outram, Jackson was clearly unable to delegate, and he insisted on interfering in matters that should have been left to the two Commissioners. He intervened in a case of capital punishment that Ommaney was handling, and quarrelled with Gubbins over the revenue collection, accusing him of lying, 'reckless disobedience' and maladministration. Days that should have been spent touring the Province, assessing the mood of the people, as Sleeman and Outram had done, were being wasted in interminable squabbling and endless written complaints to Calcutta. At the time when a firm hand, coupled with a sympathetic ear, was crucial, the three Commissioners of Awadh were publicly seen to be at each others' throats. The situation was not made easier by the fact that all three men lived together in close proximity, in the Residency complex. Both Ommaney and Gubbins had been allocated substantial houses near the Residency itself, which had become the Chief Commissioner's headquarters.

Despite internal dissension the governing of Awadh, and the maintenance of order outside the Residency, if not inside, had to go on. After the immediate problem of the animals had been solved, attention turned to the King's pensioners, his servants and other former employees. Like the animals, they too had been left without immediate provision, and many of them were owed arrears of pay. It was 'difficult to imagine anything more discreditable than the King's conduct in taking his departure from the country, with this enormous amount due to helpless people', wrote Jackson in May. 'These poor wretches were absolutely starving . . .'[26] The King had estimated that his debts, including arrears to staff and loans taken out, amounted to Rs 4,155,052 or 41 lakhs. A long list of his employees, covering nearly four pages of foolscap in the Company records, included the parasol and peacock fan-bearers, the muezzins in charge of the *taziyas* in the *imambaras*, dancing girls, artists, the bookbinders from the Sultan Press, the crews on the royal boats, carriage attendants, the aviary and menagerie attendants, news-writers, clerks attached to the old judicial and revenue departments, and municipal workers like the 'waterers of the public streets'. There were 20,000 pensioners alone who relied on annual payments for life.

Inevitably a dispute arose about where the money was going to come from to cover the King's liabilities. The King suggested that it should be taken out of the land revenue, which was estimated at 90 lakhs that spring, but this was staunchly opposed by the Financial Commissioner, who said the money should be deducted in instalments from the King's generous pension. In the end a compromise was reached. The bulk of the cash was to come from the King, but money raised by the British from the sale of his assets, including the menagerie auction, could also be used. 'A few lacs', wrote the Governor General, 'spent in closing the account without injustice, and even with liberality will be well repaid if we can thereby smooth down discontent and escape disturbance.' But, Jackson warned, it was to be a one-off payment. The servants would get a month's wages immediately, but arrears would not be considered before the last financial year. Earlier arrears would have to be claimed from the King, and 'this is the last time that the British Government will interfere in their behalf and that, if they choose to continue in the King's service, they do so at their own risk'.[27]

Company officials in the city Residency and at Mariaon, the British cantonment north of the river, had been tenants of the King before annexation, for he nominally owned and maintained all the buildings within these two extensive areas. Now the houses, barracks and gardens had all been acquired, without payment, by the new government. In the past, members of the King's staff had been provided for 'keeping in order the several Gardens and houses' at the Residency and the cantonment. With the abolition of the office of Resident, these servants were pruned to the minimum and the total monthly wages cut down to Rs 298, now that the Company was paying the bill. The Residency's Intelligence Department became redundant, as there was no longer any need to spy on the King and his Ministers. Three long-serving Indian spies were pensioned off, their work completed. Rather poignantly, an eighty-year old portrait painter, Machoo Beg, was found to have been attached to the Residency since 1806, presumably recording half a century's visitors. He had been on the royal payroll too, and was now awarded a small pension for the remainder of his life. The Chief Commissioner was allowed to retain only two out of the twelve elephants which the King had kept at the

Residency for State occasions. The other ten were to go to new government departments. The elephants' silver howdahs and trappings were
sold and two sensible, serviceable howdahs purchased instead.

Now, with the King out of the way, his animals gone, his servants,
dependants and soldiers paid up, a great spring-cleaning began. Remind-
ers of the past were swept away, and a number of innovations speedily
introduced. For people living outside Lucknow, one of the first indications
of the change in masters was the arrival of British surveyors on the old
Residency elephants. A land revenue survey was carried out immediately
after annexation and a temporary three-year settlement made with the
landowners, or with the people who seemed to be in charge of the land.
The settlement was to come into operation from 1 May 1856, in advance
of the autumn harvest. The marking out of village boundaries began and
locally recruited staff were quickly trained to measure the villagers' fields.
The Department of Public Works carried out its own survey before
submitting proposals for the land it needed. The Superintendent of Irri-
gation was busy measuring the water levels between different rivers in
Awadh, and the Superintendents of Forests were 'introducing rules for
the preservation of Forests and the felling of Timber of mature growth'.
The Company had been unaware that the King also owned land in Delhi,
until the Estates Manager wrote to Outram after annexation. They were
small estates, yielding about Rs 12,000 a year and enquiries found that the
land was 'ancestral and private property', probably acquired by Saadat
Khan, the first Nawab, during his service at the Delhi Court. The King
was therefore allowed to retain them for his own use.[28]

A further visible sign of change was the construction of the electric
telegraph line between Calcutta and Lucknow. This had appeared so very
rapidly after annexation that engineers must have been standing by, ready
with their galvanised iron rods, their forked bamboo poles and copper
wires. Less than a month later the Governor General was complaining
that excitable young officers at the Residency were sending messages to
Calcutta 'upon matters of the smallest importance and of no urgency',
demanding answers to letters which had only been received a few hours
earlier.[29] He also suspected that messages were being sent without
Outram's knowledge, and wanted a limit 'put to the use of the Telegraph'.
The Lucknow Electric Telegraph Office had been set up in the Residency
Banqueting Hall, a handsome two-storeyed building, erected about 1815,
though surely none of its former guests, even in a merry moment, could
have imagined the peculiar use to which it would one day be put.

The speedy introduction of the electric telegraph must have been particularly galling for the King, for he himself had proposed setting up a line between Lucknow and Cawnpore the previous year. He initially wanted his own private line, but if that was not acceptable, he wrote, then he was willing to pay all charges for a British-run line. He found Dalhousie was 'entirely opposed' to both suggestions, and the former Governor General had firmly vetoed any British supplies or help if the King insisted on going ahead. Dalhousie suggested that the Company should pay the cost of erection and the King should sanction the ground for it. This Wajid Ali Shah refused, saying it 'would derogate from his dignity' to have a British-funded line running through his kingdom, and in any case, he wanted the revenue from it, which would have been considerable, given its novelty value. There the matter had rested for a year.

Further communication links were vital to integrate the new province into British India. Six Indian surveyors and an overseer from the Thomason Civil Engineering College at Roorkee were needed at once for the Cawnpore Road. 'Without a Survey it will be impossible to organise the Police of the City, to lay down roads connecting the Military posts with the Civil Station or to devise those measures for developing the [re]sources of the country which are expected at our hands and which are as politically expedient as they are necessary for the improvement of the province,' explained Ommaney.[30] The Cawnpore Road, 'our only communication with the province is rapidly falling into disrepair and requires a fresh layer of kunkur along the entire line'. An Engineers Department was also needed to 'superintend the works' and help with 'the formation of Cutcherries, Treasuries, Jails and other public establishments of the capital'.

Dr Fayrer, who combined the curiously disparate jobs of Post Master and Residency doctor had been allocated the task of setting up 'new lines of road' to the various stations selected for the District Commissioners. The small Lucknow post office was now considered 'totally unadapted to the present requirements' and an adjoining building, probably the Begum Kothi palace, was taken over. The new building was to become 'the chief sorting office for letters for every town in Oude', and a list of staff required was drawn up, including writers, letter peons and *bur-khandazes* (sentries). Regulations for the distribution and sale of postage stamps, still a novelty in British India, were drawn up. 'Native currency', the silver coins bearing the Nawabs' roccoco coat of arms embellished with mermaids, *chattars* (ceremonial parasols), pennants, crowns and swords, that had been issued from a number of mints in Awadh were called in to the new Government's treasuries. They were replaced by British rupees stamped with Queen Victoria's head, though the old coins continued in circulation, and there was no devaluation of the currency.

Within the city, public establishments belonging to the former government were scrutinised and changes recommended. The Judicial Commissioner made a personal inspection of the city's four jails and found the Kotwali, the police jail, 'in a condition of squalid filth', with 250 prisoners. The 'Black Jail' held 800 men, 'some in cages' while the 'Thuggee and Dakoittee jail', attached to the Residency complex, had only thirty-two prisoners. Ommaney advised that the fourth, the Singchawali Jail, be enlarged to hold 1,000 men and that it should become the District Jail. The Commissioner for Lucknow, Major John Sherbrooke Banks, took a radical decision to establish both his office and his home outside the Residency complex, selecting an old building thought to have been Claude Martin's powder mill or arsenal. It quickly became known as 'Banks' Bungalow', and was later metamorphosed into Raj Bhawan.

Several establishments which had been financially supported by the royal family were now without their annual stipends. The Shi'a Imambara College, set up by Nawab Amjad Ali Shah in 1842, was found to be running at a loss, and salaries to staff were in arrears, although there were 205 fee-paying pupils.[31] Ommaney recommended its closure, not only on economic grounds, but because its continuation would mean that 'we should be perpetuating an educational establishment, which teaches and fosters an exclusive creed, and religious tenets to which the Government cannot subscribe'. As a conciliatory measure he proposed 'that a liberal scheme of education which shall embrace all classes, will be shortly set on foot'. The Governor General agreed with both of Ommaney's suggestions and sent him details of the education scheme that had been introduced in the Punjab.

No parallels were drawn between the exclusive Imambara College and the Christian School, founded by the former Resident, Colonel John Low. This had been established as a philanthropic measure for the 'daughters and young sons of the poorer classes of Europeans in the city who are now to be numbered by hundreds'. Of the forty-three pupils, mainly children of uncovenanted Company servants, twenty-one were Protestants and the remainder Catholics. The King had supported the school with a monthly payment of Rs 150, but that had ceased on annexation. The new Chaplain, the Reverend Henry Polehampton reported that the school could easily double its numbers, with 'local subscriptions' covering all expenses, but Government money was needed for contingencies.[32] By the time Polehampton's proposal was considered in Council at Calcutta, he was already dead, an early victim of the siege.

The sudden arrival of so many Company officials, Army officers and civilians had inevitably led to an immediate shortage of accommodation in Lucknow. The Residency complex, large as it was, could not hold an infinite number of men, neither could the cantonment. More importantly, all the new administrators had to have places where they could work. A temporary solution had been found by providing substantial tents that could be used as offices, and Rs 25,539 was allocated for them during the first year. George Christian, the Commissioner in Khairabad District, used a bungalow in his compound as a temporary *kutcheri* until a permanent one was erected. In other areas, the Company followed Colonel Weston's lead and took over *barahdaries* and palaces for offices. Rent may have been paid to the owners, but if so, there is no mention of it in Company records. Ommaney, as Judicial Commissioner, had been put in charge of *nuzool*, or government buildings, but it was not always easy to establish ownership. An ambitious proposal of his to adapt the Chattar Manzil palace to 'accommodate public Offices' was firmly rejected by the Chief Commissioner. Shortage of space in Lucknow affected not only the living (especially as wives and children now joined their husbands), but also the British dead, whose numbers were rising with the increase in population. We shall see later how this led to the opening of new Christian burial grounds.

By the end of October 1856, the King, who was now established at Garden Reach, north of Calcutta, was anxiously awaiting a message from Queen Victoria. Dalhousie had promised to inform the Queen that the royal party was going to England to seek an audience. It was a promise which was not kept. The new Governor General, Lord Canning, was not prepared to write to Queen Victoria either. Wajid Ali Shah reminded Canning that his only reason in coming to Calcutta was to get an inquiry set up to examine the unsigned, disputed Treaty. When Canning refused even to discuss the matter, the King became determined to take it up with the British sovereign herself. However, as we have seen, he deputed his mother, brother and son to travel to London, and plead his case, with ultimately tragic results. The King had been advised not to go to England by his doctors and it may have been illness that decided him against travelling back to Lucknow, or he may have felt it politically expedient to remain near the Governor General, and await the return of his relatives.

But it is more likely that he chose not to re-enter the capital until his former status had been restored, as he still believed it would be.

But the longer the King stayed away, the more steps were taken in Lucknow to erase his memory. By December 1856 it was suggested that he ought to clear out his property from storerooms in Qaisarbagh, the Macchi Bhawan, the Chattar Manzil, and other various palaces and *barah-daries*. This seemed to indicate that whatever the King thought, the British believed he was unlikely to return, that an assumption had been made about the ownership of the Lucknow palaces, and that the possessions of nearly a century should be removed from them. Ommaney reported that the roofs of the Qaisarbagh storerooms were dilapidated and dangerous, and that once the King had sorted out what he wanted, the number of storeroom guards could be reduced. Helpfully, Ommaney had already got Captain Carnegie to make an inventory of the contents of the storerooms, and soon, without apparently visiting them himself, Ommaney told the Governor General that 'this singular miscellaneous hoard has been collected by degrees and no article has ever been used from the date of its deposit. The things are in fact rotting to decay and would soon all have been utterly valueless.'[33] There were certainly some articles in the inventory which could have deteriorated, including embroidered coverings for the elephants, 'old dresses, English and Hindustanee', shawls, tents, curtains and floor coverings. But there were also palanquins, matchlocks, swords, ivories, china, glass, silver, copper, a gold throne studded with stones, another plain gold throne, wrapped up in cloth and twenty-six wooden chests of valuable stones, jewels, and crowns.

The King ignored the request to pack up his belongings, and the Judicial Commissioner did not press the matter further. But Carnegie's inventory was to come in useful six months later, during the early days of the uprising. On 28 June 1857, Major Banks, accompanied by several officers, a company of riflemen, and two cannons, entered the Qaisarbagh. Dismissing the protests of the King's treasury guards, he took twenty-two wooden chests of jewels, three jewelled crowns, a quantity of gold coins and a 'priceless' throne, into British custody in the Residency, for safe-keeping. Some of these treasures were subsequently looted during and after the siege, thus reducing the initial value of the haul, which was originally estimated at Rs 80 lakhs.[34]

A more significant sign of the King's waning influence came when Ommaney ordered the Chief Magistrate to dismiss the *chobdars*, the royal mace-bearers. Although of purely symbolic importance, these men had always formed part of the royal processions. To be appointed *chobdar* and to carry the silver stick was a high honour, and one to which men of good family would aspire. *Chobdars* were also part of the retinue of Nawabi government officers, and their presence indicated that the officers were carrying out duties sanctioned by the King. The dismissed *chobdars* were ordered to hand in their silver sticks of office, their insignia and badges. 'I sent some Insignia of office recovered by me to the Deputy Commissioner from members of the late Judiciary,' reported Ommaney in April 1857, and he intended to collect more 'still in possession of officers of the late State, which should be reclaimed'.[35] Captain Hayes, the liaison officer, more sensitive than the Commissioners, clearly recognised that this was 'not acceptable on political or legal grounds', and in this he was backed up by the Governor General, who acknowledged that Ommaney's order was likely to cause complaint. Canning also said that there was no purpose in collecting the silver sticks, a valid comment, since they were part of the former administration which had been abolished, and were therefore now deprived of symbolic meaning. Only the Chief Commissioner had the right to order the disposal of State property or the King's property, he added, indicating that although the two were still separated, both could now be disposed of by Company officials. The silver sticks were not, however, returned.

By the beginning of May 1857, the Company could congratulate itself on the transition of Awadh from an ill-governed kingdom to a well-organised province. The first land revenue collection had been made, despite protestations of hardship by many. A framework of administration had been put in place with the distribution of District Commissioners and their staff throughout the country. British wives and children moved into bungalows, bringing an atmosphere of domesticity and normality. The judicial system had been set up, and reported crime had already dropped dramatically. Land surveying had begun and important communication links established. Calcutta was now only hours away by the electric telegraph. Public building had started and former government establishments were taken over and reorganised. The King's army had been radically overhauled, old soldiers pensioned or bought off, and a promising nucleus re-employed in the Oude Irregular Force. The King, in conveniently taking himself off to Calcutta, had defused the situation in Lucknow, and it would surely be only a matter of time before *all* his palaces would be brought under the Company's authority. The remaining members of the royal family had been marginalised and were now subject to British law. The King's servants and pensioners had been provided for, albeit at a cost, but it had been done fairly. The problem of the royal animals and the menagerie had been solved. The staff at the old Residency had been rationalised, and for the first time, the British were now in control of their own buildings. An English system of education was shortly to be introduced. Customs duties had been fixed in Awadh, and profitable concerns like the saltpetre monopoly had been sold to the highest bidder. Licences would shortly be introduced legalising the manufacture of salt. Was there anything the Company had overlooked?

Raja Arjun Singh was one of many *taluqdars* against the temporary land settlement made immediately after annexation. A number of petitions were put up to the Governor General, where the complainant had been persistent enough to go over the head of Martin Gubbins, the Financial Commissioner. Though the words of the Raja's petition were probably drafted by an English-speaking lawyer, the force of his argument is not lost. 'The Majority of [my] countrymen in Oude have to complain that the officers of the British Commission in Oude, look upon that country as a conquered country like the Punjab and lie under this feeling that the rights of the People of Oude have been made subservient to the Will and Laws of the present ruling power in like Manner that the Laws and Will of a conquering power are made to take precedence over the rights and laws of a conquered nation.'[36]

On 15 June 1857 the King and his Chief Minister, Ali Naki Khan (who had finally been allowed to join him in Calcutta), together with another Minister, Raja Tikait Rai, had been arrested and confined in Fort William for the duration of the uprising. Commenting on his own downfall in verse, the King wrote: 'There was a time when showers of pearls were trodden underfoot/Now I feel the cruel sun above and pebbles underfoot.'[37] Lucknow suffered more grievously after its recapture by the British than it had done during the whole of the uprising. To people who had known the city before 1857 it was now unrecognisable, so great were the changes. Broad military roads swept through the old city and intersected those palace complexes which had not been blown up. The Macchi Bhawan was almost completely destroyed. William Russell, the Irish journalist, who had described the city as more beautiful than Rome, Athens, or Constantinople, commented sarcastically on his return in the 1870s, that 'Lucknow has been fairly improved off the face of the earth.' A sense of loss and sadness hangs about the city even today, especially among the ruined palaces, and the Nawabi families who still inhabit them, re-telling the old stories of the last King of Awadh.

According to Abdul Halim Sharar, who got the story from his grand-father, chief clerk to Janab Alia Begam, the Queen Mother, Wajid Ali Shah was persuaded by his courtiers and relatives to accept the pension which was still on offer from the Company. In agreeing to do so, no matter how reluctantly, the King had tacitly acknowledged his final defeat. He spent the rest of his life at Matiya Burj, recreating his lost capital on the banks of the Hooghly. He was said to support up to 40,000 people from the 12 lakhs he got every year. As he lay dying in September 1887 *The Statesman* newspaper reported that many of his attendants, sensing the end of an era, were helping themselves to his possessions, including the Seals of office, and taking them away by the cart-load. His funeral was, nevertheless, magnificent. The British government, always at its most generous in these situations, gave the funeral procession full milit-ary honours, lending some of its own troops from Fort William and a band to play the Dead March from 'Saul'. Colonel Prideaux, the agent to the Governor General, represented the government. The sepoys fol-lowed behind, joined by the King's own household guards, with their rifles reversed, the military sign of mourning. Sounds of grief from the crowds rent the air during the hour it took the catafalque to reach the Imambara where the King was to be buried.[38]

Neither the title of King, nor his pension, was passed down to his heirs, which partly explains the relative poverty of some of the descendants today, living in the remaining buildings of Asaf-ud-daula's Daulat Khana palace. The British government, in a repetition of their actions on an-nexation, sold off the King's Calcutta property and palaces (again, far too cheaply), and distributed the profits to each heir in cash. The Marchio-ness of Dufferin and Ava, who was in Calcutta at the time, visited Matiya Burj and noted that 'His [the King's] ladies were nearly as numerous as his animals, and they are now being despatched to their homes as quickly as possible. They go at the rate of seven or eight a day, but there is still a great number left . . .'[39]

And what of Lucknow itself? Memories of the radical physical changes made immediately after the British had regained control were fading. The broad military roads were now lined with shops and houses, and parks had been laid out over the sites of demolished buildings. Hazratganj, the 'royal road', with its Begum Kothi, Nur Baksh Kothi, Kunkurwala Kothi and Chota Imambara was becoming a street of shopkeepers, in-cluding bizarrely, two English milliners. The department store of White-away Laidlaw & Co. had set up a branch in Qaisarbagh. The Oudh &

Rohilkhund Railway Company was established in the old orchard gardens at Charbagh, and the Superintendent of Telegraphs in the Shah Najaf Road. There were now five bridges over the Gomti, including two railway bridges, eleven churches and four English hotels, the latter named, without a trace of irony, The Imperial, The Prince of Wales, The Elgin and The Royal. There were numerous colleges and schools, and the city hummed with the sound of paper mills and printing presses. Dr Führer, curator of the museum, and a man who passionately hated Nawabi architecture, was housed in the Chattar Manzil. The descendants of several Europeans who had been employed by the Nawabs were still there at the end of the nineteenth century; the Quieros family, now working on the railway, a Mr Rotton at the Telegraph Office, Mr J. Johannes and Mr W. Sangster in the Judicial Commissioner's Office and George Catania on the pension list. Somewhere across the Gomti lived the lepers and the lunatics in their asylums. British rule had less than half a century left to run.[40]

NOTES AND REFERENCES

1. The idea for this chapter developed when P.J.O. Taylor commissioned me to write a short article on Awadh for his book, *A Companion to the 'Indian Mutiny' of 1857*, OUP, Delhi 1996.
2. Oldenburg, Veena Talwar, *The Making of Colonial Lucknow 1856–1877*, Princeton 1984, p. 3.
3. 26 September 1856, Minute by J.P. Grant of 18 June, no. 381, India Political Consultations, OIOC.
4. Azhar, Mirza Ali, *King Wajid Ali Shah of Awadh*, Karachi 1982, pp. 445–6.
5. Khan, Masih-ud-deen, *British Aggression in Oudh*, Lucknow 1964, p. 90.
6. Azhar, op. cit., pp. 457–8.
7. Oude Blue Book, 1856, Enclosure 13, no. 4, pp. 291–2, BL.
8. 13–20 June 1856, no. 221, G. Couper, Secretary to the Chief Commissioner, Lucknow, to G.F. Edmonstone, Secretary to the Government of India, India Political Consultations, OIOC.
9. 27 June 1856, no. 223, Couper to Edmonstone, India Political Consultations, OIOC.
10. 13 March 1856, no. 24, Bengal Public Consultations, OIOC.
11. Azhar, op. cit., p. 464.
12. 13–20 June 1856, no. 225, letter from James Outram, dated 14 March 1856, India Political Consultations, OIOC.
13. Haider, Kamal-ud-din, *Tawareekh-i-Awadh* (Urdu), vol. 2, Lucknow 1879, p. 166.

14. 13–20 June 1856, nos 235–45, Wajid Ali Shah to Edmonstone, India Political Consultations, OIOC.
15. 13–20 June 1856, no. 174, Minute from Lord Canning, dated 13 March 1856, India Political Consultations, OIOC.
16. Ibid.
17. 18 July 1856, no. 163, Couper to Edmonstone, letter dated 10 June 1856, India Political Consultations, OIOC.
18. 26 September 1856, no. 380, India Political Consultations, OIOC.
19. Ibid., no. 381.
20. 13–20 June 1856, no. 178, Couper to Edmonstone, India Political Consultations, OIOC.
21. On his accession, Wajid Ali Shah re-organised his Army, issuing new arms and uniforms, and recruiting more men. New regiments included the *Akhtari* (Star-like) and the *Nadiri* (Excellent). Older regiments included the *Atish-fishan* (Volcano), the *Fateh Mubarukh* (Auspicious Victory), the *Gulabi* (Rose-like) and the *Suleimani*.
22. Op. cit., ref. 20.
23. Haider, op. cit., p. 170, says: 'There were 87,000 employees of all religions in the Army at the time of disbandment . . . and 14,000 civilian staff.'
24. Steel, Flora Annie, *On the Face of the Water*, London 1897, p. 1.
25. Haider, op. cit., p. 171.
26. 27 June 1856, letter from the Chief Commissioner, Lucknow, to Edmonstone, dated 22 May 1856, India Political Consultations, OIOC.
27. Ibid.
28. 13–20 June 1856, no. 226, India Political Consultations, OIOC.
29. Ibid., no. 170.
30. Ibid., no. 206, Couper to Edmonstone, letter dated 3 March 1856.
31. 31 October 1856, no. 109, Couper to Edmonstone, India Political Consultations, OIOC.
32. 31 August 1856, no. 171, letter from the Reverend Polehampton dated 6 May 1857, India Political Consultations, OIOC.
33. 15 February 1857, no. 139, India Political Consultations, OIOC.
34. Haider, op. cit., p. 210. On his departure from Lucknow, Wajid Ali Shah had taken *some* jewels with him, which he deposited in the Company's Treasury at Calcutta. After his release from Fort William he requested their return, and they were delivered back to him in February 1860. An investigation in 1917 (Political & Secret Memorandum LPS/18 D225, OIOC) found no proof that they had subsequently passed out of the custody of the King or his family. The Memorandum also states that no property of the King was sent to England after annexation, which is true. Nothing was sent officially by the Government, but no tally could be made of the looted items from the palaces that entered Britain unofficially, and which were sufficient, in some cases, to pay off family debts.

35. 24 April 1857, no. 406, India Political Consultations, OIOC.

36. 13 February 1857, no. 165, Petition of Raja Arjun Singh to the Governor General, India Political Consultations, OIOC.

37. I am indebted to the Nawab Jafar Mir Abdullah of the Sheesh Mahal, Lucknow, for this couplet and many interesting stories about his eminent family background.

38. *The Statesman*, Calcutta. Articles dated 15 and 23 September 1887.

39. Beechey, G.D.S., *The Eight Child or George Duncan Beechey, Portrait Painter 1797–1852*, Mss. in the OIOC (IOL Photo EUR. 106), p. 120.

40. Details from O'Rourke & Hayward's Resident, and Street Directory of Lucknow and Barabanki. *The Only Complete List of all the European and Eurasian Residents Both Civil and Military*, Lucknow 1895, BL. O'Rourke & Hayward described themselves as 'Auctioneers, Commission, House, Press & Furniture Agents' with offices in Lalbagh.

CHAPTER SIX

Bones of Contention

'The Union Jack on Lucknow Residency was lowered at 20 hours on 13 August.' (Telegram to Rear-Admiral Viscount Mountbatten of Burma, from Sir Francis Wylie, Provincial Governor, Lucknow, 14 August 1947 at 2.45 p.m.)[1]

Union Jacks were descending all over the Indian subcontinent fifty years ago at Independence, but the hauling down of the Residency flag got a special mention because it was the only one in the British Empire which was never lowered at sunset. This was in commemoration of the flag of 1857 which had frequently been shot at by the besiegers of the Residency, and just as often patched and repaired and run up again. The symbolic importance of this flag in Empire mythology cannot be over-estimated. Lord Tennyson eulogised it as 'Banner of England':

O Banner of England . . .
Never with mightier glory than when we had reared thee on high
Flying at the top of the roofs in the ghastly siege of Lucknow—
Shot through the staff or the halyard, but ever we raised thee anew,
And ever upon the topmost roof our banner of England blew . . .

Generations of flags had flown from the flagstaff at the top of the remaining Residency tower after the recapture of Lucknow on 16 March 1858 by Sir Colin Campbell, when the Union Jack was again run up over the shattered building. In the following ninety years of British rule (only a little longer than the eighty-one years of Nawabi Lucknow), the flag 'acquired an almost mystical significance. The pock-marked Residency ruins were preserved with religious care, and the Residency grounds where hundreds of the victims of the siege lay buried under lawns and flower beds, became something of a shrine . . .'[2] By 1947 the flag had been changed over 200 times because of wear and tear.

As Independence Day approached, discreet measures were put in place by the departing British officials to ensure that their second, and final retreat from the Residency would be more dignified than the first. On 19 November 1857 the evacuation of the survivors of the six-month siege had begun. The hungry, ragged procession, Indians and Europeans, took a circuitous route to the Dilkusha Palace while Campbell's relieving force provided covering fire. So quietly and quickly had the survivors left that the besiegers were taken by surprise. The Residency compound was left empty until mid-day on 23 November, when it was realised that its defenders had gone. Then a 101-gun salute was fired in celebration and looting began in earnest. 'The bodies of the brave men and women who fell during the siege and were buried there, were, after the final relief, torn from their graves by the mutineers and scattered about, the whole place was dug up in the mad search for treasure, so that on the re-occupation [by Campbell] not a trace of the graves, and indeed hardly a vestige of the original order of things remained,' wrote Darogah Abbas Ali, seventeen years later.[3] The reburial of the siege victims, who included Sir Henry Lawrence, the Chief Commissioner, was quietly shrouded from public knowledge. It would have added intolerable grief to the burden of the bereaved. Tombstones were erected (perhaps not always over a grave), shrubs planted, and paths laid out in the Residency cemetery. The entrenchments on the 33-acre site were filled in, and the makeshift, but effective, barricades dismantled. Trees were re-planted, lawns laid down, outhouses demolished, major buildings shored up and made safe, though not restored. They were to remain as they were, bullet and cannon holes visible, a testament to the siege and the stubborn defenders. The whole area became a pleasant public garden.

Now in 1947, the custody of the Residency, the icon of Empire, was passing into Indian hands. There was a mad proposal that the whole site should be blown up, as the Macchi Bhawan had been in July 1857, 'to stop it falling into Indian hands', and a very real fear that it would, at the least, be desecrated.[4] More practical counsels prevailed, some of which have only come to light fifty years later, in commemorative publications to mark Indian Independence. Don Stokes, a young officer at the time, described how he was called to the office of the Assistant Director of Electrical and Mechanical Engineers (ADEME) in Lucknow in July 1947 and 'in some secrecy, told that with the approach of Independence, there was a real possibility of the Union Jack . . . being desecrated. I was given the task of making secure the tower from which it flew. I measured the entrance to assess the materials required. As all my workshop personnel were Indian, I had to be very cautious in giving instructions for the cutting and preparation of the timber and metalwork. When it came to the "on-site work", the ADEME rustled up three or four British Other Ranks (BORs). We set off from our various locations to rendezvous at the Residency. All went well, and it was not long before we had completed our task, fitted the padlocks and delivered the keys to the ADEME.'[5]

The Residency flag was lowered for the last time two days before Independence, at 8.00 pm, when dusk had fallen, by the Residency caretaker, Mr Ireland. Later that night a group of British sappers, led by Major-General Alfred ('Tiger') Curtis, climbed the spiral stairs of Flagstaff

14. Mr Ireland, the Residency caretaker,
with the last Union Jack, 13 August 1947

Tower, 'cut the steel flagstaff from its base, hacked out its masonry foundations, re-cemented the hole flush with the tower floor, and dragged the rubble down the tower steps'.[6] At midnight on 14–15 August a 'jubilant mob' approached the Residency 'intent on taking down the famous Union Jack and raising the new flag of an independent India . . . there was a near riot when they discovered that they had been forestalled'.[7] It was the Chief Minister of the United Provinces, Pandit G.B.

Pant, who called out the police and 'saved' the Residency this time. The stories that still circulate today about the final resting place of the last flag are an echo, over a century and a half, of the sacred qualities invested in it. Like a piece of the true cross of Christendom, at least six 'last flags' are known. The truth is, as Penderel Moon wrote, 'Various applications were made for the custody of the flag before it was agreed, with the King's approval, that it should be hung at Windsor Castle.'[8] There it remains today, framed and hung in the Royal Library.

Apart from the gesture at the Residency, the leaving of the British from Lucknow was far less dramatic than their coming. On the surface the city seemed very different from that first entered by the British in February 1856, lost the following year and re-captured the next. Lucknow's status had initially suffered a reverse in 1877 when Awadh was amalgamated with the North-Western Provinces, and the capital shifted to Allahabad, but Lucknow rallied at the turn of the century and re-established itself as the symbolic centre in political, cultural and religious terms. It was no longer isolated geographically the development of the railway complex in the former Nawabi garden of Charbagh, to the south of the city, made Lucknow an important junction. The bridging of the Ganges at Cawnpore in 1872, replacing the old crossing of boats, eventually linked Lucknow to Calcutta.

Thanks to Sir Harcourt Butler, District Commissioner and later Lieutenant Governor from 1918 to 1922, substantial plans for the city's development were drawn up and begun.[9] Lucknow University, designed by Sir Swinton Jacob, was built in another former Nawabi garden, the Padshah Bagh, north of the Gomti. It incorporated Canning College, which itself had started in 1864 as a modest venture in the Amin-ud-daula palace, later moving to the Lal Baradari, the former throne room. More than half the cost of the University was met by the *taluqdars* and rajas of Awadh. Jacob also built the King George and Queen Mary Medical Hospital and College on the site of the old Macchi Bhawan Fort, blown up in 1857 on Sir Henry Lawrence's orders. *The Pioneer* newspaper, on which Rudyard Kipling had worked as a cub reporter, moved into new premises, imaginatively commissioned from a modernist American architect, Walter Birley Griffin. The Municipal Committee and the Lucknow Improvement Trust had been set up, though both were under investigation in the 1940s for malpractice and corruption, a not unfamiliar complaint, especially where Lucknow's buildings were concerned.[10]

But however much Lucknow had been physically altered, first by Robert Napier's radical 'town-planning' of 1858, and later by these subsequent developments, it was not a British-created city, like Calcutta or New Delhi. Once the British had gone, it was found that old Lucknow was still there. Many of the street names, usually the first to go on Independence, remained largely unchanged because they referred to precolonial sites like the Shah Najaf, Qaisarbagh and the Akbari Darwaza. Others, like the East India 'Kampani' Bagh (pre-1858) and Victoria Park (post-1858) were assimilated without fuss.

There were changes at Independence of course, though nothing like those at annexation, almost a century earlier. The Chattar Manzil Palace, built around Claude Martin's town house on the Gomti, which had housed the United Services Club, no longer echoed to the dance music of Anglo-Indian bands. It was later to become the Central Drug Research Institute. Aminabad Park, a pleasant, open area, became encroached by shops, known as the Refugee Market, as Hindus displaced during Partition settled there. Government House, known earlier as Banks' Bungalow, and which reputedly stood on the site of Martin's old powder mill or arsenal, was renamed Raj Bhawan. In the Dilkusha cantonments British officers packed up and left their spacious mid-Victorian bungalows, as Indian officers moved in. The 'European-style' hotels changed hands, but not names. The Carlton Hotel continued to offer tiger hunting for big game enthusiasts. Within the year the majority of Britons in civil and military posts had gone home. But there was something they could not take with them and that could not be repatriated—the bones of all those who lay in the European cemeteries of Lucknow.

It has been estimated that nearly two million Europeans, the majority of them British, were buried in the Indian subcontinent during the 300 years before 1947. To mark these often short lives, in a country where 'two monsoons' were reckoned as the average life-expectancy of a newcomer, the most elaborate funerary monuments were erected. Far grander than anything seen in Britain, there were domed, pinnacled and columned rotundas the size of small houses, gothic follies fit for a country estate, enormous pyramids, and huge rusticated columns. More modest tombs had draped urns, obelisks, or broken columns, to signify a life cut short. Only during the last twenty years has a serious attempt been made to evaluate these funerary monuments in the subcontinent and to place their architectural, historical and social importance in context, providing a valuable source of material for colonial historians in India and Europe. In 1976 an Englishman, Theon Wilkinson, published a small volume appropriately entitled *Two Monsoons,* describing a melancholy journey through the cemeteries with their crumbling monuments and tombs damaged beyond repair. His book was the inspiration for a new organisation, the British Association for Cemeteries in South Asia (BACSA), based in London, which undertook the enormous task of recording and photographing graveyards, particularly in the subcontinent. Modest sums of money were provided for repairs where feasible.[11]

It was difficult, or even impossible for Britons to imagine what would happen to their dead once they had left India. They had compiled meticulous local burial records, although the cemeteries and graveyards surrounding the cantonments and towns, with their poignant inscriptions, had inspired comparatively little creative writing or art. Individual tombs of particular historical or architectural merit like that of Job Charnock, who founded Calcutta, or Sir George Oxinden, Governor of Bombay, were noted, and there had been early photographic studies of South Park Street, Calcutta, the most magnificent necropolis in India. But even before 1947 some cemeteries had lapsed back into the wilderness, and others were only mentioned when disputes arose over whose responsibility it was to maintain them. Perhaps the high death rate among the British in India had inured the survivors against that maudlin sentimentality over death found in Victorian England's novels and paintings.

Thus it was not surprising that late in 1947 the Commonwealth Relations Office in London issued this statement: 'It has been tentatively agreed that cemeteries which cannot be suitably cared for should be levelled as soon as possible in order to avoid the possibility of desecration later. Hard as this may be, it seems the best course to pursue.' This negative proposal was immediately challenged in a letter published in the *Daily Telegraph* from a former Indian chaplain, the Reverend B.G. Fell, under the headline 'Our Graves in India—Need They Be Levelled?' in which were set out the arguments against their destruction, which have continued, in one form or another to be repeated during the fifty years since Independence.[12] European cemeteries had, before 1947, been maintained by several offices—the Public Works Department, the Military Engineering Service and the Railway Board, at an estimated cost of £45,000 annually.

Within these cemeteries were a number of endowed graves, where a capital sum of money had been invested, usually by relatives, or the deceased themselves, to provide an 'income' for maintenance and repair. The endowment of graves seems to be a feature peculiar to British India. The system was started in the 1880s, for civilian and military officers, the government undertaking the care of graves of the ordinary soldiers. Endowments were made 'in perpetuity', to endure forever, but even when they were set up, were often of pathetically small amounts, like Rs 10, that took no account of the inflation that would soon outstrip any possible interest on such meagre sums. Endowment money was usually handed over initially to the priest in charge, who remitted it to government, who in turn passed it on to the Public Works Department. Annual lists of endowments were published, and the system seems to have worked well, given the enormous number of graves involved.[13]

At Independence, the new government of India had, not unreasonably, asked Britain to provide a sum of money as an interim payment to maintain all endowed monuments 'except the most simple' for six months, until a longer-term solution could be worked out. A powerful argument against the Commonwealth Relations Office proposal of wholesale levelling was that it would clearly involve the loss of endowed graves where money had been invested in good faith, for their long-term maintenance. By the spring of 1949 it seemed that a compromise had been reached, after a solid two years work collating British burial records and endowments from all over India. The Secretary of State for Commonwealth Relations, Philip Noel-Baker, told the House of Commons that the European cemeteries formerly maintained by the pre-Independence Government of India had now become 'the responsibility of the United Kingdom Government'.[14] It would, he admitted, be impossible to maintain *all* the cemeteries. Some were 'merely groups of graves, often by the roadside, in remote places'. Many dated 'from a distant past and have had no burials in them for generations'. 'Nevertheless the Government are doing what they can to secure that, where cemeteries cannot be maintained their preservation will be safeguarded so far as local circumstances permit. In such cases the aim of His Majesty's Government would be to secure that they should revert to nature in a dignified and decent manner.' This was subsequently endorsed by the Government of India. The attempt to maintain, in a foreign country, considerable areas of land which would be 'forever England' seems fraught with difficulties to us today, but we should look at it in the context of the times. The Indian subcontinent was the first to slip out of the embracing net of Empire. There were no precedents for guidance. The fact that arrangements for the cemeteries were still being worked out two years after Independence shows that their future had not been a priority at the time, though ironically they are today one of the most enduring and interesting monuments to British rule.

Hopes were pinned on another European legacy—'It is on members of the Christian congregations resident in India and Pakistan that the local task of caring for Christian graveyards must now primarily devolve.' Though admitting that church congregations were now depleted or non-existent, it was reported that some 300 voluntary local cemetery committees existed in March 1949. These were made up by the clergy, businessmen, the United Kingdom Citizens' Association and the Anglo-Indian Association. Six Regional Trustee Boards covering the whole of India were set up to liaise between the local committees and the British High Commission and to supervise their work. Money for the endowed graves was passed on to these regional boards.[15]

On British withdrawal the Anglican churches in the subcontinent had merged with other religious groups like the Methodists and the Baptists, to form two major groupings—the Church of North India and the Church of South India. (The Catholics maintained a separate pan-Indian structure but the local cemetery committees often included Catholic members, to reflect Catholic burial plots, separately consecrated, within non-denominational cemeteries before Independence.) Now the two Churches of North and South India pledged to maintain the cemeteries 'in a suitable manner' with the help of income from endowments and burial fees, where cemeteries were still in use. The High Commission would, at first, top up the financial shortfall by 'small subventions'. 'Closed' cemeteries, where burials no longer took place, would be maintained in the same way if they were considered historically important. (The Lucknow Residency cemetery came into this category.) Other closed cemeteries would be 'attended to at intervals . . . for as long as funds will last'.

Parliament was asked to approve a lump sum for this purpose and to assist the Churches of North and South India. The endowment capital for private graves, where they could be ascertained, was to be transferred to the British High Commission. It was acknowledged that it would not be practicable always to apply it as intended and in such cases, local records of endowed graves were to be maintained but the money diverted to the maintenance of open cemeteries, subject to the wishes of people who had paid for endowments. The 'lump sum' allocated was £50,000, only a few thousand more than the annual pre-1947 amount for maintenance. Had it been invested, even this modest amount would have provided a small return, but in fact it was disbursed as requests came in. By 1959 it was exhausted and the Regional Trustee Boards wound up.[16] The Churches of North and South India and the voluntary local cemetery committees were thrown back on their own resources. What happened next, certainly in Lucknow, is generally a sorry story, redeemed in small part by the efforts of the Archaeological Survey of India and a few individuals, but illustrating how some, at least, of the city's dead were not allowed to rest in peace.

The growth of Lucknow, like that of other Indian cities, can be traced by its cemeteries. The European dead were generally not buried in or near churches, because it was considered unhealthy to do so; and in places outside the Presidency towns of Mumbai, Chennai (Madras) and Calcutta, European settlement and the need for burial grounds frequently preceded the building of churches. Since many churches in India were raised through public subscription, there had to be a reasonable number of Europeans before enough money could be collected for a place of worship. The first Anglican church in Lucknow was not built until 1839, in the Mariaon cantonment, and earlier worshippers used a large room in a Nawabi-owned house in the city Residency.[17] Land for cemeteries therefore had to be bought, or gifted, and was invariably selected on the outskirts of towns, outside the city walls, but not too far away for burial parties to walk at night. As the population increased, these sites were swallowed up, and once-isolated walled areas for the dead now became encircled by the living. South Park Street Cemetery in Calcutta had been set out on the very periphery of the city in 1767, in marshy fields and patches of dacoit-haunted jungle, but by the time it was closed it the 1830s it was almost in the middle of town. In theory, all European cemeteries can be dated by their consecration, thus providing a useful guide to a town's growth.

The earliest European cemetery in Lucknow was long ago swallowed up in development around the Chowk area. Neither its name nor its location have been discovered, but it undoubtedly existed, because an English 'factory' had been established in the mid-seventeenth century by the East India Company, in the Farangi Mahal area.[18] The factors had been sent by the Company to trade in dereabauds, a kind of muslin made in Lucknow, as well as sugar and indigo, all precious commodities for the European market. The fortified factory thrived at first, and a separate house was hired for Company staff, but by 1653 the difficulties of sending goods on the long journey to Surat led to the official closure of this early enterprise, though it struggled on for another two years. Certainly during the decade of its existence some of its English staff would have died and been buried locally, but their only memorial today is the name of their house, the 'Foreigners' House'.

Estimates put the number of known cemeteries in Lucknow at about twenty-five, including several small sites where only one or two graves remain. (A complete list will be found in Appendix A.) Some, of course, are connected with the 1857 uprising and the recapture of the city the following year, but the majority are those of the ordinary Christian inhabitants of Lucknow, the English, the European, the Anglo-Indian and, latterly, the Indian Christian. E.A.H. Blunt, an ICS officer who compiled the book *Christian Tombs and Monuments in the United Provinces* (1911), was incorrect in claiming that 'Almost all the Lucknow tombs belong to the Mutiny period.'[19] There were however scant records of early burials. Mordaunt Ricketts, the British Resident, admitted in 1828 that Burial Registers had not been kept before his time (nor baptism and marriage registers either). Ricketts forwarded a quarterly return to Calcutta for the beginning of that year, but this was because his own small son, Frederick, was among the dead. Burial services were conducted by friends of the family because there was no permanent clergyman in Lucknow until 1832, when the Reverend Greenwood was appointed. Before that Anglicans had to rely on a visit every three months from the clergyman at Fatehgarh. Burial Registers between 1832 and 1857 were kept in the Residency, together with the church plate. Carefully preserved during the siege by the Reverend James Harris, they were left behind through the carelessness of his clerk Mr Weston when the siege was lifted. 'It is shocking to think of the Communion-plate falling into the hands of the heathen enemy,' mourned his wife, but the Registers were an irreparable loss.[20] When the parish system was introduced in Lucknow after 1858, registers were kept by the local minister, but these too can be elusive. Inscriptions are missing on nearly all the early tombs, rendering accurate identification impossible, but a few independent surveys and family records exist that can pinpoint the cemetery, if not the tomb, where a person was buried.

Europeans began to settle again in Lucknow after 1775, when the Nawabi Court was transferred from Faizabad by Asaf-ud-daula. The earliest identifiable European tomb in Lucknow is that of Major General Claude Martin, who died in September 1800. Not only is it by far the grandest, but it is the largest European funerary building in India, a unique treasure called Constantia, now La Martiniere College for boys, near the Dilkusha. The story of the adventurous Frenchman's life has been told before, and the building he erected often described, in fiction, architectural surveys, and on film.[21] Here we shall look only at the tomb, thirty feet below ground level in the basement of the magnificent baroque palace, built to his own design. Martin left very specific instructions for his own burial. His body was embalmed, most probably in alcohol, and deposited in a leaden coffin, placed inside another of wood. The coffins were covered with a substantial masonry core, covered with marble slabs. The inscription read simply 'Here lies Major-General Claude Martin born at Lyons the 5th day of January 1735. Arrived in India a common soldier and died Lucknow the 13th September 1800. Pray for his Soul.' Around the tomb stood four life-size sepoys, probably fashioned from plaster, with bowed heads and muskets reversed, as a sign of mourning. These were erected by Joseph Quieros, Martin's steward, as a tribute to his late master.

Neither the sepoys, nor the elaborate tomb, were proof against an attack by grave robbers that took place when the British lost control of Lucknow. The boys and masters of the school had been evacuated to the Residency at the start of the siege, after an initial attempt to make Constantia impregnable, as Martin himself had designed it to be. At some point it was occupied and its wooden fittings torn out, though the fine interior decoration escaped much damage. 'General Martin's tomb has been broken to fragments and his old bones dug up and scattered to the winds,' wrote the Residency chaplain's wife on 23 November 1857, after the relief of the Residency.[22] Others reported that his body had been thrown into the adjoining Gomti. After the recapture of Lucknow the new Commissioner, Colonel Abbott, restored 'the scattered bones . . . to their resting place', but because the report of the reburial cannot now be traced, it is conjectural how much, if anything, was re-interred. The tomb had clearly been so badly damaged that it had to be entirely reconstructed, and both the lettering and the quatrefoils around the sides date stylistically from the 1860s. The tomb is the focus of a moving ceremony, held annually on 13 September, Founder's Day, and the date of Martin's death, at his Farhat Baksh home. Wreaths made from flowers grown at La Martiniere are placed around the tomb, and a short service held during which the participants offer a prayer for his soul, as he requested.

The oldest cemetery which can be identified was already in existence by 1805, when a Mr Braganca 'seized by force' the graveyard and church belonging to Catholic priests and began charging Rs 20 for burial plots in it.[23] This was the Catholic cemetery of Qaisarpasand, in Qaisarbagh, opened long before the development of the Qaisarbagh palaces, when the wooded area stood isolated, well east of the city. Nearly twenty years later, in 1824, it was restored to the Agra Catholic Mission and its priest, the Reverend Father Adeodatus, by the Nawab Ghazi-ud-din Haider. The Nawab's gift was probably prompted by his Anglo-Armenian wife,

Mariam Begam Saheba, who although a convert to Islam during her marriage, and who had changed her name from Mary, later became a devout Catholic. She was the daughter of an Armenian widow, Mary Minas and Dr James Short, of the East India Company. Mariam Begam was also known, not impolitely, as Vilayati Begam, the foreign wife (an echo of the Black Princess), and it was probably for her that Vilayati Bagh, south of La Martiniere was created, with its exotic English flowers.

Little is known about Mariam Begam's life in the Chattar Manzil palace. She was one of several wives, and was married in 1822 when she was about fourteen years old.[24] She was still a young woman when she was widowed in 1827, clearly a favourite, because she was left well provided for on the Nawab's death. Her pension of Rs 2,500 per month came from the interest on one of the large loans made 'in perpetuity' to the Company by Ghazi-ud-din Haider, and was administered through the British Resident. Not trusting his own officials, Mariam Begam wrote that the Nawab 'had me placed under the immediate protection of this Honourable Company . . . I was always treated and guarded with the greatest attention and respect and honour due to my rank and position under the protection of the Government' and added that 'in consideration of my privileges from Government, I place all my relatives and dependants under the immediate protection and guardianship of the British Government . . . trusting that my legatees will be treated in a like manner as myself . . .'[25] She continued to live in the palace after her husband's death, though now as a Christian. According to Mesrovb Seth, who wrote a history of the Armenians in India, Mariam Begam had one of her rooms fitted up as a chapel, where divine service was held. It was here that she welcomed an Armenian Bishop from Julfa, who gave Holy Communion to her and her servants. In return she presented him with a set of expensive robes.

The position of a foreign wife at the Court, though privileged, was not without its difficulties, particularly in widowhood, and towards the end of her life she made several applications to the East India Company to be allowed to leave Lucknow, not granted until she was on her death-bed.[26] In fact she seems to have been something of a political pawn, and one suspects an untold story behind her life. How did the young girl catch the eye of the Nawab, and what concessions did he make, or was pressed to make, in order to marry her? Her generous financial settlement was closely tied up with his loan to the Company. Her marriage, in turn, allowed her to offer support to her relatives. In her will she left a monthly pension of Rs 800 to her brother Joseph Short, whom she had 'brought up from his infancy under my care and protection like my own son', 'maintenance and clothing to my other imbecile brother John Short and my youngest sister Eliza, she is attacked with severe palpitation, if her husband and son may not support her . . .' Did she agree to marry the richest man in Awadh because she knew this would enable her to maintain her family? At this distance we can only speculate.

Through a clause in the loan treaty the British Government guaranteed to pay these pensions to her relatives 'forever' down the generations and descendants of her youngest brother Joseph were still being paid, through the Government Wasika (Pension) Office up to Independence. Mariam Begam also left Joseph her house, Bunyad Manzil, her jewels, cash and Indian and Abyssinian slaves. Money was left to Father Adeodatus 'for the purpose of repairs and lighting and charities of the Roman Catholic chapels', one of which stood adjacent to the Qaisarpasand cemetery. She charged Joseph with erecting her tomb there, and after her death, on 5 April 1849, from tuberculosis, he put up a substantial domed kiosk over a handsome marble tombstone. On the anniversary of her

15. The tomb of Marian Begam, Qaisarpasand
Cemetery, 1998. Renovation is in progress

death her relatives would meet there to burn incense and candles. Hers was the most prominent tomb in the cemetery, nearest the entrance, and the only one to be desecrated during 1857, when the marble tombstone was broken up, leaving the brick core beneath exposed. The adjoining chapel was also destroyed at the same time, its bells torn out of the belfry, the church ornaments and sacred vestments stolen, the priest's house ransacked and two adjoining mission houses wrecked. After 1858 a piece of land in Hazratganj was given in compensation for the loss, and the old Catholic church of St Joseph's built on it.[27]

By the early years of this century residential buildings had surrounded the Qaisarpasand cemetery, which was only protected in places by a low wall, like an English country churchyard. Today it is mainly hidden from public view behind a substantial modern wall and is surrounded by stalls selling re-conditioned tyres. It has no identifiable entrance from the street, but once inside the anonymous gateway it is a pleasant, lightly wooded area, with a substantial number of obelisk tombs visible through the trees. Apart from Mariam Begam's tomb all the other inscriptions have vanished except that which marks the burial place of a baby, James Green, who died on 1 April 1860, aged six months, and separately, a member of the Delmerick family who worked for the Nawabs. But this ground holds much of Lucknow's Anglo-Indian history too. Somewhere here lie the bones of Joseph Quieros, the Spanish nobleman who worked for Claude Martin, and later, Saadat Ali Khan and Ghazi-ud-din Haider. Here too will lie the musical Braganca family, their fellow musicians the Catanias, Casanova the King's painter, and every Catholic of note who died in Lucknow.

As in most cemeteries a chowkidar and his family were in residence in a hut inside the wall, and claimed it as an hereditary right. The fertile ground provided a rich grazing ground for goats. Recently (1998) the Catholic church decided to build a shelter for street children inside the cemetery, and although this was fiercely opposed by the chowkidar's family, building went ahead.[28] The *pukka* shelter adjoins Mariam Begam's tomb, but in compensation, her tomb and all the others have been whitewashed and the cemetery cleared of debris. Encoachments are however still continuing.

The curiously named Lat Kallan-ki-Lath cemetery in Aminabad contained the most grandiose funerary monuments of old Lucknow, the upcountry equivalent of South Park Street Cemetery in Calcutta. The site pre-dates the development of Hazratganj by Nawab Saadat Ali Khan, and it remained isolated until the 1840s, when it was developed by Amin-ud-daula, the Chief Minister. The odd name came from the tomb of the only British Resident to die in office, Colonel John Collins, who was in post for less than a year before his sudden death on 18 June 1807. It is a play on words, a 'Lat Sahib' being a great English official, as 'King' Collins (his nickname) certainly was, while a lath is a column or obelisk. The huge tomb consists of a square plinth supporting a tapering column, the lath, and measures sixty feet from base to pinnacle, easily the tallest monument in Nawabi Lucknow. It was built from *lakhori* brick, covered with *chunam* (stucco) and appears not to have had a metal core, being pyramid-like at the top. Collins himself had been described in life as 'cold, imperious and overbearing' and his tall, pompous tomb accurately reflects, in brick, these characteristics. The tomb was designed and paid for by the Nawab Saadat Ali Khan, as a tribute to Collins, and its inscription is the only one that remains today. The Nawab had been careful to obtain permission from the East India Company before erecting the monument, and it was tactfully agreed that something 'constructed according to the form of European architecture' would be more suitable than an 'Asiatic Model'.[29]

Around the first tomb stood smaller, but no less elaborate memorials, one rather like a Hindu temple, with *chattris* on top. There was a canopied *barahdari* to one side where coffins rested before the funeral service. Among those known to have been buried here, although all inscriptions except that of Collins had gone by the end of the nineteenth century, was the infant son of the Resident Mordaunt Ricketts, Frederick, who died in 1828, aged five months old. The cemetery also contained the tomb of Lieutenant Colonel R. Wilcox, the English astronomer to the Nawab, and builder of the Royal Observatory in Lucknow, the Taronwali Kothi, who died in October 1848. Curiously, Wilcox's tomb was the only one here to be desecrated during the uprising of 1857, though this may have been a personal grudge, rather than an anti-British one.[30]

Although Lat Kallan-ki-Lath was known as the Protestant cemetery and Qaisarpasand as the Catholic, segregation between the two sects was not as rigid as the names suggest. Mr Crank, one of the Residency chaplains (and headmaster at La Martiniere), had reported that he conducted few marriages among the European residents of Lucknow because the majority were Roman Catholics, who had their own priest, and of course their own cemetery. But the new chaplain, the Reverend Hyacinth Kirwan, who replaced Crank in 1852 and who had a particularly rigid interpretation of his faith stated that nearly half of those interred at the City Burial Ground (Lat Kallan-ki-Lath) before it was consecrated in 1823, were Catholics, and that 'some of the same denomination have been buried there since'.[31] He said that the Nawab Saadat Ali Khan had intended the cemetery for Christians of all denominations, and that it had been properly consecrated by a Bishop. Kirwan placed considerable emphasis on the act of consecration (which often, of necessity, took place years after a cemetery had been opened, when a touring Bishop could carry it out), because he was anxious to block the burial of unbelievers in 'his' cemetery. Catholics were acceptable, but special permission had to be sought when Mr Campagnac, a 'Dissenter' wanted to bury his child there. One of the Residency clerks, a Mr Joyce, was refused permission to erect a tomb over his child's remains, because he was a Baptist, but Kirwan really exceeded himself when, in February 1856, he forbade the burial of the unbaptised child of Mr and Mrs Symes, who were Baptists. While he argued that the burial could not take place in consecrated ground, the body began to decompose, and it was only after intervention by the Resident William Sleeman, that it was interred. Kirwan was later severely censured by the Acting Archdeacon when this incident was reported to Calcutta.[32] The cemetery was enlarged in January 1857 to accommodate soldiers of Her Majesty's 52nd Regiment, now stationed in Lucknow, and for 'Christians of other persuasions', as the delicate phrase went, to avoid future arguments.

The cemetery was closed after 1858 and remained in reasonable condition until the 1990s, protected behind high brick walls and massive gateposts, though at some point it had lost its handsome iron gates. Only Collins' tomb could be identified, but forty or so brick and stucco tombs remained intact and the cemetery was a pleasant area filled with trees and shrubs, a breathing place in the congested city. Its destruction came about suddenly in 1992, though encroachment had already started when a chowkidar and his family set up home inside the walls. One day neighbours found bamboo screens erected around the whole cemetery and a demolition crew inside dismantling the tombs and uprooting the graves.[33] Police were called several times, but demolition continued as soon as they had gone. It is always hard to get accurate information when the 'bhumafia', as they are called, move in, but in this case it seems that the cemetery was sold to Christian buyers at giveaway prices, who in turn sold it to other, mainly Muslim, purchasers. Today the cemetery houses, behind its *lakhori* walls, twenty or so houses, and two small factories, effectively bricking up the Collins tomb, the only one that was too substantial to demolish. Some of the stolen gravestones have been used to pave the narrow alleys between the *pukka* houses.

Three months before his death, John Collins had reported to the East India Company in Calcutta that a new site had been found to house the British cantonment. It was to be built some four miles north of Lucknow, across the river, at Mariaon. The first troops had been cantoned nearer the Gomti, opposite the Daulat Khana palace of Asaf-ud-daula. But with the increase in numbers, at the Company's insistence, a larger, less congested area had to be found. Once the site was chosen and measured out on 8 March 1807, building started immediately and the first inhabitants, the Indian sepoys, were in place by the start of the monsoon. While the sepoys lived in huts, easily and quickly erected, substantial bungalows were put up for the British officers, each with a garden compound and out-buildings for kitchens, stables and servants' quarters.[34] At first Mariaon was exclusively a military area, with a parade ground and armoury, but segregation between civilians and soldiers quickly broke down and during the half century that followed, it became a paradigm of a small colonial town.

Mordaunt Ricketts, the Resident between 1822 and 1830, was particularly fond of Mariaon and got a substantial 'country house' built there, where he lived exclusively for the last three years of his term of office, in preference to the city Residency. Other Residency officials followed, and officers brought their wives and children to live with them in the pretty, cottage-style bungalows. The amenities for a comfortable life soon followed. There was a Company Bagh, where the cantonment band played in the evening, a 'Grand Parade', a little library, an Ice-Club, a few 'Europe' shops, a cricket ground, a race-course, and entertainments in the Resident's 'theatre' and ballroom. A small church had been built, predating the city Residency's church by several years. There was also a good-sized cemetery, for the pure air of the cantonment, which had attracted many, was no protection against endemic disease and sudden death.

The firing of the cantonment on Saturday, 30 May 1857, by the sepoy regiments was the first shocking warning to the British that the great uprising had reached Lucknow. 'The whole of the cantonment has been burnt to the ground; some few houses have escaped burning, but every one ransacked and pillaged,' wrote Mrs Harris from the relative safety of the city Residency the next day. 'If Sir H[enry] Lawrence had not sent all the women and children out of cantonments, we should inevitably, every one of us, have shared the fate of our countrywomen at Delhi and Meerut.'[35] There was no attempt to defend Mariaon, it was simply abandoned on 29 June. The little church was destroyed, the roof fired, the window panes and door frames torn out and the memorial tablets wrenched off the walls and smashed.

For years the only reminder that this had once been the site of a respectably-sized cantonment was the oddly named Bailey Garad [sic] cemetery, officially closed shortly after 1858. The Bailey Garad, not to be confused with the city Residency gateway of a similar name, stood isolated in fields whose names recalled a vanished world—the *gend ghar* (sports field), the kamasariyat (the store house) and the *golghar*, literally translated as ballroom, but which probably means a racket court and not a dance hall. During the 1980s, with the expansion of Lucknow, the residential suburb of Aliganj was built over the old cantonment site, although the cemetery remains at present unencroached upon. It is the only one of the Lucknow cemeteries of which we have a pre-1857 photograph, showing an impressive variety of early nineteenth-century tombs, some edged with low iron railings. A matching pair of fine tombs topped with urns, clearly identifiable today, perhaps marks the graves of a family who were not separated in death. It is still possible to stand exactly where that early photographer stood and mark the decay of nearly 150 years. All the railings have gone, as well as the inscriptions, but a surprising amount remains, including some of the urns on top of the tombs. Even the box tombs are still there, the *lakhori* bricks retaining traces of stucco around the rubble cores that topped the graves.

16. The Mariaon Cemetery, Lucknow, 1995

It is likely that George Duncan Beechey lies here, for he was a long term resident in the cantonment, who died in 1852. Whether any of his three Indian wives joined him, we do not know.[36] After his death, his bungalow was allocated to the Reverend Henry Polehampton, who complained that the old artist was still to be sensed around the place, possibly mourning his many paintings lost at sea in 1851. Only one name is known here, from records, though the little tomb cannot be identified. It is sometimes difficult to appreciate today how great was the extent of child mortality among the British in India. It was, of course, no greater, than the mortality among Indian children of the same period, but more frequently reported in letters home. Cholera, typhoid, smallpox and dysentery were no respecters of race, and babies and young children were particularly susceptible. Lack of knowledge about the importance of postnatal care and nurture felled many within days of birth. The eye becomes weary in scanning inscriptions that survive elsewhere, recording infant deaths, often several in one family, year on year. But the numbers should not obscure the anguish behind these very frequent tragedies. The account of the burial of the baby son of the Reverend Polehampton and his wife Emily has quite rightly been described as 'one of the most moving letters, in its honesty and simplicity'.

Henry Polehampton, with his wife, left England in January 1856 to take up his post as Chaplain with the East India Company and chose Lucknow on the advice of his brother-in-law, the artist Henry Salt, who had sketched many of the buildings there. The newly-married couple settled into a pretty little bungalow in the cantonment, with their spaniel dog, Chloe, and their well-tended garden. Their first child, Henry Allnutt, was born at the end of that year and survived for only three days. Henry borrowed 'a little closed carriage' to carry the baby to the Bailey Garad cemetery, after 'the cruel task of taking him away from his mother. She begged to have him a little while longer . . . and wept over him in a manner which made me feel more than I ever felt in my life. Then she had the coffin put where the cradle had been and placed him in it herself, and put some little dark red roses which grow in great luxuriance in our garden and of which she is very fond, in his hands and on his breast, and then she bravely covered him up, and I carried him out and fastened down the coffin out of her hearing. I cannot tell how I suffered at seeing all this. Captain [Fletcher] Hayes and Dr Partridge took the coffin, carrying it slung at each end with a white cloth and I read the service. I had had a brick grave made close by the side of a beautiful little tomb under which Mrs Forbes' little girl lies. Captain Hayes threw a rose in upon the coffin. We stayed and saw the grave arched over—and then I left my first born to lie there, till the sounding of the Archangel's trumpet.'[37] Seven months later, Henry himself was dead, a few days after being wounded by a musket ball during the siege of the city Residency. As a mark of respect he was buried in a coffin, apart from the mass graves, where the dead were simply sewn up in their bedding and interred.

The Residency cemetery, as we have seen, came into existence unplanned during the siege of 1857. Of the estimated 3,000 Europeans and

Indians who took shelter behind the barricades in June of that year, less than a thousand left in November, though an uncounted number of Indians, mainly servants, had slipped away during the summer. European burials had not previously taken place in the residential complex, though interestingly there is a Muslim tomb by the side of the path leading to the Residency itself, that of Qasim Syed Shah Baba, according to an attendant chowkidar. This is likely to pre-date the development of the site by the East India Company, for the complex was by no means exclusively British, incorporating a mosque and Indian-owned houses. The siege cemetery was not consecrated until December 1864, when the depredations of the grave-robbers had been made good, corpses reburied and memorials erected. A large mass grave was delineated by low brick walls and a plaque put up stating: 'Within this enclosure are buried the remains of over one hundred of the brave defenders of the Residency who were killed during the early part of the siege. Their names are not recorded.'

Many of those buried, or reburied, in individual graves are known by name, others, including non-commissioned officers and men, by their regiments. Some officers and men who had died during the evacuation of the Residency and had been temporarily interred at Alambagh to the south of Lucknow, were reburied after the recapture of the city in 1858. Among those who lie here are Brigadier General Sir Henry Lawrence, who had replaced Coverley Jackson, acting Chief Commissioner in April 1857 and who died on 4 July at the beginning of the siege. He had been mortally wounded on the morning of 2 July when a shell fired from beyond the barricades burst in the Residency, nearly amputating his leg. On his death-bed he named Major Banks, the Commissioner for Lucknow, as his successor, but Banks himself was killed two weeks later. The inscription on the marble tomb reads 'Here lies Sir Henry Lawrence who tried to do his duty. May the Lord have mercy on his soul.' Also buried here are Ommaney, the Judicial Commissioner, who died on 8 July, leaving a wife and six children, and Thornhill, the Assistant Commissioner, fatally wounded after the first, unsuccessful attempt to relieve the Residency. Of the Commissioners appointed on the annexation of Awadh and subsequently besieged, only Martin Gubbins had survived. Another memorial stone records the Reverend Hyacinth Kirwan, who died of smallpox on 3 April 1858, at a field hospital somewhere outside the city.[38]

Although the cemetery was effectively closed before it was consecrated, members of the original Residency garrison and their families were still interred here. Edward Hilton, who as a boy of seventeen, had endured the siege, and later became the official Residency guide, lived into his eighties, and he was buried here in December 1922. The last burial was that of Frederick Lincoln, in November 1934, whose father had been a civil judge in Lucknow. Because the cemetery was of particular historic importance, its upkeep was maintained before Independence by the Public Works Department, and it passed, without dispute, into the care of the Archaeological Survey of India in 1948. Not only has it been well maintained since, but tombs have been well restored too, as stucco work has crumbled. But the problems of guarding an historic site were highlighted when thieves removed the iron railings around the tomb of Sir Henry Lawrence sometime in the early 1980s, and these have not been replaced.

Around what was in 1857–58 the outskirts of the city are a small number of isolated graves, marking the advances and retreats of the British troops. Of necessity soldiers were sometimes buried where they fell, the site marked and a proper tomb erected later. Captain Augustus Otway Mayne, for example, is buried near the spot where he was murdered on 14 November 1857, just outside La Martiniere School. His box tomb, surrounded by a low wall, lies today adjacent to the Golf Course, presenting a unique hazard for golfers. Unusually, for the frantic days of fighting, his death and burial were recorded in some detail. Mayne and his party came across a naked sadhu, his face painted red and white, 'his body smeared with ashes. He was sitting on a leopard's skin counting a rosary of beads.' One of the soldiers volunteered to 'try his bayonet on that painted scoundrel' but was prevented by Mayne who said, 'Oh, don't touch him; these fellow are harmless Hindoo yogis, and won't hurt us.' At these words the man pulled out a blunderbuss from under the leopard skin and shot Mayne through the chest. The sadhu was immediately bayonetted to death, and Mayne's body put in a *dhoolie*, a kind of palanquin, to await burial the following day. Lieutenant Frederick Roberts (later Lord Roberts) described how he and his adjutant Arthur Bunny 'chose a spot close by for his grave, which was dug with the help of some gunners, and then Bunny and I, aided by two or three brother officers, laid our friend in it just as he was, in his blue frock-coat and long boots, his eyeglass in his eye as he always carried it. The only thing I took away was his sword, which I eventually made over to his family. It was a sad little ceremony. Overhanging the grave was a young tree, upon which I cut the initials "A.O.M."—not very deep, for there was little time: they were quite distinct however, and remained so long enough for the grave to be traced by Mayne's friends, who erected the stone now to be seen.'[39] The grave was surrounded by iron railings and a chain link, which later disappeared, together with the inscription. A new tablet, with the original wording, was erected recently by the local military authorities.

The Alambagh was a 'country house' built by Wajid Ali Shah for his wife, Khas Mahal, on the Cawnpore Road, five miles or so to the south of the city. It stood some way back from the road, in a large walled garden, approached through an impressive gateway. Early photographs show the fields and woods that lay between it and the city. Before the first attempt to relieve the Residency, in September 1857, the Alambagh was captured by British troops and held as a valuable strategic outpost, from which forays could be launched into the city. It was here that the evacuees from the Residency were brought after the second, successful attempt to free them. During the four months from November to March 1858 when the city remained out of British control, the only British troops in Awadh were stationed at the Alambagh, because its location, on the Cawnpore road, meant it could be supplied from that cantonment, which had been recaptured in July 1857.[40] It was peculiarly suited as a defensible military area and withstood six determined attacks that winter by soldiers under the command of Begam Hazrat Mahal, the queen who was left behind. Those same features which had protected the privacy and safety of Khas Mahal, were now adapted by her husband's opponents. The house itself was not unlike a small castle, completely surrounded by high walls, and with four sturdy brick towers at each corner. One of these towers had been used as a semaphore post to signal to the Residency during the final days of the siege, when 'a blue light from the Alumbagh' confirmed that Sir Colin Campbell and his troops had arrived there. The electric telegraph, so desired by Wajid Ali Shah, and so quickly laid after his dethronement, was an early victim of the siege. Its wires were melded into crude, though effective bullets, the iron pipes through which they were threaded became, with a little adaptation, gun barrels, and the supporting posts were a handy supply of kindling.

General Sir Henry Havelock had entered Cawnpore a day too late to save its European inhabitants from death, and he went on to Lucknow in the first, unsuccessful, attempt to relieve the Residency. Three days after the second, successful relief, he was struck down with dysentery. He was carried in a palanquin from the Residency to the Dilkusha, now in British hands, and died there on 24 November. Without arguing his soldierly skills, it is correct to say that Victorian England made Havelock its chief hero of 1857. Just as the Residency flag came to symbolise the courage of the defenders, so Havelock, dying just as those defenders were finally freed, became a perfect representation of the gallant soldier that was so badly needed during the dark winter of 1857–58. He was the militant Christian personified, a Baptist, converted by his father-in-law, and whose last words to his soldier son were 'Harry, see how a Christian can die.' Nearly every town in England of any pretension commemorated him in some way or another. London alone has twelve roads, avenues and terraces that bear his name and his statue stands in Trafalgar Square on Admiral Nelson's left-hand side. When the news of his death reached the United States, flags were flown at half-mast, in a unique tribute to an English General.

It was not surprising therefore, that his tomb should reflect the man who lay beneath it. Havelock's body was taken from his tent at the Dilkusha to the Alambagh, and interred there on 25 November, near one of the few trees that had survived the fighting outside the garden walls. A small engraved plate was hammered into the tree-trunk to mark his flat tomb-stone and the tree and grave were surrounded by a low brick wall.[41] This was how it remained until the 1860s, when his widow and family had a substantial plinth and obelisk erected over the grave, with a long inscription inset on a marble tablet. The General's son, Major General Sir Henry Marshman Havelock-Allan who was murdered in the Khyber Pass in 1897 was commemorated in a similar plaque on the other side of the plinth. The obelisk, surrounded by decorative iron railings became the centrepiece of the Alambagh cemetery, surrounded by the graves of other soldiers who had died during the siege and re-capture of Lucknow. Paths and flower beds were laid out symmetrically, and the area bounded by a substantial pillared wall.

The site remained as a pleasant, yet melancholy garden, well into living memory, but its destruction began as the city extended southwards. Unlike Lat Kallan-ki-Lath, there was no sudden encroachment, but a gradual process of stripping away. The garden walls that had shielded the British soldiers were demolished and the Alambagh house fell into serious disrepair, its roof and interior ceilings gone, although fine stucco work around the rooms remained until well into the 1970s, showing that it had been a handsome building. Khas Mahal, the queen for whom it had been built, had tried to reclaim it in 1859, when a list was drawn up of property belonging to the ex-royal family and their courtiers, but it had been declared *nazool*, that is, government property, and it does not seem to have been used again. The iron railings around Havelock's tomb were sawn off and stolen, and the surrounding graves were reduced to rubble cores, then disappeared. The cemetery wall became broken down in places, allowing entry to people and animals, the flower beds and shrubs died through lack of regular maintenance, and by 1994 only one other tomb remained apart from the central memorial. This was a well-preserved tombstone to Lieutenant Dundas Gordon, 'killed at his post' in January 1858, aged twenty-four years, a victim of one of the unsuccessful attacks on the Alambagh. A year later the tombstone had vanished, and the grave and its contents scooped out. Only a shallow depression marked where it had been.

It seemed inevitable that the Havelock memorial and tomb would share the same fate, especially as crude walls were already creeping up around it. But a spirited campaign by Havelock's great-great-grandson, Mark Havelock-Allan, QC, dramatically halted the encroachment in 1997. It was established that just like the Residency, the Alambagh cemetery, as an historic site had, after Independence, passed from the custody of the old Public Works Department to that of the Archaeological Survey of India (ASI). This British-created body had initially come into existence in 1870, with the appointment of Major General Alexander Cunningham as its first Director General, although there had been earlier attempts at archaeological excavations and some conservation work in Delhi and Agra.[42] It was the whole-hearted support of Lord Curzon, Viceroy from 1899 to 1905, which gave the ASI its status, and extended its remit far wider than the simple surveying of archaeological sites. Under the Protection of Monuments Act all listed public buildings and sites carry the dark blue and white enamel board of the ASI. The fact that these boards, especially in remote areas, are defaced or damaged, does not alter the status of a site. It is easy to criticise the ASI where ruined buildings under its protection are being systematically robbed of their bricks, like the once splendid Barowen, to the west of Lucknow, which has been considerably reduced during the last twenty years, but the task of policing every isolated monument in India is plainly impossible, given the hunger for land and accessible building material. In the 1960s eleven cemeteries were handed over to the Catholic Diocese of Lucknow, with the approval of the British High Commission, which explains why former Protestant cemeteries like Lat Kallan-ki-Lath were under Catholic protection at the time of their destruction.

In the Alambagh case it emerged that the local Christian Burial Board, originally set up in 1948 to safeguard the Lucknow cemeteries, had not only claimed a site which had never been in its care, but had also 'sold' plots of land in the cemetery, in December 1992, to local traders for a reputed Rs 5 lakhs. What those who 'bought' the land either did not know, or knew, but ignored, was that British cemeteries cannot be sold, for they are the property of the Government of India. While it is true that the British High Commission has delegated authority to local cemetery committees for those graveyards not protected by the ASI, these cemetery committees or Burial Boards are specifically forbidden to sell cemetery land, or to use it for purposes other than burials, without prior permission from the High Commission. Once the illegal 'sale' of 1992 had come to light, the explanation for the *kutcha* walls that had been cobbled together, and the piles of bricks that appeared in the Alambagh, became clear. The cemetery was being marked out according to the plots people thought they had bought. The tomb of Lieutenant Dundas Gordon lay in the middle of one such plot, and had therefore to be removed before building could begin. It seemed only a matter of time before the Alambagh would become another lost site, like Lat Kallan-ki-Lath, with the Havelock memorial surrounded by new houses.

To its credit, after some high-level intervention by Mark Havelock-Allan, and sustained local publicity, the ASI did move in to safeguard what remained of the Alambagh cemetery.[43] The illegally constructed walls were demolished, the cemetery's boundary re-defined by a barbed-wire fence, new sign boards erected, the missing iron railings around the Havelock obelisk replaced and chowkidars posted. Much has, of course, gone forever. Lieutenant Dundas Gordon's tomb can never be re-established, but the campaign to save the cemetery from a profit-making land scam is a successful example of what can be done, even at the eleventh hour, when the ASI utilises its considerable power.

It was, however, unable to prevent the destruction of another protected burial site at Bargawan, four kilometres south of Alambagh, in 1983. This contained the graves of soldiers who had fallen during the attacks on the Alambagh, in the winter of 1857–58, and was marked by a nearby obelisk memorial. Here the ASI were up against another official organisation, the Lucknow Development Authority, who shamefully exhumed the dead, providing the newspapers with grisly photographs of skeletons and broken coffins.

Near the Bara Imambara lies the Macchi Bhawan cemetery whose recent rediscovery (1998) could provide another fruitful source of contention. This cemetery appears on a Revenue Survey map of 1862–65, as a substantial, enclosed area, lying in open land immediately outside the walls that surrounded the courtyard of the Imambara. It must have been set up directly after annexation in 1856, when the flood of Company officials and their families moved in, and the existing cemeteries quickly became overcrowded. There is no record that Wajid Ali Shah gave, or sold, this piece of land to the Company, and it is unlikely that he would have sanctioned the use of such a prominent site at the most dramatic entrance to Lucknow, and immediately adjacent to the Imambara. The cemetery so neatly fulfills the British criteria of being outside the city walls, but conveniently accessible, that it is likely to have been established in the first wave of reforms, in the interregnum between annexation and revolt. In this same area lies a small Methodist cemetery, which marks the presence of the American mission which was housed in the Asafi Kothi after 1858.

To its embarrassment, the ASI had 'mislaid' the Macchi Bhawan cemetery, although it was a protected monument and thus under its care. It was found only when the Christian Burial Board attempted a similar scam to the Alambagh cemetery, and began offering plots within it for sale.[44] Residents living nearby complained, and the ASI began its own investigations, uncovering the coffin of Jane Ricketts, 'beloved wife of Sergeant James Ricketts' who died of cholera in 1873. It is estimated that there were another hundred or so burials in the cemetery, now partially occupied by huts and grazing animals. Today the entrance is marked by two boards, the newly-installed notification of a protected monument by the ASI, and that of the local Burial Board, facing each other as opponents in another cemetery stand-off.

Not every story has an unhappy ending, however. Like the Havelock memorial, individual tombs *can* be saved, sometimes with help from abroad. The grave of Walter Birley Griffin in the Nishatganj cemetery, north of the Gomti, is a case in point. How Griffin, a pupil of Frank Lloyd Wright and the man who drew up the plans for the Australian capital, Canberra, came to rest in Lucknow, is a story that began in hope, but ended in tragedy. The Chicago-born architect had won a competition in 1912 to design the new capital, but disputes led to his dismissal eight years later when the enormous project of 25 square miles was less than half-realised. He remained working in Australia, but through a friend who had got a job on *The Pioneer* newspaper in Lucknow, was asked, initially, to prepare some preliminary sketches for a new library at Lucknow University, on the old Padshah Bagh site. He was invited to India and after visiting Bombay, Agra and New Delhi, itself a new capital, arrived in Lucknow in November 1935.

Griffin wrote warmly of the city and its people to his wife Marian, a gifted artist. He felt particularly at home here, because both he and Marian had become Theosophists, the movement begun in America by Madame Helen Blavatsky in the 1870s, but which flourished in India under her successor, Annie Besant. The Griffins subsequently became Anthroposophists, an offshoot of Theosophy, developed by the philosopher Rudolph Steiner. After only a month in Lucknow, Griffin decided to set up a permanent office in India, and his wife joined him here in May 1936.[45] He was immediately commissioned by Desmond Young, then editor of *The Pioneer*, to design a new building for the newspaper, to house its reporters and its presses. Sketches and ideas for many other projects in India, the majority sadly unbuilt, flew across his drawing board during the short, creative period that he spent in the city. He was commissioned by leading figures in Lucknow including the Raja of Mahmudabad and the Raja of Jehangirabad to design a mosque, a library and museum, none of which were realised, though the drawings survive. He designed and supervised the building and landscaping for the United Provinces Exhibition of Industry and Agriculture (the Lucknow Exhibition), which was erected in the old Kampani Bagh at the top of the Chowk. With its pavilions of covered bamboo and woven reed frames, brilliantly lit at night, this was a deliberate reference back to the temporary structures erected by the Nawabs for wedding celebrations, like that described by Abu Talib Khan for Wazir Ali's marriage. But Griffin's masterpiece, the Pioneer Press building, begun in December 1936, was a monument to Modern Movement architecture, with its simple, striking lines and subtle detailing.

It was during a visit to Cawnpore, to inspect the steel to be used for re-inforcing the Press, that Griffin fell ill with appendicitis.[46] He was taken to the King George Medical Hospital in Lucknow and operated on, but died there after surgery on 11 February 1937, at the age of sixty-one. He was buried in Nishatganj cemetery, which had been opened in 1887, in Plot 11, No. 63, unmarked by a tombstone. Whether his widow Marian did not have time to get one erected before her return to Australia, or whether the couple's beliefs precluded any kind of memorial is not known. It was not until 1988 that a simple black and granite stone was erected over his grave by the Australian Institute of Architects, bearing only his name, date of birth and date of death.[47] The Pioneer building was demolished several years ago and replaced by an undistinguished tower block that houses the press in the basement.

Today's travellers coming into Lucknow by rail from Calcutta run alongside the Bandariabagh cemetery just before entering the station at Charbagh. Also known as the Military, or Cantonment cemetery, this was established after 1858 when the new Dilkusha cantonment was built. Inside the Gothic gatehouse is a large board, with a fading list of its endowed graves. The names show that both civilians and soldiers are buried here, lieutenants, captains, colonels, majors and sergeants, all equal now in death. Yet there was a division between soldiers who died during the First World War and those who died during the Second, for the bodies of the latter, seventy in all, were exhumed after the War and re-interred in the Commonwealth War Graves cemetery at Delhi cantonment. The 103 men who died between 1914 and 1921 were allowed to remain here, although the majority of their graves are today in a pitiable state, with fallen headstones and smashed gravestones. Twenty or so of the graves have simply disappeared, only a gap in the regular lines indicating where a burial had taken place. In another part of the cemetery suspicious gaps among the rows of civilian tombs from the 1940s usually indicate that the site is being prepared for a new burial, though the fate of the original owner cannot be ascertained.

Holes in the boundary wall, cattle grazing among the tombs, trees cut down for firewood, washing lines hung around, are all indicators of an ill-kept cemetery. Because Bandariabagh is still open for burials of Anglo-Indians and Indian Christians, its condition has attracted substantial criticism from these communities. Their concerns were increased when it was discovered in October 1992 that a portion of the cemetery had been 'leased' out for Rs 50,000 by officials of the Christian Burial Board.[49] Illegal leasing, or selling, of cemetery land is usually the first step to encroachment, because no one wants to pay money for land that is not capable of producing a profit. Encroachment can range from complete demolition of tombs and the building of a housing colony in their place, as happened in Lat Kallan-ki-Lath, to allowing small traders to erect booths, which by sleight of hand, spread like fungi. Those who believe they have bought or leased plots in cemeteries run the risk of losing their 'investment' when the legality of the transaction is challenged, which is what happened at Bandariabagh. At present the cemetery remains unencroached, but damaged and vulnerable.

Describing the Lucknow cemeteries in 1994, the Indian author E.I.L. Jackson wrote: 'The Government of India gave an assurance to the UK Government "that these cemeteries will be adequately safeguarded against destruction and desecration as any property belonging to Government themselves".' (Letter from the Under-Secretary to the Government of India, writing to the Chief Secretaries, to Provincial Governments and Chief Commissioners, 28 January 1949.)[49] 'It is a pity that the assurance which the Government of India had given to the Government of the UK has not been kept. While arrangements exist and have been considerably improved for safeguarding their own property from destruction, they have failed to make adequate arrangements for safeguarding these cemeteries and tombs. As a result of their failure to do so, during the preceding years encroachments have been freely made on the lands of the cemeteries and thieves have freely robbed and taken away priceless artefacts and other objects from the tombs . . . Much resentment prevails among the members of the Christian minority community in Lucknow on account of these unfortunate happenings.'[50]

There is no doubt that much of interest, and worthy of respect, has been irretrievably lost from the Lucknow cemeteries since 1947, mainly by human depredations. What is equally clear is that this is a cause for concern not only among the Christian community, most closely affected, but for other citizens too. The destruction of Lucknow's old cemeteries has received widespread coverage and condemnation in the English language newspapers and magazines. The desecration of a place of burial is an offence under Section 297 of the Indian Penal Code, punishable by imprisonment or a fine. The Christian Burial Board has abrogated its role as guardian of the cemeteries, and the ASI has not always acted swiftly enough to prevent the destruction of protected monuments in its care. Safeguards which were put in place by the British on their departure from India in 1947, and willingly accepted by the Government of India, have broken down, particularly badly in Lucknow, a city often careless of its extraordinarily rich heritage.

NOTES AND REFERENCES

1. Moon, Penderel, *The Transfer of Power 1942–7*, HMSO, London 1983, vol. XII, p. 725.
2. Pemble, John, *The Raj, the Indian Mutiny and the Kingdom of Oudh 1801–1859*, Harvester Press, Sussex 1977, p. 255.
3. Abbas Ali, Darogah, *The Lucknow Album*, Calcutta 1874.
4. Telephone interview with Lieut. Col. A.A. Mains, 22 April 1998, who was Area Intelligence Officer in Agra in 1947.
5. *Indian Army Association Journal*, 'The Last Flag', Kingston-upon-Thames, August 1997, p. 51.
6. Tuker, Francis, *While Memory Serves*, Cassell, London 1950, p. 417.
7. Farwell, Byron, *Armies of the Raj*, Viking, London 1989, p. 356.
8. Moon, op. cit., p. 725.
9. Graff, Violette, ed., *Lucknow: Memories of a City*, chapter by Francis Robinson 'The Re-emergence of Lucknow as a Major Political Centre, 1899–early 1920s', OUP, Delhi 1997, pp. 196–212.
10. Graff, op. cit., p. 220.

11. Wilkinson, Theon, *Two Monsoons*, Duckworth, London 1976. British Association for Cemeteries in South Asia (BACSA) at 76½ Chartfield Avenue, London, SW15 6HQ, England.

12. *The Daily Telegraph*, London, November 1947.

13. Interview with Theon Wilkinson, 10 May 1998.

14. Parliamentary Debates, House of Commons, 28 February 1948 and 18 March 1949, p. 176.

15. Ibid., p. 178.

16. Lucknow Cemetery file in the BACSA Archives, OIOC.

17. Llewellyn-Jones, Rosie, *A Fatal Friendship: The Nawabs, the British and the City of Lucknow*, OUP, Delhi 1985, p. 112.

18. Foster, William, *The English Factories in India 1637–1641*, Oxford 1912, p. 278.

19. Blunt, E.A.H., *List of Inscriptions on Christian Tombs and Tablets of Historical Interest in the United Provinces of Agra and Oudh*, Allahabad 1911, p. 217.

20. Harris, G., *A Lady's Diary of the Siege of Lucknow*, John Murray, London 1858, p. 169.

21. See Llewellyn-Jones, Rosie, *A Very Ingenious Man: Claude Martin in Early Colonial India*, OUP, Delhi 1992, and the Channel Four film 'Stones of the Raj' by William Dalrymple, August 1997, on La Martinière.

22. Harris, op. cit., p. 170.

23. 26 June 1805, no. 126, Bengal Foreign Consultations, OIOC.

24. Information from Mrs Rachel Speirs, whose husband was the great-grandson of Joseph Short, Mariam Begam's brother.

25. Seth, Mesrovb, *The Armenians in India from the Earliest Time to the Present Day*, Calcutta 1937, pp. 564–8.

26. 14 June and 28 June 1850, India Political & Foreign Consultations, OIOC.

27. Amelia Short, sister-in-law of Mariam Begam erected a mural tablet to her memory in the old church of St Joseph's, Hazratganj.

28. Letter to the author from Father Ignatius Martiz of the Catholic Diocese of Lucknow, 9 March 1998.

29. 4 August 1807, no. 43, Foreign Political Consultations, National Archives, New Delhi.

30. Llewellyn-Jones, *A Fatal Friendship*, op. cit., p. 72.

31. 30 November 1855, no. 63, India Political Consultations, OIOC.

32. 15 February 1856, no. 88, India Political Consultations, OIOC.

33. *The Pioneer*, Lucknow, 'History Buried Under Decay', by Sudipta Dev, 22 October 1995.

34. Llewellyn-Jones, *A Fatal Friendship*, op. cit., pp. 118–19.

35. Harris, op. cit., p. 31.

36. Letter to the author from Dr G.D.S. Beechey, great-grandson of George Duncan Beechey, 5 December 1991. Dr Beechey says that one of the artist's wives, Houssiana Begum, was the daughter of the Nawab Ghazi-ud-din Haider.

37. Polehampton, the Reverend Henry, *A Memoir, Letters and Diary*, London 1858.
38. Blunt, op. cit., pp. 235–6.
39. *Chowkidar* (Journal of the British Association of Cemeteries in South Asia), vol. 6, no. 3, 1992.
40. Taylor, P.J.O., *A Companion to the 'Indian Mutiny' of 1857*, OUP, Delhi 1996, p. 8.
41. Archer, Mildred, *Visions of India: The Sketchbooks of William Simpson 1859–62*, 'Havelock's Grave, Alambagh, near Lucknow, 2 December 1860', Phaidon, Oxford 1986, p. 8.
42. Guy, Alan & Boyden, Peter, ed., *Soldiers of the Raj*, National Army Museum, London 1997. Chapter by S.L. Menezes, 'The Legacy of the Undivided Indian Army in the Sub-continent', p. 190.
43. *The Pioneer*, Lucknow, 'For Havelock's Honour, Great Great Grandson Comes Calling', by Sudipta Dev, 3 March 1997.
44. *The Hindustan Times*, Lucknow, 'How to Forget History, Courtesy the Land Mafia', by Shirin Khan, 19 March 1998.
45. Johnson, Donald, *The Architecture of Walter Birley Griffin*, Macmillan, 1977, pp. 126–56.
46. Information from Dr Monty Foyle, March 1988, who had interviewed a former employee of Griffin at the Old Pioneer Press.
47. *Chowkidar*, op. cit., vol. 5, no. 1, 1988.
48. Copy of the lease dated 16 October 1992 in the author's possession.
49. Copy of the letter in the author's possession.
50. *The Pioneer*, Lucknow, 'Save Lucknow's Historic Tombs, Cemeteries', by E.I.L. Jackson, 10 May 1994.

The Lucknow Cemeteries

References in italics immediately after the name indicate that the site is marked as a cemetery on the 'Survey of India Lucknow Guide Map' (First Edition) 1:20,000 published by the Government of India in 1973, from a survey carried out in 1970–71. (author's collection).

'Vanrenan' indicates that the cemetery appears on the Revenue Survey map compiled by Lieut. Col. D.C. Vanrenan and Capt. A.D. Vanrenan between 1862 and 1866 (covering a smaller area than the Lucknow Guide Map, above), published by the Office of the Surveyor General of India, Calcutta 1870 (National Archives, New Delhi).

1. **Alambagh Cemetery** *E10* Alambagh Marg, Chandranagar
   Earliest burial November 1857. Last burial *c.* 1858
   Only the Havelock tomb and memorial remains
   caretaker Archaeological Survey of India

2. **Bandariabagh (Military/Cantonment Cemetery)** *1 8* Mall Avenue
   Opened 1859, consecrated 3 December 1859. Open (1998)
   5 acres, 229 endowed graves, 103 First World War graves, some destroyed
   caretaker Christian Burial Board.

3. **Bargawan Cemetery** *E12* East of the Lucknow-Kanpur Highway
   1857–58
   Memorial column remains, graves destroyed 1983
   caretaker Archaeological Survey of India

4. **Chiria Jhil Cemetery**, *I 5* Sapru Marg (formerly Oliver Road)
   post 1858
   Two sections, Catholic and Protestant
   part caretaker Catholic Diocese of Lucknow

5. **Constantia (La Martiniere)**, Dilkusha
   September 1800, destroyed 1857, reconstructed *c.* 1860
   Tomb of Major General Claude Martin
   caretaker La Martiniere College

6. **Dilkusha tombs**, Dilkusha Garden
   1857–58
   Six tombs dispersed among the gardens
   caretaker Archaeological Survey of India

7. **Lat Kallan-ki-Lath** *G6 (Vanrenan)* Aminabad
   Opened 1807, consecrated 1825 (?), destroyed 1992
   Only the tomb of John Collins, British Resident, survives
   caretaker Catholic Diocese of Lucknow

8. **Lotan Bagh**, near Musabagh
   1858
   Isolated grave
   caretaker Archaeological Survey of India

9. **Macchi Bhawan Cemetery** *(Vanrenan)*
   c. 1856
   Only one grave remaining
   caretaker Archaeological Survey of India

10. **Mariaon Cemetery (Bailey Garad***)***, Aliganj
    c. 1807–*c.* 1858
    caretaker Archaeological Survey of India

11. **La Martiniere Park**, Dilkusha
    1857–58
    3 graves
    caretaker La Martiniere College

12. **Musabagh**
    1858
    Isolated grave
    caretaker Archaeological Survey of India

13. **Nishatganj Cemetery** *J4* Paper Mill Colony Road
    Opened 1887, consecrated 1 October 1889
    2 acres, 900 endowed graves, open (1998)
    caretaker Christian Burial Board

14. **Qaisarbagh tombs**, near the tomb of Saadat Ali Khan
    March 1858
    Memorial to 14 officers and men and some graves
    caretaker status unknown

15. **Qaisarpasand Cemetery** *(Vanrenan)* Qaisarbagh
    pre 1805, closed *c.* 1861.
    Contains the tomb of Mariam Begam
    caretaker Catholic Diocese of Lucknow

16. **Residency Cemetery** *G4 (Vanrenan)*
    1857–1934, consecrated 26 December 1864
    Numerous identified graves, mass grave of over 100 defenders
    Regimental memorial inscriptions, including 2 to Indian officers
    and sepoys killed fighting for the East India Company
    caretaker Archaeological Survey of India

17. **Sikander Bagh,** Ashok Marg
    November 1857
    6 graves, now vanished
    caretaker Archaeological Survey of India

18. **Wilayati Bagh**, south of La Martiniere,
    1858
    Three graves
    caretaker Archaeological Survey of India

Index